·ᴥ· Rooted in Hope ·ᴥ·

Twelve Practices for Resilience Building Educators

By Katie McDonald, M.Ed., LMSW

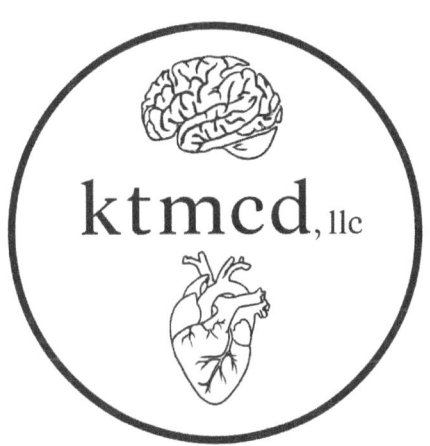

ktmcd, llc

ISBN 979-8-218-79665-5

First edition 2025

❧ contents ❧

❧ acknowledgments ❧

This project grew out of lived experiences, hard lessons, and enduring hope—the memories of which are deeply rooted in relationships that must be acknowledged.

To my daughter—Your curiosity, courage, and honesty keep me grounded. You teach me every day what it means to listen deeply and love fully.

To my people — J, K, C, and my SQBs. Thank you for keeping me grounded and loving me through every moment. I am honored to do life with you.

To my RUSTIC T-I group—Thank you for challenging me to think deeply and lead bravely. Your work in trauma-responsive schools has not only shaped these pages but also the way I see the work ahead. You are all the real deal- living and breathing this work every day.

To the OG— Jim Sporleder. Nearly ten years ago, you trusted me to work alongside you on this journey, and I am honored to carry on your legacy.

To my Miss Honey— Lynn, thank you for seeing me, guiding me, and inspiring me.

To the 2014 Kansas Teacher of the Year Team— In so many ways, this project would never have happened without our year together. Thank you for your friendship and encouragement.

To the Ducks— It was an honor to work alongside you in the Pond of Misfit Educators. I will forever be grateful for our time together reimagining and redesigning education.

To my former students— I am so proud of all that you have accomplished. Thank you for teaching me more than I ever dreamed of teaching you.

To the educators, students, and families whose stories and resilience inspired this journey— your honesty, vulnerability, and strength remain at the heart of this project.

To you, reader—Thank you for joining me. I hope these words meet you where you are and offer the encouragement you didn't know you needed.

And to every teacher, caregiver, and healer doing the invisible work—this one's for you.

❧ preface ❧

Life doesn't ask if you're ready. It rushes in, loud, fast, unrelenting, until one day you look around and think, How did I end up here? I've asked that question more times than I can count. Sometimes it arrives as a quiet ache; sometimes it's laced with awe, gratitude, and the unexpected beauty of survival. This isn't the life I expected, but in many ways, it's more than I ever thought possible.

As you begin this book, I think it's important that you know my story to help you hear my heart in these pages. It's a story of transformation —of holding space for both pain and possibility. It's about living with trauma and still reaching for purpose.

As educators, we don't just shape minds; we help grow a student's capacity for hope. How do we nurture belief in a future that hasn't unfolded yet—especially when many of us are still healing our pasts?

For me, it began with books. Within their pages, I encountered characters who mirrored my pain and exemplified resilience. They whispered the message I most needed: *"You are not alone."*

I was a Matilda, searching for my Miss Honey. And while my world wasn't ruled entirely by Miss Trunchbull, there were enough "I'm big, you're little; I'm right, you're wrong" moments to make me crave the quiet protection of a gentle adult. However, I didn't find that person in my own K-12 experience.

What I found instead was routine, escape, and invisibility. I loved school, not because I always felt seen or challenged, but because the rules stayed the same, the expectations were low, and, most importantly, no one interrupted me when I was reading.

Books became the adults I could trust—offering adventure, wisdom, and, most of all, hope. Through stories, I practiced courage, learned empathy, and imagined a life where someone might actually see me.

When I wrote a bleak little story in fourth grade, what I needed was a teacher to notice the cry for help between the lines. Instead, I learned to hide. I quickly realized my teachers weren't looking. I finished elementary school pained and scared, invisible to the very adults I needed. Research tells us one caring relationship makes a child 30 times more likely to be engaged in school—yet sixth grade came and went without a Miss Honey.

When I was in seventh grade, my mom married John. To give you a picture in your head, imagine Clint Eastwood, but he's drunk and not quite as handsome. Initially, John was kind and fun, making our lives exciting. Soon, John drank at least a 30-pack of Natty Light daily and would have bouts of rage. I can still hear the cans popping - 24 hours a day. He smelled like green olives, as if his insides were pickling.

My sisters adored him, but he hated me—and I him. He crushed my mom's light, called me names meant to break me, and dreamed aloud of my death. She stayed.

By ninth grade, the weight of trauma had hollowed me out. I was medicated on Prozac, flirting with the idea of swallowing the bottle. On the outside, I looked intact; inside, I was empty. Still, no one noticed.

So I kept borrowing hope from literature. I found grit in Scout, solace in Jo March, and stubborn wonder in Esther Greenwood. Hope, I would later learn, isn't a mood; it's the belief that we have both the will and the way to reach our goals. It lengthens our life expectancy, strengthens our health, and, for me, it became a thread I could follow through the dark.

The first time I recall feeling hopeful, I stood in the doorway of her bedroom as my mom ran downstairs. "Watch him," was the only direction she had given. From the doorway, I watched as John's body convulsed, lifting from the bed, his eyes rolling into the back of his head. As I stood there watching him seize as a result of alcoholism, a great sense of peace washed over me. I didn't attach the word hope to it then, but I know now that it was precisely what it was. I clearly understood that the future would be better than the past.

I'm sure I had felt hope before, but I can't conjure those moments in the same visceral way I can the memory of that night. He moved out shortly after that night. Three months later, my mom packed up and drove away to be with him. My sisters and I moved in with our dad. He was steady but unable to ease the sting of abandonment. I understood why she left—she was hopeless—but knowing didn't dull the pain of watching her drive away.

Losing my mother and home made me wary of attention I didn't want and of teachers who might miss me just as others had. So I turned inward, chasing distraction where I could and solace in books. Stories became my companions: The Little Prince taught compassion, the Brontës hinted at love, L'Engle wrinkled time, and Orwell, Huxley, and Bradbury gave me the courage to question authority. Their characters let me borrow hope and glimpse doors I couldn't yet open.

My mom returned in my junior year, John trailing close behind. She seemed stronger; he appeared weaker. That year, he died by suicide. For a fleeting moment, I felt hope—maybe the worst was finally over. But the weight of years pressed back in. Outwardly, I was the model student; inwardly, I was unraveling, proof that trauma doesn't always look like acting out.

After graduation, I spent the next two years wondering why I failed, pretending to have the time of my life. Still, no adult noticed. Later, I would learn about fight, flight, and freeze—the nervous system's survival responses. I hadn't fought or fled; I had numbed, shut down, frozen.

Then the world split open on a quiet September morning as the towers fell. Fear returned, raw and familiar. Beneath it, hope stirred again—an unlikely companion reminding me there had to be more. I left home. I waited tables, lived on baked potatoes, and started over. In the space created by leaving, fear loosened its grip and possibility crept in.

A year later, I walked into a kindergarten classroom as a paraeducator and met my Miss Honey. She saw my pain and chipped away at the armor with kindness, boundaries, and belief. She asked the question that changed everything: "How do you want your story to be told?" With her help, I applied to college, navigated financial aid, and stepped onto a path I hadn't believed I deserved.

I carried that hope into my own classroom. Hired six weeks into the year as an overflow second-grade teacher, I inherited a class that other adults had pieced together: eleven IEPs, thirteen English learners, a child who was legally blind and partially deaf, and one with explosive behaviors. By week two, I'd seen a knife, confiscated pornography, and broken up fights.

Fear felt like the baseline again. So I reached for the one thing that had always steadied me: literature. We filled our room, our brains, and our souls with the words of others. We found ourselves in the stories of Esperanza Rising; we borrowed hope from The Little Engine that Could, traveled to other worlds, laughed, cried, argued, and became a family. By year's end, every student had made significant growth. Behavior incidents went down. Attendance went up. Connection worked.

The following year, about four weeks in, there was a knock on my classroom door. I opened it to find two of my boys with tear-stained faces. One dared to ask me a simple question: *"Did you know?" "Know what?"* I responded. *"They are moving us again,"* and then his words hit like a ton of bricks: *"Why do teachers keep getting rid of us?"* The community we had built, our tiny, hard-won sense of safety and trust, was decimated overnight. That rupture was its own kind of trauma. Attendance dropped. Behaviors spiked. The kids weren't acting out because they didn't care; they were grieving. So was I.

The following year, my principal moved me to 4th grade. I asked for my kids back—those who had been displaced—and she agreed. We picked up where we left off, reading over 1,000 books together, not just dreaming of who they wanted to be, but of what problems they wanted to solve. They knew we were partners. If they needed to borrow hope, I had plenty to share.

Despite their history and environment, they began to believe their future could be brighter than the present. Yet as their hope grew, mine dimmed. Early that year, a parent confided that her son had been abused and begged me not to tell anyone else. I promised to love and protect him, and I carried that secret all year.

By May, I was drained—physically, emotionally, spiritually. I knew the statistics: one in three teachers leaves within three years. I didn't want to be one of them, but I wasn't sure how much I had left to give.

I returned to my hometown to teach, engaged and expecting a baby. It felt like coming full circle—but I was running on empty. I slipped into compliance, mistaking privilege for protection, and overlooked the hidden scars of students who masked their pain like I once had. Looking back, I knew there were children that year who needed more from me. In response, I made healing myself a priority.

So here I am today, not without scars, but no longer afraid. I've come to understand that hope isn't something that only visits in moments of fear; it's something I can carry with me, always. My suffering didn't break me; it built me. It shaped my perseverance, strengthened my character, and taught me how to find light even in the darkest corners. I believe in the power of education and in the profound ability of educators to be bearers of hope, especially when it feels out of reach.

I've accepted I won't be "the one" for every child. But here's what I also know: one relationship can change everything. Just one adult who truly sees a student—who offers connection over correction, presence over perfection—can alter the course of a life.

 And thankfully, it doesn't fall on a single teacher. Across a child's K–12 journey, there are countless opportunities for them to find their "one." What would it look like if we worked together to ensure every student did?

If you're reading this, you probably became an educator because you love kids—or because someone once saw the light in you before you could see it yourself. But love and talent alone don't sustain us. What sustains us is a mindset—a way of being that allows us to hold trauma and transformation in balance. For me, the throughline has been to remain rooted. Rooted in courage. Rooted in compassion. Rooted in Hope.

That phrase carries deep meaning for me, personally and professionally. Being rooted in hope means choosing possibility when things feel broken. It means building a life and a practice on resilience, intention, and connection. It's the work of editing the story we inherited and designing the one we will live. The chapters ahead weave research and lived experience into a framework for educators who want to become bearers of hope—especially when it feels out of reach.

To teach is to dedicate your life so others may learn how to live. That's what we do here: we learn how to cultivate hope—in ourselves first, and then, inevitably, in our students. May this book be a hand on your shoulder and a light at your feet. May it help you become someone's "one."

Rooted in Hope. Always.

✦ introduction ✦

Why this book? Why now?

It has been said that we live in one of the most stressful times in human history.[1] We could spend our time discussing what has changed in society, pointing fingers at what or who is to blame, or reminiscing about the good old days, but that won't change the fact that stress is impacting our children. The adversity that many of our youth undergo before ever setting foot in a classroom is increasing. For those children, their brains may be wired for fear, and their perception of how they fit into the world is often shaped by disconnection and a focus on survival. We can no longer expect our students to adapt to a system that doesn't fit their needs. It is time to adjust the system to fit our students.

As the awareness of trauma's impact on learning has grown, many school systems have begun pursuing what it means to be trauma-informed. Unfortunately, this pursuit is often reduced to surface-level solutions: a keynote speaker shares how a teacher changed their life, or a consultant—usually years removed from the classroom—delivers a one-day training that boils it all down to "build relationships." The irony? Neither takes the time to build a relationship with *you*. I say that with humility, because I've been both that speaker and that consultant. What I've learned is this: relationships *do* matter. No single speaker, book, workshop, or conference will make you, or your school system, trauma-informed.

This book won't pretend to be the answer. It cannot sit beside you after a hard day or help co-regulate a student mid-crisis. It isn't a substitute for real, human connection. What it *can* do is offer a framework, rooted in relationship, reflection, and sustained commitment. It doesn't offer quick fixes, because trauma doesn't heal on a timeline. The approach in these pages is relational at its core, not in the cliché sense of "just build relationships," but in the deeper truth that lasting change happens through trust, consistency, and presence. That's why this isn't a checklist. It's an invitation into a different way of thinking, feeling, and responding, one that honors both the science of the brain and the soul of the classroom.

I offer this book not as a prescription, but as a companion—something to return to, wrestle with, and build upon alongside your team. Because becoming trauma-informed is not a destination, it's a journey. It's not a certification to earn or a policy to post. It's a process that requires time, trust, and transformation. It will ask you to examine your own experiences, beliefs, values, and behaviors. It will stretch both your heart and your brain, and not always at the same pace. At times, it may leave you disillusioned or exhausted. Growth lives there too. The kind that reshapes not only how we teach, but how we lead, live, and connect with students and with each other.

Often, this process takes an individual 1-2 years of consistent focus and a system 3-5 years to entirely change. I know...that timeline can feel overwhelming. You might already be thinking, *How can I possibly keep up with one more initiative?* That's okay. In education, we've been conditioned to expect quick fixes: fast policy shifts, new programs each year, and ever-changing expectations. This isn't that. What you'll find in these pages isn't a pendulum swing or a passing trend. It's a framework that has the power to create lasting change for yourself, your students, and your school culture.

This is not another professional development book filled with abstract theories or glossy stories that feel more like movie scripts than real-life classroom experiences. This book is different. Yes, I'll share the science. Yes, I'll offer vignettes and strategies. But the real power of this book will come from *you*. Each chapter will prompt you to reflect on your own beliefs, practices, and personal story. You'll complete exercises that help shift both heart and mind. Most importantly, you'll be challenged to take what you learn and put it into action, imperfectly, bravely, and with intention.

Rooted in Hope: A Framework for Healing, Growth, and Well-Being

ROOTED IN HOPE is the framework that will guide this journey. It's a practical research-based model for healing, growth, and well-being, especially for those impacted by Adverse Childhood Experiences (ACEs). It supports recovery through relationships, builds on Protective and Compensatory Experiences (PACEs), and promotes secure attachment.

I created Rooted in Hope because I know, both personally and professionally, that healing doesn't happen in isolation, and transformation doesn't come from quick fixes. It comes from safe, consistent relationships and from environments that honor both pain and possibility. This framework anchors everything I do: my consulting, my clinical work, and this book. It's a reminder that hope isn't passive or abstract. Hope is a skill, a mindset, and a choice. It's something we can model, teach, and build for ourselves, our students, and one another.

Rooted in Hope rests on twelve core elements:

Resilience, Origin, Openness, Trust, Empowerment, Discernment, Intentionality, Neuro-Informed Practice, Hope, Ownership, Purpose, and Engagement

These elements emerged from my journey as a trauma survivor, educator, therapist, and consultant. They weave together research and real life. They provide a flexible, human-centered structure for individuals and systems to become trauma-responsive, neuro-informed, and authentically connected. Let's walk through the framework together.

RESILIENCE is the enduring capacity to move forward and grow through suffering.

ORIGIN acknowledges the influence of early experiences on shaping our worldview.

OPENNESS fosters a willingness to be vulnerable and helps us to stay curious, willing to adapt, and embrace new perspectives.

TRUST is developed through secure attachments and relationships, as well as within oneself, creating a safe space for vulnerability and emotional growth.

EMPOWERMENT encourages us to take initiative, believe in our agency, and move toward change.

DISCERNMENT helps us respond wisely in complex situations with clarity, rather than reactivity.

INTENTIONALITY brings focus and purpose to each decision, ensuring deliberate and meaningful actions.

NEURO-INFORMED PRACTICES deepen our understanding of how the brain and nervous system influence behavior, learning, and healing

HOPE reminds us that the future can be better than the present, and that we have the power to shape it.

OWNERSHIP fosters personal responsibility and self-awareness.

PURPOSE connects us to our "why," the deeper reason we show up and keep going.

ENGAGEMENT emphasizes the importance of active participation in life, relationships, and communities to cultivate a sense of belonging and shared resilience.

How to Read This Book

You are not just reading this book. You're becoming part of a movement, a movement rooted in science, shaped by story, and powered by hope. While this book is grounded in the *Rooted in Hope* framework, it doesn't present each of the twelve elements one at a time, in clean, even chapters. Instead, these core concepts are woven throughout the content. Like roots beneath the surface, they show up in various ways, sometimes obvious, sometimes subtle, yet always present, always guiding.

You'll revisit certain elements more than once. You might see Resilience in the context of your own story, and then again in how you support a student. You'll explore Trust as both an internal feeling and a systemic design principle. These concepts are not checkboxes. They are lenses. They are tools. They are invitations.

I invite you to fully engage with this book, not just read it. Throughout these pages, you'll find reflection prompts, action steps, and pause points, and I encourage you to respond right where you are. That might mean jotting down your thoughts in the margins, grabbing a separate journal, or covering these pages with sticky notes, much like a well-loved lesson plan binder.

Now, I know what you're thinking: "We were taught not to write in books!" I get it. Somewhere along the way, maybe in elementary school or during a librarian's stern warning, you absorbed the sacred rule: books must remain pristine. Well, consider this your permission slip. Scribble. Highlight. Doodle. Engage. This is your learning journey, and it should look like it. Whether you're dog-earing pages or typing out reflections on your Notes app, your active participation will deepen the work we're doing together. You're not just reading this book, you're living it.

In addition to the hard copy you are reading right now, you will find supplemental material, templates, activities, and other resources on the book's companion website: katiemcdonald.org/book-companion, QR codes throughout the book will link you to these resources.

A Widening Circle: How This Book Is Organized

This book is about you. Not just your students. Not just your school. You.

You are the focus, your growth, your reflection, your journey. This isn't a manual to fix kids. It's a guidebook for the kind of educator you're becoming. One who leads with both clarity and compassion. One who is willing to reflect, unlearn, and rebuild. Perhaps, along the way, this journey will offer you healing as well.

The book unfolds in four distinct parts, each expanding the focus from science to the self, to the student, and finally to the system. Think of it as a widening circle of impact. Each layer builds on the last, helping you connect the personal and the professional, the inner and the outer, the individual and the collective.

Part Five is where theory becomes action. Throughout Parts One through Four, you'll complete short reflections at the end of each chapter. At the close of each Part, you'll also be directed to a larger, culminating reflection located in Part Five. These reflections are designed to connect your insights across the book, ultimately tying everything together in a practical, personal way.

You don't need to memorize all twelve facets of the *Rooted in Hope* framework. They'll become familiar as you move through the book. You'll feel them reflected in your own experiences. You'll see them take root in your practice. Let this book meet you where you are. Use it for reflection, discussion, or action. As you go, remember: you are not alone. The work of healing and growth is a shared endeavor, and it's worth doing.

Rooted in Hope begins by exploring how trauma, stress, and resilience shape the nervous system, and how this science is applied in real classrooms with real children. From there, the book turns inward, inviting educators to engage in deep personal reflection through tools. These practices help illuminate how our nervous systems, beliefs, and histories impact what we see and how we respond.

Once grounded, we move outward using the ROOTED IN HOPE framework to identify and support students of concern through the Student in Need of Connection (SiNoC) process, teacher self-assessment tools, and trauma-responsive practice shifts. Later chapters guide readers through creating healing learning spaces, implementing co-regulation strategies, and building whole-school systems that center safety, belonging, and agency. This isn't a behavior management book—it's a call to return to the kind of work that changes lives, beginning with our own.

Let's begin.

✺ part one ✺
Understanding the Roots

For the past decade, many school systems have offered professional learning on trauma-informed practices. You've probably attended a workshop or two, maybe even several. Still, the reality is that not all trauma training is created equal, and few go far enough to explore both the depth of the science and the complexity of applying it meaningfully in classrooms, systems, and our own lives. That's why Part One of this book is dedicated to building a shared foundation. Before we explore strategies, we need to ground ourselves in a shared understanding.

In this section, we'll look at two sides of the same coin: the science of adversity, what it tells us about difficult events and their potential effect on our brains, bodies, and ability to relate and learn, and the science of healing, which we can draw upon to build resilience in our students and ourselves.

First, we'll unpack the research behind the Adverse Childhood Experiences (ACE) Study and examine how stress and trauma impact the brain and body. Then, we'll explore what makes resilience possible, how protective factors, supportive relationships, and intentional practices create the conditions for growth. Together, these chapters will establish the context for the Rooted in Hope framework and why it matters, not just for students, but for all of us.

❧ one ❧
The Science of Adversity

We are living in an era of unprecedented stress, one that profoundly impacts the emotional, physical, and neurological development of people at every age, especially children and youth. In this climate, none of us are immune. We all carry burdens, some visible, some silent. We all need support from one another to stay grounded, resilient, and whole.

However, some people carry an additional, often invisible, load. Chronic stress or trauma embedded in our earliest relationships and environments are burdens that shape how we behave, connect, and learn. The Adverse Childhood Experiences (ACE) Study, conducted in the late 1990s by the CDC and Kaiser Permanente, was a groundbreaking research project that helped shift the national conversation.[2] For the first time, researchers had identified a clear and measurable link between early-life adversity and long-term health outcomes.

The study outlined ten common adverse experiences, ranging from various forms of abuse and neglect to household dysfunction, that, when experienced in childhood, significantly increase the risk for mental health challenges, chronic illness, substance use, and difficulties in school and relationships. Its findings revealed something educators already felt in their classrooms: what happens to us in childhood doesn't stay in childhood.

Trauma rewires the brain, primes the nervous system, and alters the way we interpret and engage with the world. For children, especially those with high ACE scores, school can be a battlefield or a lifeline. Teachers are often placed in a unique position, either to reinforce harm or to interrupt it with compassion, consistency, and co-regulation.

As educators, caregivers, and human beings committed to others' growth, we can no longer ask students to simply conform to rigid expectations without first understanding what they carry. This chapter offers a foundation for recognizing the spectrum of stress and trauma, not to diagnose, but to deepen insight. With this understanding, we can begin shaping environments that meet people where they are and support growth from that place.

Trauma exists along a continuum.

To truly support those who have experienced adversity, we must move beyond a black-and-white view of trauma. Trauma is not a single event or a simple diagnosis; it lives on a continuum. A person's response to stress can vary significantly based on biology, environment, developmental stage, and the presence (or absence) of support. What is tolerable for one individual may be overwhelming for another.

The American Psychological Association defines trauma as:

"Any disturbing experience that results in significant fear, helplessness, dissociation, confusion, or other disruptive feelings intense enough to have a long-lasting negative effect on a person's attitudes, behavior, and other aspects of functioning. Traumatic events include those caused by human behavior (e.g., rape, war, industrial accidents) as well as by nature (e.g., earthquakes) and often challenge an individual's view of the world as a just, safe, and predictable place."[3]

By understanding trauma as a spectrum, from manageable stress to toxic stress to complex trauma, we can begin to recognize the full range of experiences that shape behavior, emotional regulation, and learning. This more nuanced understanding equips us to respond with empathy and design environments that honor both struggle and strength.

Stress, in itself, is not inherently harmful and is, in fact, necessary for growth and development. However, when stress ceases to be intermittent, which allows for recovery when it is intense, frequent, and/or prolonged, it becomes toxic and harmful. For children, toxic stress is defined as the extreme, frequent, or prolonged activation of the body's stress response without the buffering presence of a supportive adult. It is the combination of feeling overwhelmed by stress and isolated from any support community.[4]

When a child experiences toxic stress over an extended period, it can cause lasting damage to the structure and function of their developing brain. This response may result in symptoms such as intrusive thoughts, hypervigilance, avoidance behaviors, and emotional dysregulation. Post-traumatic stress often stems from acute experiences like accidents, natural disasters, or violence and can significantly impact an individual's daily functioning and sense of safety.

Complex traumatic stress impacts an individual's core sense of self, disrupting emotional regulation, the ability to form secure relationships, and one's overall worldview. It is characterized by deep feelings of powerlessness, mistrust, and difficulty processing emotions due to the cumulative effects of toxic stress and repeated trauma.[5] It's essential to recognize the subjectivity of these categories; what is tolerable stress for one individual might become toxic for someone with less access to support.

Perception is Reality

It's essential to remember that a person's perception of stress is their reality. As adults, we often forget the immense weight children and teens carry as they navigate the world. It is common for adults to dismiss a young person's feelings by saying things like, "If you think life is stressful now, just wait until you're an adult." This perspective can be harmful for two reasons: first, it offers little hope for a brighter future, and second, it fails to acknowledge what we know about the brain and stress from the beginning of life. The experience of stress is complex and often relative to a person's developmental age and maturity. However, this complexity does not account for the profound impact of adverse childhood experiences or unbuffered stress. Children come into our classrooms daily, often carrying a mix of stressors, some developmentally appropriate, while others are burdens too heavy to bear, regardless of age.

Stressors Ages 5-12

Children between the ages of five and twelve face numerous stressors that can significantly impact their emotional and physical well-being. Understanding these stressors is crucial for providing the necessary support they require.

Some of this pressure stems from school itself. Academic expectations can weigh heavily on children, especially when their self-worth becomes entangled with grades. The fear of making mistakes may cause them to hesitate, hold back, or avoid tasks altogether. Transitions, such as starting a new grade, switching schools, or adjusting to a different teacher, can exacerbate this uncertainty, eroding the fragile sense of stability that many students rely on to feel safe. For some, difficult relationships with teachers become another layer of stress, especially if they've already learned that adults might not always be trustworthy.

Social pressures add another dimension. Navigating friendships, managing peer dynamics, or simply trying to find a sense of belonging can be overwhelming. Some children struggle to form or maintain friendships. Others experience the pain of being left out or pressured to conform. Bullying, whether direct or subtle, leaves deep emotional scars. Constant comparisons to peers chip away at self-esteem, reinforcing the lie that they'll never be "enough." For students who feel socially awkward or shy, the daily demand to engage can become exhausting.

At home, the challenges don't always fade. High parental expectations can translate into an internalized need to be perfect. Sibling conflicts, shifting family dynamics, or the pressure to meet adult standards can create emotional exhaustion long before a child even arrives at school. Some children face bigger disruptions, such as a divorce, a move, the loss of a loved one, or the arrival of a new family member. Others live with chronic financial insecurity, food instability, or parents facing job loss—each one a silent stressor that shapes how safe a child feels in the world.

Then there are the stressors that often go unseen: the child who feels unloved or unnoticed, the one who can't find the words to express what's wrong, the student who gets through the day on too little sleep or too many obligations, the child whose sadness shows up as anger, whose anxiety shows up as apathy, whose fear shows up as defiance.

Adolescent Stressors

As adolescents and young adults navigate the complexities of increasing independence, identity formation, and societal expectations, they encounter a myriad of stressors that can profoundly impact their emotional and mental well-being. Understanding these challenges is essential in providing support during this critical developmental stage.

Some stress comes from seismic life changes. A move to a new city or school may look like a fresh start, but to a young person, it can feel like the ground shifting beneath them. Familiar routines vanish, friendships get left behind, and belonging suddenly feels far away. Even without a change of zip code, many adolescents struggle to answer the fundamental question: Who am I, and where do I fit in? That search for identity can feel urgent and disorienting, especially when it's layered with questions about gender, sexuality, or cultural acceptance in spaces that don't always feel safe or affirming.

At the same time, teens face relentless pressure to perform, conform, and succeed. From classrooms to social feeds, the message is often: Be extraordinary. Be beautiful. Be productive. Be someone. The strain of measuring up to academic expectations, athletic standards, societal beauty norms, and family hopes can fracture a young person's confidence. Self-esteem falters under the weight of comparison, especially when social media floods their attention with curated lives that always seem better, easier, or more perfect than their own.

Many young people are also learning how to manage complex emotions, but often lack the necessary tools to do so. Emotional regulation, a process still developing in the adolescent brain, becomes even more challenging when sleep is scarce, routines are overwhelming, and the pressure to be everywhere and do everything never lets up. Between academic loads, jobs, sports, clubs, and friend groups, many are simply exhausted. Sleep deprivation is often the norm, not the exception, and with it comes an increase in anxiety, irritability, and disconnection.

Layered onto all this are the silent stressors that often go unnamed. Chronic health issues or invisible illnesses can make each day feel like a battle. Some young people are deeply affected by global instability, climate change, political conflict, or humanitarian crises, feeling helpless in the face of large-scale problems. Others carry the weight of responsibility at home, whether it's helping support their family financially or managing the emotional labor of a complex household. Family dynamics may be shifting, including divorce, remarriage, and blended families, and many are navigating those changes without the support they need.

Social life, so often seen as central during adolescence, is not always a source of joy. Romantic relationships introduce intense emotions, and breakups can bring waves of self-doubt. Friendships are crucial but complicated—the desire to belong often clashes with the fear of rejection or exclusion. Peer pressure, around sex, substances, or fitting in, can quietly erode a student's sense of agency. When conflicts arise at home or school, or when a young person feels misunderstood by adults, feelings of isolation grow.

The truth is, adolescence is not just a transitional stage. It's a full and complex season of life, and for too many young people, it's marked not only by discovery but also by distress. When we take the time to look beyond the surface, we see that behind every student's behavior is a young person trying to navigate a world that often feels overwhelming, with too much to handle and too little support. They don't need perfection from us; they need presence. They need safe spaces to fall apart and be put back together. They need adults who listen, honor their voice, and help them carry the load.

Adult Stressors

We adults are not immune. We bring our stresses into the classroom; we're human, after all. Adults encounter many stressors as they navigate the complexities of managing careers, relationships, finances, and personal well-being. Understanding these stressors is crucial for providing support and resources to help them cope effectively. Adulthood often carries the illusion of stability, careers, families, and routines that suggest things have finally fallen into place. Just beneath the surface, many adults are quietly managing a complex web of stressors that span finances, relationships, health, and identity.

Financial concerns sit at the heart of much adult stress. Job security isn't guaranteed, and even for those who are steadily employed, the rising cost of living, inflation, and unexpected expenses — such as car repairs or medical bills — can destabilize even the most carefully planned budgets. Student loans linger, mortgages loom, and the pressure to save for retirement competes with the urgent need to cover day-to-day expenses. Add in the high cost of raising children, and many adults are left feeling like they're always one step behind, no matter how hard they work.

In the workplace, stress manifests in various forms. Some adults are stuck in jobs that no longer fulfill them, facing limited growth opportunities and feeling stagnant. Others are chasing promotions and career milestones that never seem to arrive. Even for those who enjoy their work, interpersonal conflicts, heavy workloads, and burnout can gradually erode their sense of purpose and well-being. The balancing act between professional and personal life becomes an unrelenting performance—one where there's rarely time to rest, much less reflect.

Outside the workplace, family responsibilities bring their emotional weight. Parenting comes with a constant sense of urgency, from managing schedules to navigating the emotional needs of children. For many, the stress doubles as they also care for aging parents or extended family members. Marriages and relationships may shift or dissolve, while dating in adulthood introduces new uncertainties. In the flurry of family and career, social connections often suffer, friendships fade, and isolation can set in quietly.

Health, both mental and physical, is another layer adults must carry. Chronic conditions, aging-related issues, and the sheer pressure of trying to maintain a healthy lifestyle in the face of limited time or resources can feel like an uphill battle. Anxiety and depression are common companions, often exacerbated by sleep deprivation, worry about mortality, or the burden of constantly "keeping it together."

All of this unfolds in a broader social context that often intensifies the stress. Political and societal tensions, expectations to present a polished life, and the relentless influence of social media can make it feel like everyone else is thriving while you're just surviving. The quiet voice of comparison can be loud: "Am I where I should be by now?"

"Why do I still feel like I'm falling short?" That internal narrative is only strengthened by imposter syndrome, the fear of not measuring up even in spaces where you're already succeeding.

Then there's the existential weight, questions about meaning, purpose, and whether the life you've built aligns with who you really are. Adults often struggle to balance personal ambitions against societal expectations, striving to be independent while still fulfilling family and community obligations. It's no wonder so many carry a sense of restlessness or fatigue beneath their responsibilities.

The truth is, being an adult is not about having it all figured out. It's about learning to hold complexity—joy and worry, strength and doubt, responsibility and longing—all at once. For many, it's about realizing that the most courageous thing isn't always having the answers, but simply continuing to show up.

Recognizing these stressors is vital for employers, family members, and friends to support adults navigating these challenges. By understanding that an adult's perception of their stress is their reality, we can foster a more empathetic and supportive environment that acknowledges their struggles and helps them find balance and fulfillment.

To better understand the spectrum of stress and trauma, consider generating a list of experiences that fall into the categories of stress, toxic stress, and trauma. You might go back through the previous section and reflect personally on where stressors from your own life fall along this continuum, or you might think more broadly.

Stress	Toxic Stress	Trauma
Feeling of being overwhelmed by mental or emotional pressure	*Strong, frequent, and/or prolonged adversity that causes feelings of overwhelm, powerlessness, and isolation*	*An event, series of events, or set of circumstances that has lasting adverse effects on an individual's functioning and mental, physical, social, emotional, or spiritual well-being*

Going Beyond ACEs

The ACE Study got the ball rolling—and that mattered. It gave many educators, healthcare providers, and policymakers language and data to advocate for change. However, it also came with limitations. For example, the study focused primarily on individual pathology rather than systemic or relational factors. It did not account for protective factors, cultural contexts, or the resilience of children in the face of adversity. Perhaps most dangerously, it inadvertently led to a simplistic assumption: that high ACE scores equal broken kids, and low ACE scores mean safety.[6]

As we build on this foundational research, we must move beyond those early assumptions. Trauma is more than a checklist of past harms. It is a disruption of connection—within the body, in relationships, and across systems. Understanding this complexity enables us to approach our students and ourselves not with pity or panic, but with clarity, compassion, and a commitment to repair.

Today, 55% of Americans report experiencing no ACEs, roughly 25% report at least one, and nearly 10% report three or more, a critical threshold where the risk for long-term negative outcomes begins to rise sharply.[7] Acknowledging that the original ACE study doesn't encompass all potential traumas is crucial. Other impactful events, often referred to as "lowercase t trauma," include moving from a familiar neighborhood, bullying, losing loved ones, or living with developmental pressures.

Chronic mental health issues are also a source of toxic stress for many children. Early diagnosis and treatment are vital, yet access to these services remains inconsistent, particularly for children in poverty. One in five children living below 100% of the federal poverty level has a mental, behavioral, or developmental disorder, yet access to treatment is often limited. According to the Centers for Disease Control (CDC), national US data from 2021-2022 show that 1 in 7 children ages 3-17 have been diagnosed with a mental health or behavior disorder. Of those children, nearly 80% with depression and almost 60% with anxiety receive treatment, while roughly 50% of children with a behavior disorder receive help.[8]

Trauma affects neurotypical brain development, leading to challenges in cognitive performance, emotional regulation, and behavior. Students with three or more ACEs are three times more likely to experience academic failures, five times more likely to have attendance issues, and six times more likely to exhibit behavioral problems.[9]

For educators, the ACE Study offers a vital lens for understanding student behavior. It shifts the question from

"What's wrong with this student?" to *"What might have happened to them?"* and ultimately, *"What do they need to feel safe, supported, and ready to learn?"*

The impact of adverse experiences can continue throughout the lifespan, and often leads to long-term health issues, and individuals with four or more ACEs are at significantly higher risk for adverse health behaviors and chronic diseases. These outcomes are well-documented in long-term studies conducted by the CDC and Kaiser Permanente, including:[10]

- Thrill-seeking behaviors
- Overachieving/perfectionism
- Missed work
- Smoking
- Substance use
- Lack of physical activity
- Depression
- Suicide attempts
- Cancer
- Broken bones
- Severe obesity
- Heart disease
- Diabetes
- Stroke
- COPD
- STDs

The ACE Study was a watershed moment. For many educators and practitioners, it offered the first clear, evidence-based connection between early adversity and long-term outcomes, mental health, chronic disease, educational challenges, and relationship struggles. Its strengths are undeniable. It provided a data-driven foundation that sparked new conversations across schools, healthcare, and policy. It framed adversity not as a personal failure, but as a public health issue. By doing so, it created a powerful call to action: prevention and early intervention.

However, like all foundational studies, it came with limitations that need to be named. The original participant group lacked racial and ethnic diversity, with over 70% being white, middle-class, and college-educated, which limits the generalizability of the findings.[11] It focused on ten predefined adversities, omitting key experiences such as racism, poverty, displacement, or exposure to community violence. It centered the individual experience of trauma, without examining the broader structural and historical forces that often create those experiences. It also failed to explore protective factors, which allow some children to thrive in the face of adversity.

These gaps invite us to expand. The ACE Study offers a starting place, not a finish line. There is a tremendous opportunity to integrate its findings with more culturally responsive and neuro-informed frameworks. We can partner with community resources, elevate resilience as much as we assess risk, and shift our focus from "what happened to you" to "what's possible for you now?" Perhaps most importantly, we can use this data not just to understand trauma, but to transform the systems that perpetuate it.

Yet there are threats we must be cautious of. If misapplied, ACE scores can become labels, reducing children to numbers and overlooking their strengths. There's a real risk of pathologizing minoritized communities, especially when the data is interpreted without cultural humility or contextual understanding. Overgeneralization can fuel bias, and even with the best intentions, schools and systems may face resistance from constrained resources, overwhelmed staff, or leaders unwilling to shift from compliance to care.[12]

To move forward, we must hold both truths: the ACE Study was a vital breakthrough *and* an incomplete map. Our job now is to fill in the missing pieces, with nuance, equity, and relationship at the center. As educators, we must avoid using ACE scores as a label or limit. Instead, we should view them as a starting point for empathy and understanding, rather than a complete picture of a child's identity or potential. Trauma-informed education means not only recognizing adversity but also honoring the resilience that accompanies it. It calls us to be curious, not conclusive, to see students as more than what has happened to them, and to help them see themselves the same way.

There are meaningful opportunities to expand the ACE framework in ways that better serve all students. This includes integrating culturally responsive practices that honor the lived experiences and strengths of diverse communities, intentionally emphasizing resilience over risk, and building strong partnerships among schools, mental health professionals, and community organizations. These collaborations help create a more holistic, trauma-responsive ecosystem around our students.

Real challenges remain. Resource limitations, whether in terms of time, staffing, or funding, can hinder implementation. The overgeneralization of ACE findings can lead to oversimplified views of trauma, or worse, the unintentional labeling of students. Perhaps most pressing: the risk of educator burnout. Being trauma-informed does not mean becoming trauma-absorbed.

So, what can educators do? First, remember that you are not alone in this work. Trauma-responsive education is most sustainable when it's shared. Advocate for team-based approaches and push for systems that support you, not just your students. Prioritize professional development that incorporates both trauma and resilience science, particularly through a culturally responsive lens. Above all, set boundaries that protect your well-being. A regulated, resourced adult is the most potent intervention any child can have.

◈ reflection ◈

The ACE survey[13] provides one lens into how early experiences may have shaped your development, relationships, health, and coping mechanisms. It helps connect the dots between past and present, offering insight into patterns that may otherwise remain unnamed.

Although the survey is brief, it can evoke strong emotions or trigger difficult memories. Please take a moment to check in with yourself before beginning. If you choose to move forward, be gentle with what comes up. You don't need to process it all at once, and you don't need to do it alone.

If you feel overwhelmed at any point, consider stepping away, journaling your thoughts, or reaching out to a trusted person or mental health professional for guidance and support. This is not a diagnostic tool, and your score does not define you; it's simply one window into your story. You are more than your ACE score. And you are not alone.

Instructions: Place a check mark next to each ACE that you experienced before your 18th birthday.

1. Did you feel that you didn't have enough to eat, had to wear dirty clothes, or had no one to protect or take care of you?

2. Did you lose a parent through divorce, abandonment, death, or other reason?

3. Did you live with anyone who was depressed, mentally ill, or who attempted suicide?

4. Did you live with anyone who had a problem with drinking or using drugs, including prescription drugs?

5. Did your parents or adults in your home ever hit, punch, beat, or threaten to harm each other?

6. Did you live with anyone who went to jail or prison?

7. Did a parent or adult in your home ever swear at you, insult you, or put you down?

8. Did a parent or adult in your home ever hit, beat, kick, or physically hurt you in any way?

9. Did you feel that no one in your family loved you or thought you were special?

10. Did you experience unwanted sexual contact (such as fondling or oral/anal/vaginal intercourse/penetration)?

Your ACE score is the total number of checked responses:

Do you believe that these experiences have affected your health?

                      Not Much   Some   A Lot

❧ two ☙
The Science of Resilience

One of the noted criticisms of the ACE study and trauma-informed schools movement is its focus on a deficit model and the fact that half of the population reports experiencing no traumatic experiences in their childhood.[14] This is why I have shifted my focus from helping schools implement trauma-responsive frameworks to supporting the idea that our schools should prioritize building resilience. Throughout the text, you will find that I use the terms trauma-responsive and resilience-building interchangeably. Being resilient is a quality that all people will need in life, regardless of the level of stress or trauma they experienced in childhood.

Resilience is not merely bouncing back from adversity; it is the enduring capacity to move forward and grow through suffering, rooted in safe, stable relationships that provide support and encouragement. This strength builds upon lessons from past struggles, fostering perseverance and character, and is sustained by a hopeful vision of the future.

Resilience encompasses a belief in the possibility of healing and the existence of paths to overcome trauma and stress. The combined influence of inner growth derived from past challenges and the nurturing presence of trusted relationships enables one to face future hardships with courage and optimism. In the face of adversity, resilience becomes a source of strength, sustained by the belief in a hopeful future and supported by nurturing relationships.

Building Resilience

Building resilience isn't just about surviving hardship; it's about strengthening what surrounds and supports us. Research on Protective and Compensatory Experiences (PACEs) suggests that certain conditions can buffer the impact of trauma, allowing individuals to heal and thrive. At the heart of resilience are stable, supportive relationships—connections that offer trust, safety, and emotional security.

Resilience also grows through meaningful community, a sense of belonging, and purpose that reminds us we're not alone. Safe, predictable environments play a vital role too, providing the stability we need to take risks, make mistakes, and grow without living in a constant state of fear. Ultimately, resilience is built through opportunities, moments that allow us to learn, contribute, and succeed. These moments fuel confidence, agency, and the belief that we are capable of shaping our own story.

Hope: The Science of Resilience

When we talk about building resilience, we have to talk about hope. Not the vague, fluffy version. Not the empty optimism that says *"everything happens for a reason."* I'm talking about real hope, the kind that has grit, direction, and power.

Hope is the science of resilience; it's the measurable, teachable force that fuels our ability to endure, adapt, and grow in the face of adversity.[16] While resilience is the outcome we seek, hope is the engine that drives it forward, combining the belief that the future can be better with the motivation and strategies to make it so.

The most hopeful people I've met are often those who have had every reason not to be. They've seen darkness and still choose to believe in light. They've been dismissed, yet they still fight to be seen. They've survived, and now they want to do more than just survive. I know this not just as an educator or a therapist, but as someone who's lived it. In the preface of this book, I shared a piece of my story, the years I spent looking for someone to notice, to name the pain, to see the scared girl behind the silence and the stories. I needed someone to say:

"I see what you've been through."

"It makes sense that it hurts."

"You can still shape what comes next."

That's what hope after harm requires. Not just blind positivity, but grounded presence. Not just inspiration, but someone who *stays*. Educators can be that someone. *You* can be that someone. We help rebuild a person's internal hope map, the set of beliefs that tells them a better future is possible and accessible. We do this not by handing out empty encouragement, but by setting small, achievable goals and celebrating each step. This helps others see more than one path to success and use coaching self-talk that reminds them, "You have what it takes."

Dr. Shane Lopez, one of the leading researchers on hope, taught us that hopeful people hold two core beliefs:

The future will be better than the present.

I have the power to make it so.[17]

Hopeful people don't pretend the path will be smooth. They just believe there are many ways to get to where they're going, and that none of them will be free from obstacles. Roadblocks do not deter them; they plan around them. That's what makes hope a strategy, not a wish.

Hope is far more than a fleeting feeling or naive optimism; it's a powerful, research-backed force that profoundly impacts our lives, our happiness, and our success. People with high levels of hope tend to live longer and healthier lives. They experience less stress, recover more quickly from illness, and have stronger immune systems. Hope serves as a protective factor, enabling the body and mind to regulate more effectively under pressure. It supports mental well-being and contributes to emotional resilience, particularly during life's most challenging periods.

When it comes to happiness, hope is one of the strongest predictors of well-being. It offers a steady sense of purpose and direction, rather than just temporary good feelings. Hopeful people are more satisfied with their lives, experience greater joy, and report lower levels of depression. Unlike toxic positivity, which ignores real struggle, hope allows people to acknowledge pain while still believing in possibility. It helps us focus on what we can influence and provides a sense of agency, even when things feel hard.

Perhaps most compelling of all: hope directly influences success. In schools, workplaces, and personal growth, hope is more predictive of achievement than intelligence, test scores, or even socioeconomic status. According to Dr. Lopez, hopeful individuals set meaningful goals, believe in their ability to achieve them, and persist through challenges by finding multiple pathways forward. They don't just wish, they work. They problem-solve, they adapt, and they keep going, even when things get tough.

In every setting, whether we're supporting a student, leading a team, or navigating our healing, hope changes how we show up. It shifts our mindset from "what's wrong" to "what's possible." In the face of trauma, it becomes not just a comfort but a strategy. When we believe the future can be better and that we have the power to shape it, everything changes.

Where Does Hope Come From?

I had the honor of learning from Dr. Lopez during my undergrad years at the University of Kansas. One day in class, he led us through a simple yet powerful exercise to explore the origin of hope within us.[18] I never forgot it, and now, I'd love for you to try it, too.

Here's how it works: Raise both hands in the air. Now, on the count of three, point to where your hope comes from. Is it your head, the thinking, planning part of you? Your heart, the seat of emotion and compassion? Or something holy, whatever you find sacred or beyond yourself? You only have two hands, so you'll have to choose your top two. Ready? 1... 2... 3.

Where did you point? Take a moment to reflect on why, and what that says about the way you carry hope in your life. Most people instinctively know. Some point to their temples, some to their chest, and some even raise both hands to the sky. This simple exercise reminds us: hope is personal. It's shaped by our background, our culture, our story. However, regardless of where it begins, hope only becomes real when it motivates us to take action.

Hope Has Three Parts

Hope isn't passive. It's built from a three-part process that gives us direction, momentum, and purpose. These three components, defined by Dr. Lopez, are:

Goals – The clear targets we want to hit. These are specific, meaningful, and motivating.

Agency – The belief that *I* can make progress. It's the inner voice that says, "I've got this."

Pathways – The ability to find alternate routes when things get hard. Hopeful people are flexible problem-solvers. When one door closes, they build another one.[19]

When we combine goals, agency, and pathways, we move forward, even when the road is hard. Hope becomes a motor that powers resilience. The best part? We can teach this to others. In education, hope is not a soft skill. It's a core strategy. It's how we help people envision a better future and believe they have the tools to achieve it. It's how we restore dignity, purpose, and strength. In a later chapter of this book, we will revisit the use of hope as a strategy for yourself and others, because whether you're a student, a teacher, a parent, or a leader, you need hope. Not someday. Now. The good news? You can build it, choose it, and share it, one action at a time.

Resilience and Hope as the Antidote

Trauma disrupts our sense of safety, predictability, and connection; it teaches the nervous system to prepare for danger rather than possibility. It shrinks the world, narrowing our focus to survival. In this way, trauma is a thief of the future, but hope and resilience are the antidotes. Hope gives us back what trauma tries to take: belief in a future that can be different from the past. It fuels the internal engine that says, *"I can keep going. I can make a way."* Resilience is what carries us there, not just bouncing back, but growing through hardship with strength built from within and bolstered by relationships.

Together, hope and resilience push back against the isolation, helplessness, and fear that trauma creates. They rewire our brains for connection. They help us imagine, plan, and move toward something better. They aren't just innate traits; they are skills, mindsets, and practices that can be taught, modeled, and nurtured in classrooms, therapy offices, staff meetings, and homes.

This is why Rooted in Hope centers not on the pain of trauma but on the power of transformation. Trauma may shape someone's origin story, but hope and resilience shape what comes next. When we intentionally build protective environments, teach agency, model belief, and invite new ways forward, we become part of the solution that interrupts the cycle of trauma within our students, our systems, and ourselves.

Hope isn't just a feeling; it's fuel. It's what gets us up and in the door after a hard week. It's what helps us imagine what's possible when everything around us feels broken. More than optimism, hope is the belief that the future can be better *and* that we play a role in making it so.

Over the years, I've seen that the educators who last—and more importantly, the ones who still *love* what they do—are not necessarily the ones who avoid burnout or hardship. They're the ones who keep their hope alive. That doesn't mean toxic positivity or denying reality. It means refusing to let discouragement write the final chapter. Hope sustains us by:

Giving us something to look forward to.
Reminding us of our purpose during tough seasons.
Helping us reframe challenges as part of growth, not proof of failure.
Connecting us to others with shared vision and values.

⊶ reflection ⊷

Hope doesn't always come easily, especially when the world feels heavy, uncertain, or overwhelming. The truth is, hope isn't something you either have or don't. It's something that can be nurtured, cultivated, and restored over time. If your roots in hope feel shallow or shaky right now, that's okay. You're not doing it wrong. You're human. That's precisely what this book is about: helping you strengthen those roots.

When have you felt most hopeful in your life?

What helped you get there?

What people, practices, or beliefs sustain your sense of hope today?

When hope feels hard to access, what tends to get in the way?

For me, hope looks like _____, sounds like _____, and feels like _____.

If you'd like to learn more about your level of hope, you can use the QR code to take the Hope Scale.

Book Companion Resources

- Hope Scale

৯ৎ three ঽ৶

Neuro-Informed - Understanding the Brain and the Nervous System

When we know *why* a student is shutting down, *how* trauma impacts regulation, or *what* builds resilience in the brain, we stop guessing. We start responding with intention instead of reaction. That clarity makes room for compassion. To make this shift, we must first understand what we're up against and what we're working with. Being *neuro-informed* equips us with the knowledge and insight to stop blaming behavior and start building capacity. It helps us see what's underneath the surface, and why so many students can't just *"try harder"* or *"make better choices"* without support.

Neuro-informed practices are grounded in a deep understanding of how the brain develops, learns, and responds to stress. They begin with recognizing how the nervous system reacts under threat, particularly in students who have experienced trauma. When the brain perceives danger, whether real or perceived, it shifts into survival mode, which impacts a student's ability to think, regulate emotions, and engage socially.

Being neuro-informed also means understanding how the brain learns best: through safety, repetition, engagement, and relational connection. Learning is not just cognitive; it is deeply neurological and emotional.

Finally, neuro-informed educators are attuned to executive function skills, such as impulse control, working memory, flexible thinking, and planning, which are essential for academic success and often delayed or disrupted by chronic stress. When we teach with the brain in mind, we stop blaming behavior and start building capacity.

All three components — understanding stress responses, the learning brain, and executive function — are essential to neuro-informed practice. We will focus specifically on the first and last: how the brain and nervous system respond to stress, and how that impacts the development of executive function skills. These areas are critical for building trauma-responsive, relationship-centered classrooms.

While the science of how the brain learns academically is foundational to instructional design, it is outside the scope of this book, which is not intended as a manual for curriculum or pedagogy. Instead, this work centers the relational, emotional, and regulatory needs of students as the starting point for meaningful engagement and healing within schools.

The Value of Understanding Neuroanatomy

This chapter examines the key regions of the brain, their functions, and how trauma, stress, and self-regulation strategies can influence our neurological and emotional experiences.[20] This understanding is foundational to effective interventions that foster resilience.

The brain's intricate structure and interconnectivity reveal how profoundly our biology influences our emotions, behaviors, and ability to adapt. Each region, from the instinctive brainstem to the reflective prefrontal cortex, plays a vital role in our survival and growth. Yet, trauma and stress can disrupt these functions, leaving us vulnerable to miscommunication within our brains and heightened reactivity to the world around us. Understanding these processes and adopting strategies to strengthen and regulate key brain areas can foster resilience, self-awareness, and greater control over our thoughts and emotions. This knowledge reminds us that while the brain is deeply complex, it is also incredibly adaptable, capable of healing, and equipped to help us thrive.

Understanding neuroanatomy is essential for teachers, not only to support their students but also for their well-being. Teaching is demanding, often requiring educators to manage stress, regulate emotions, and respond effectively to challenges. By understanding how the brain functions, particularly how stress and trauma can dysregulate key areas such as the amygdala, hippocampus, and prefrontal cortex, teachers can better recognize their emotional triggers and implement strategies to remain regulated and calm.

This self-awareness enables them to model emotional resilience and self-regulation for their students. Additionally, a deeper understanding of neuroanatomy enables teachers to identify why students struggle with focus, behavior, or learning in stressful situations. With this insight, teachers can create resilience-building classrooms emphasizing safety, connection, and strategies to help students re-engage their "thinking brain" for optimal learning. Understanding the brain empowers teachers to foster a healthier environment for themselves and their students, promoting academic success and emotional well-being.

Teaching students about the brain, its development, and how it responds to stress empowers them with knowledge that fosters self-awareness, emotional regulation, and resilience. When students understand that their brain develops over time and that specific parts have distinct roles, they can better comprehend their emotions, behaviors, and reactions.

For example, knowing that the prefrontal cortex, responsible for decision-making and impulse control, isn't fully developed until the mid-twenties helps students give themselves grace during challenging moments. Similarly, understanding how the amygdala triggers fight-flight-freeze responses in times of stress can help students recognize when they're overwhelmed and use strategies to calm down and re-engage their thinking brain.

This knowledge also destigmatizes the effects of stress and trauma, teaching students that these responses are natural and that their brain is wired to protect them. By learning about grounding techniques, mindfulness, and other effective strategies, students acquire tools to manage stress more effectively. Additionally, when students understand how learning strengthens the brain through neuroplasticity, they may feel more motivated to embrace challenges, knowing they are building resilience and growing their capabilities.

Ultimately, teaching students about their brains equips them with lifelong skills to manage stress, regulate emotions, and achieve academic and personal success.

Let's start with a review of the structure of our brains.

Basics of Neuroanatomy

Our brains are marvelously complex organs designed to keep us alive, safe, and thriving in an ever-changing world. Each part of the brain has a unique role, contributing to our ability to process emotions, solve problems, and respond to challenges. From the instinct-driven brainstem to the reflective prefrontal cortex, understanding how these parts function and interact can empower us to take control of our emotions, behaviors, and overall well-being.[21]

Amygdala – The Alarm System

Deep in the brain sits the amygdala, constantly scanning for danger. It's like a smoke alarm; when it senses a threat, it takes over and sets off the body's fight, flight, or freeze response. You might notice your heart racing or your hearing sharpening. This response is automatic and designed for survival. For people who have experienced trauma, the amygdala may become overactive, sending false alarms even during everyday situations like a raised voice or a sudden sound.

Hippocampus – The Timekeeper

Next to the amygdala is the hippocampus, the brain's memory organizer. It helps determine whether something is happening now or is just a reminder of an experience. The hippocampus asks, "Have I been here before? Was I safe?" If it isn't functioning correctly, as is common in people who've experienced trauma, it may send mixed signals, causing the amygdala to react even when the threat is no longer real. That's why a smell, sound, or image can trigger a strong emotional response without warning.

Cingulate Cortex – The Emotional Regulator

Acting as a buffer between emotion and logic, the cingulate cortex helps manage frustration, problem-solving, and emotional highs and lows. Think of it as a warm blanket around the amygdala, calming fear so the brain can think clearly. It helps you pause before reacting and recover from emotional surges, whether it's from anger, sadness, or even joy. When overloaded, it may become more difficult to regulate or make sense of your emotions.

Brainstem – The Survival Center

The brainstem is in charge of your most basic life functions: breathing, heart rate, and sleep. It kicks in immediately during danger to prepare your body for action or stillness. For those with a history of trauma, the brainstem can become hyper-alert, triggering frequent fight, flight, freeze, or even collapse. This can lead to emotional shutdown or dissociation. It's a primitive but powerful part of the brain that keeps you alive in crisis, but struggles with chronic stress.

Insula – The Awareness Hub

The insula helps you notice what's happening inside your body, such as tightness, chills, nausea, and what those sensations might mean emotionally. It helps name and interpret emotions, such as fear or excitement. When overwhelmed, the insula may either numb these sensations or magnify them, leaving a person disconnected or overly reactive. Grounding practices can help recalibrate this part of the brain.

Prefrontal Cortex – The Thinker

The prefrontal cortex is responsible for reasoning, planning, impulse control, and focus. It's like air traffic control, helping all the brain's systems work together. Under stress, this part often "goes offline," making it difficult to think clearly or stay calm. It's also the last part of the brain to fully develop, which is essential to keep in mind when working with children and teens. The good news? It can be strengthened through practice, routines, and connection.

The Thinking Brain: Top-Down Control

When a student is in a regulated state, they can access the prefrontal cortex, the most advanced and intentional part of the brain. This region governs reflection, reasoning, decision-making, and emotional control. It's what allows a student to pause, consider consequences, and engage in problem-solving. In this regulated state, often referred to as "top-down control," the brain's chemical environment is also balanced. Stress hormones like cortisol and adrenaline are in check, while oxytocin, the hormone associated with trust and connection, is present, creating an internal climate where learning can take root.

I'm sure you've learned by now that the prefrontal cortex is the last structure in the brain to develop fully. For a neurotypical biological female, full development typically occurs around age 23. In contrast, for a neurotypical biological male, it occurs between 25 and 27.[22] That means children and teens, even in the best of conditions, don't always have full access to this part of the brain. Instead, they rely more heavily on the limbic system, also known as the relationship brain —a region that is more reactive, emotional, and sensitive to stress. That's why impulsivity, emotional outbursts, and split-second decisions are developmentally normal, especially when stress is high or support is low.

Understanding this changes how we respond. I think back to times in my classroom when I said something along the lines of *"You are ten years old! You should know better!"* However, I might see that same student later walking a long way home after school without a coat, carrying their ziplock bag of Food 4 Kids weekend rations, and heartbreakingly sigh, *"She's only ten years old."* We stop asking, *"Why aren't they acting their age?"* and start asking, *"What part of their brain are they operating from right now, and what do they need from me to return to regulation?"* It's not about expecting perfect logic from a developing brain. It's about providing the connection, structure, and co-regulation that enable higher-level thinking.

The Relationship Brain: Midbrain Control

The limbic system, also known as the emotional brain, regulates the emotional and social aspects of behavior. While still dysregulated, individuals operating from this state may begin to show readiness for connection and regulation. The amygdala, responsible for processing fear and emotional responses, is overactive in trauma, leading to heightened anxiety, shame, or rage. The hippocampus, critical for processing context and differentiating past from present, is impaired, causing people to feel like they are reliving trauma. Individuals may oscillate between emotional dysregulation and moments of connection or trust-seeking. At this stage, relationships play a pivotal role in fostering regulation.

When students begin to shift out of the survival brain, they don't immediately enter a calm, regulated state; instead, they move into what we can think of as the relationship brain.[23] At this stage, the amygdala, the brain's emotional alarm system, remains overactive. Fear, shame, or anger can be easily triggered, and students may oscillate between moments of dysregulation and brief attempts to reconnect or regain trust. It's fragile ground, but also fertile. Because at this stage, relationships become the most powerful intervention we can offer.

Supportive adults play a critical role here. Students don't need us to fix everything; they need to know we're present, attuned, and emotionally responsive. When we help downregulate negative emotions, such as fear or frustration, and upregulate positive emotions, like curiosity or joy, we begin to build safety at a nervous system level.[24] This is the groundwork of co-regulation. However, missteps, such as ignoring a student's emotional cues, rushing them to calm down, or failing to follow through, can reinforce mistrust and send them right back into dysregulation. Trust is fragile, and in resilience-building classrooms, connection isn't a bonus; it's the bridge.

The Survival Brain: Bottom-Up Control

When a person is experiencing an overload of stress, the brain will typically begin to operate from the brainstem, governed by a "bottom-up" approach. In this state, a person's basic instincts take precedence over higher reasoning. Stress hormones, such as cortisol, flood the body, signaling the need for fight-or-flight or freeze-or-fawn responses.

For some people who have experienced high levels of trauma, getting stuck in this part of the brain may cause everyday events to feel dangerous due to an overactive fear response. Their responses may appear instinctual, including acting out, difficulty focusing, restlessness, or withdrawal. Even when transitioning into a safe environment, the primitive brain docs not turn off for some people who have experienced trauma. Hence, the person stays continuously in survival mode, making it challenging to think, learn, or form secure attachments.

When a child is operating from the survival brain, their responses aren't calculated; they're instinctual. You'll see it in the classroom as acting out, zoning out, restlessness, or complete shutdown. Even routine moments, such as transitions, tests, or behavior corrections, can feel threatening because the nervous system remains in a heightened state of alert. The hippocampus, the part of the brain responsible for distinguishing past from present, often misfires, making students feel like they are *back inside* the traumatic experience, not just remembering it. In this state, thinking clearly, learning new content, or forming secure relationships simply isn't possible because survival comes first.

The implications for learning and behavior are profound. A traumatized child in survival mode is not "refusing to learn." They are neurologically *unable* to access the parts of their brain needed for regulation, reasoning, and retention. When school policies rely on punishment, such as suspensions or exclusionary discipline, we risk exacerbating the very trauma we're trying to address. Even in physically safe environments, the survival brain can stay active, prolonging dysregulation unless adults intervene with presence, co-regulation, and consistent relational safety.[25]

Brain Basics

Understanding the brain's three levels and their roles in trauma and regulation is critical for trauma-responsive and resilience-building practices. This knowledge enables us to recognize where a child operates, whether in survival, relational, or executive function mode, and tailor our responses to support regulation and healing.

So, how do we determine which brain a student is operating from? Observing the body and behavior of an individual can provide clues:

Surviving Brain	Relationship Brain	Thriving Brain
Low sensory processing	Distrustful	Able to process logically
Impulsive	Clingy	Has self-awareness
Heart rate difficulties	Heightened emotions	Able to show empathy
Abnormal breathing	Replaying trauma	Normal heart and respiration rate
Irrational	Hiding	Executive Functioning intact
Difficulty processing logic	Aggression	

A child whose nervous system is regulated and is in the thinking brain will appear calm, engaged, and open to learning. A dysregulated child in the relationship brain might seem emotionally reactive, seeking connection, but struggling with trust. A child who is highly dysregulated is in survival mode.

Dysregulation takes many forms. It may manifest outwardly as fight (anger, aggression) or fawn (over-compliance, people-pleasing). It may also manifest as inward behaviors, such as flight (avoidance, running away) or freeze (shutting down, withdrawal). Each response signals an unmet need, not a deliberate choice to be disruptive. Recognizing these cues enables us to tailor our interventions, meeting children where they are to guide them toward self-regulation.

Physical signs of dysregulation include:

Increased respiratory rate	Sensitivity to sound	Rapid speech
Pupil dilation	High started reflex	Chronic stomachache
Tension in the body	Crying	Chronic headache
Sweating	Yelling	Shaking
Withdrawn	Physical Aggression	Avoidance
Delay in responding	Hiding	Defiance

How Stress Is Processed Differently

Stress does not show up in the same way for everyone, and there are notable biological differences in how neurotypical males and females process stress. These differences are general patterns, not absolutes, but they can help us understand what we see in classrooms.[26]

Neurotypical males tend to process stress more visually and spatially. When aroused by stress, their brain activity often shifts toward the visual cortex, which can heighten sensitivity to movement, threat cues, or changes in the environment. A slammed book or a sudden gesture may be enough to keep the stress response activated. Neurotypical females, on the other hand, often process stress with more integration across visual and verbal centers, which can make them more attuned to facial expressions, tone of voice, and relational signals during stress.[27]

Neurotypical males typically experience a surge of adrenaline and cortisol that primes the body for prolonged fight-or-flight. Their heart rate and blood pressure may remain elevated for a longer period, and they may require more physical activity or time to metabolize stress hormones before regulation can return. Neurotypical females often experience an initial spike but metabolize stress hormones more quickly, which is why they can appear to calm faster.[28] Their bodies may also lean toward a "tend and befriend" response, seeking connection or conversation as a form of stress relief. [29]

For neurotypical males, stress can temporarily suppress emotional expression. They may look withdrawn, shut down, or mask feelings behind anger or avoidance. Neurotypical females, in contrast, may show more visible emotional responses—crying, verbalizing frustration, or reaching out for support—because their stress response is more relationally oriented.[30]

These biological differences don't determine destiny, but they do shape patterns. In schools, this means that a male student's silence or simmering anger may not necessarily indicate he is "fine," and a female student's tears may not necessarily mean she is "overreacting." Both are experiencing stress in ways consistent with how their nervous systems are wired. The role of the adult is not to judge the reaction, but to recognize the pattern and provide regulation strategies that match the need.

Research indicates that there are biological differences in the time it takes a neurotypical male and female nervous system to recover after a crisis. On average, a neurotypical biological male requires more time to return to baseline once dysregulated—sometimes up to 90 minutes—because his stress response is more easily re-triggered and tends to linger in the body. A neurotypical biological female, in contrast, typically moves through the stress cycle more quickly, averaging around 20 minutes, although this can vary. These differences are not about strength or weakness; they are rooted in how the brain and nervous system process and metabolize stress hormones.[31] For educators, the key takeaway is that regulation cannot be rushed, and support strategies may need to be paced differently depending on the student in front of you.

The Window of Tolerance

The variability across the trauma continuum is tied to the concept of the Window of Tolerance. A term introduced by Dr. Dan Siegel, this concept is widely used in trauma-responsive work to explain the differences in individuals' abilities to handle stress without becoming dysregulated.[32]

A person operating from their thriving brain generally has a larger window of tolerance, allowing them to manage higher stress levels without slipping into hyperarousal (acting out) or hypoarousal (shutting down). On the other hand, someone functioning from their survival brain has a much narrower window of tolerance and may become dysregulated much more easily.

Understanding the Window of Tolerance is essential in resilience-building education and caregiving, as it helps create environments and interventions that expand students' capacity to regulate their emotions and engage meaningfully with their environment.

"The width of the window of tolerance within a given individual may vary, depending upon the state of mind at a given time, the particular emotional valence, and the social context in which the emotion is being generated...Within the boundaries of the window, the mind continues to function well. Outside the boundaries, function becomes impaired."

-Dr. Dan Siegel[33]

When children are outside their Window of Tolerance, they may enter the Escalation Cycle—a sequence of emotional and behavioral stages that unfold when stress or trauma overwhelms their ability to self-regulate. Understanding the stages of this cycle is essential in supporting children and preventing further dysregulation. Here's a walkthrough of the stages of the Escalation Cycle.[34]

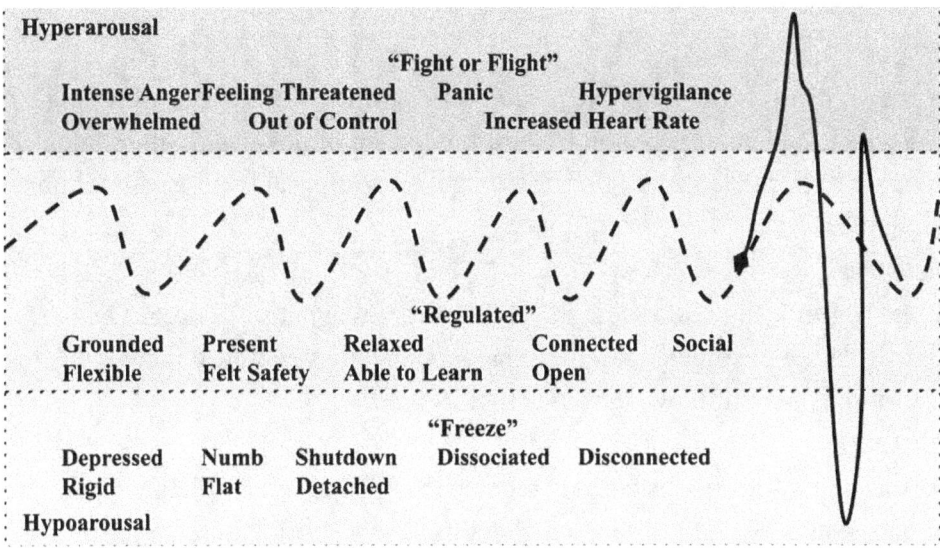

The Escalation Cycle

Regulated

Regulated is the baseline state where stress levels are low or tolerable, and the individual feels safe, supported, and regulated. Needs are met, and the brain operates in its optimal, thriving mode. This state does not just mean calm or compliant. It is more accurately described as being in a state where a person's energy matches the task. For example, a child laughing loudly and doing cartwheels in class is not regulated to participate in math class, but the same behavior is appropriately regulated for recess.

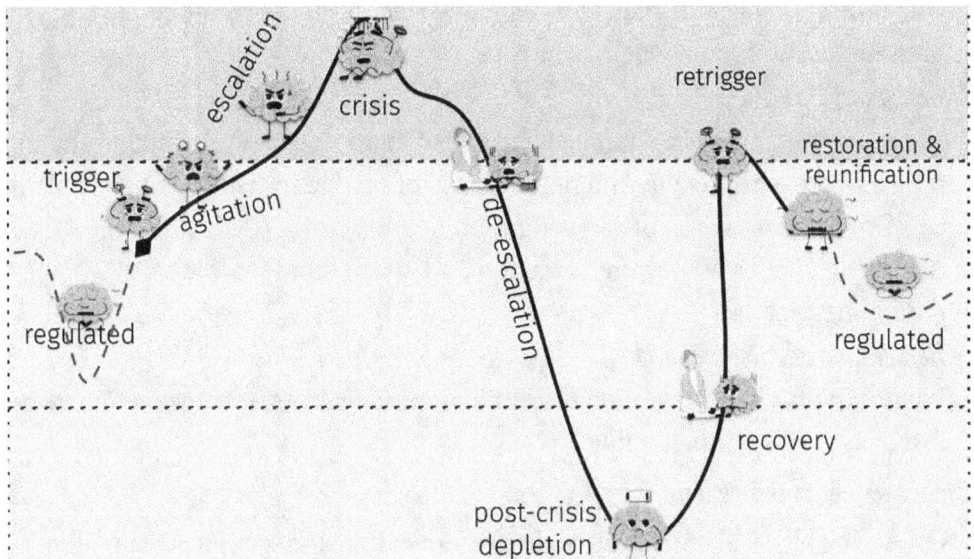

Trigger

A trigger disrupts the child's regulated state, putting them at risk of dysregulation. Triggers can include repeated frustrations, a lack of positive reinforcement, sensory overload (e.g., noise or bright lights), or internal issues such as hunger or fatigue.

Agitation

If the trigger is not addressed, the child becomes agitated, and signs of dysregulation become apparent. Behaviors include whining, complaining, resisting transitions, or withdrawing from activities.

Escalation

At this point, the child is entirely outside their Window of Tolerance, and the situation may escalate to severe behaviors such as hitting, screaming, or aggression.

Crisis

Crisis is the peak of escalation, where behaviors are most intense and dysregulation is at its highest. The child operates entirely from their survival brain.

Deceleration

After the crisis, the child's behavior begins to subside. They may appear confused, withdrawn, or emotionally overwhelmed.

Post-Crisis Depletion

At this stage, the child is emotionally and physically drained. They need time to recover and re-establish a routine.

Recovery

Once the child has returned to a regulated state, it's time to reflect, teach, and prepare for future challenges.

Retrigger

There is a possibility of slipping back into hyperarousal as the child prepares to return to the learning environment. This is often due to feelings of guilt, shame, and fear of how the restoration and reunification process will unfold.
Acknowledge this as a normal reaction and take a moment to do a breathing or grounding exercise.

Restoration and Reunification

Finally, focus on reintegrating the child into the learning environment and fostering a sense of belonging.

Using Brain Awareness to Respond

Observing physical and emotional cues, educators and caregivers can identify which part of the brain an individual is operating from. Then we can tailor our responses to help restore regulation and foster healing.

Yes, our brains can heal. The discovery of neuroplasticity in the 1960s changed the long-held belief that the brain was fixed after early adulthood. We now know that the brain continuously forms and strengthens neural pathways in response to experience. Trauma strengthens the circuits of fear, hypervigilance, and emotional reactivity.[35]

However, repeated, relational, positive experiences, especially in the presence of safety and consistency, can literally build new pathways for self-regulation, connection, and resilience. Every time we model calm in the face of chaos and offer connection instead of control, we're not just changing behavior; we're helping to rewire the brain. That's the promise of resilience-building education: *not just reacting to dysregulation, but actively building the neural foundation for healing and growth.*

Visit the book companion site for additional materials related to this chapter.

Book Companion Resources

- Printable Escalation Cycle
- Resources for teaching students about neuroanatomy

☙ reflection ❧

Being neuro-informed means moving beyond reacting to behavior and instead recognizing the brain's signals for stress, survival, and connection. When we understand how trauma impacts regulation and executive function, we gain the clarity to respond with compassion rather than blame. This knowledge empowers us to create classrooms where safety, connection, and co-regulation become the foundation for healing and learning.

How does understanding the brain's stress responses shift the way you view student behavior in your classroom?

Which part of the brain (survival, relationship, or thinking) do you see most often in your students, and how do you typically respond?

What strategies help you stay regulated so you can model calm for your students when their nervous systems are overwhelmed?

When I think about being a neuro-informed educator, I realize I need to give more attention to _____ so that I can better support my students' regulation and resilience.

❧ four ❧
Culturally-Responsive Teaching

Seeing Culture as Capacity, Not Deficit

If we are to discuss relationships, trauma, and learning, we must also address culture. Every child who walks into our schools is shaped by culture. So is every teacher. The question isn't whether culture is present. It's whether we're honoring it or ignoring it.

Culturally responsive teaching isn't about food fairs or flag days. It's not a set of holidays to celebrate or words to pronounce correctly. It's not about having "diverse books" on the shelf and never actually using them. As Zaretta Hammond writes in *Culturally Responsive Teaching and the Brain*, culturally responsive teaching is

"An educator's ability to recognize students' cultural displays of learning and meaning making and respond positively and constructively with teaching moves that use cultural knowledge as a scaffold to connect what the students know to new concepts and content in order to promote effective information processing. All the while, the educator understands the importance of being in relationship and having a social-emotional connection to the student in order to create a safe space for learning."[36]

Culture Is How We Learn

Culture is the software of the brain. It shapes how we process information, communicate, and interpret trust and authority. To ignore culture is to disconnect from the most powerful tool we have to reach students: their identity. Students' prior knowledge, schema, values, and even survival strategies are all culturally shaped. Culturally responsive teaching doesn't erase those. It starts there.

Lisa Delpit, in *"Other People's Children,"* challenges us to recognize how dominant-culture norms often remain unnamed in school systems but are nonetheless treated as the gold standard. Students who don't speak, act, or learn like the dominant group are often seen as different. They're seen as deficient. Delpit says,

"We must learn to be humble enough to listen and brave enough to confront our assumptions."[37]

This work begins by shifting our lens from *"what's wrong with this student?"* to *"what strengths is this student bringing that I haven't learned to recognize yet?"*

It's Not Just About Kindness. It's About Power.

Culturally responsive educators don't just build relationships. They build agency. They know that trust isn't earned through charisma; it's earned by seeing, valuing, and empowering students. It's about breaking the cycle of compliance and passivity by providing students with tools to think critically, question, and lead. Hammond calls this "the warm demander": the teacher who builds deep, authentic relationships *and* holds students to high expectations because they believe in their brilliance.[38] Culturally responsive teaching is not soft. It's rigorous. It's demanding. It's equity in action.

When Bias Hides in Plain Sight

Let's name it: bias lives in all of us. It's not a flaw. It's a function of the brain. Our nervous system categorizes what we've seen, experienced, and internalized to help us navigate the world. That doesn't make us bad people, but it does make us responsible. When our biases, especially the ones we don't even realize we hold, start shaping how we interpret, talk about, and interact with others, that bias becomes a barrier. Often, it shows up in the form of microaggressions.

Microaggressions are the subtle slights, comments, or behaviors, intentional or not, that send a message: You don't fully belong here. You're not quite right. You're not safe. Dr. Derald Wing Sue defines microaggressions as:

"everyday verbal, nonverbal, and environmental slights, snubs, or insults, whether intentional or unintentional, which communicate hostile, derogatory, or negative messages to target persons based solely upon their marginalized group membership."[39]

That might sound academic—but here's what it sounds like in a school:
"You're really articulate for a kid from that neighborhood."
"I don't see color; I treat everyone the same."
Assuming a child needs help with English based solely on how they look.
Praising one student's "leadership,"
        while calling another "aggressive" for the same behavior.

Microaggressions can be based on race, gender, language, ability, religion, sexual orientation, or any aspect of identity that's been pushed to the margins. They hurt, especially because they often come from people in power who *mean well.* There are different kinds. Microassaults are the obvious ones: slurs, derogatory comments, and intentional exclusion. Microinsults are subtler; they may come in the form of backhanded compliments, assumptions, and dismissive tones. Microinvalidations cut deep. They negate someone's lived experience, feelings, or identity. Saying things like *"That's not racism"* or *"You're being too sensitive"* lands hard, especially when it's chronic.

Here's the hard truth: *anyone* can commit a microaggression, even those of us who've also been on the receiving end. It's not just about power; it's about unexamined habits, unchecked assumptions, and unspoken messages.

Culturally Responsive and Trauma-Informed: Two Sides of the Same Coin

Bias doesn't just affect equity. It affects regulation. It affects how safe a child feels, and how safe *we* feel in response to them. Being trauma-responsive means recognizing that stress impacts behavior. Being culturally responsive means acknowledging that identity is also a crucial aspect of one's being. We can't have one without the other. We can't call ourselves trauma-informed if our systems consistently send Black and Brown students to the office more often than their white peers for the same behavior.

We can't call ourselves student-centered if our classroom visuals and curriculum ignore the families we serve. We can't claim empathy while using deficit language, such as *"those parents," "that group," "these kids,"* in staff meetings. We absolutely can't call it *"discipline"* when it's actually discomfort with difference.

From Traditional to Transformational Culture

In a traditional school culture, success is competitive. Kids win alone. Families participate on our terms. Differences are tolerated at best, while at worst, they are ignored. Equity is often treated as a bonus, rather than a baseline. In a culturally responsive school, success isn't a solo act. It's shared. When one student rises, we all rise. There's no hoarding of praise, opportunity, or second chances, because the goal isn't just individual achievement, it's collective thriving. Families aren't viewed as problems to manage. They're seen as partners, holders of wisdom, insight, and love. The mindset shifts from *"How do we deal with them?"* to *"How do we work with them?"*

Before we change systems, we have to understand where we're operating within them. The Cultural Competence Continuum, outlined below, offers us that roadmap.[40] This isn't a ladder you climb to feel better about yourself. It's a mirror you hold up to examine how your beliefs, assumptions, and actions affect the children and families you serve. Where we land on this continuum, individually and collectively, shapes the emotional climate of our classrooms and the moral credibility of our schools.

Cultural Destructiveness

"We are all that is important."

At this stage, cultural differences are not only rejected, they're attacked. This can look like policies that punish students for speaking their home language. It can sound like slurs, jokes, or offhand comments that justify harm against "other" students. It thrives in silence. It's rare in schools, or at least we hope it is, but its residue can still show up in who gets access, who gets removed, and who gets blamed.

Cultural Incapacity

"We take care of our own."

You may not be explicitly harmful here, but you're still centering your own comfort and culture. You help "your" kids and tolerate "the others." You may apply resources and grace unevenly without realizing it. Expectations drop, referrals rise, and students from marginalized backgrounds feel it, even if they never say it out loud.

Cultural Denial / Indifference

"I don't see color."

This is where many well-meaning educators get stuck. You believe in fairness, but confuse it with sameness. You pride yourself on treating all students the same, without recognizing that *same* isn't *equitable*. You might say things like, "All kids have a chance here," or "We just focus on character, not culture." Here's the problem: When we ignore identity, we ignore reality. Kids don't get to opt out of their lived experiences just because we don't know how to talk about them.

Cultural Pre-Competence

"We're trying."

Here, you've started to realize that your approach isn't working for every student. You've read the books. You've been to the training. You know the language of equity, but you haven't yet embedded it into your practice. You're moving, but inconsistently. You care deeply, but systems remain unchanged. The commitment is real. The action is still forming. This is a vital stage—but we can't stay here. Students can't wait for us to get brave.

Cultural Competence

"We act on what we believe."

At this stage, awareness becomes action. You recognize your cultural lens and how it shapes your teaching, interpreting, disciplining, and connecting. You actively seek input from students and their families. You analyze your data, then take action based on it. You stop asking kids to adapt to school and instead adapt school to serve *them better*. You stop mistaking compliance for success. You start seeing equity as rigor.

Cultural Proficiency

"We are all connected."

This is not a destination, it's a daily practice—a way of being. You hold culture in high esteem. You co-create systems that respond to, reflect, and celebrate difference. You no longer ask, "How can we fix them?" but instead, "How can we change us?" You operate from a place of both humility and power. You know that inclusion doesn't mean everyone gets to come to the table; it means everyone helped build it.

Every student, *every* student, can name at least one adult in the building who sees their potential and believes in them, even on the days they can't see it themselves. Teachers aren't just skilled in differentiating lessons. They know how to differentiate *connection*. They learn each student's rhythms, regulation needs, communication style, and cultural context. They adjust, not because it's convenient, but because it's necessary.

And diversity? It's not an occasional celebration. It's not a checkbox. It's the norm. It's woven into the fabric of the school. It's expected, honored, and protected.

❧ reflection ❧

Let's be honest. Most of us move around this continuum depending on the day, the student, or the situation, but we all have a home base—where we return when we're stressed, defensive, or tired.

This reflection isn't about shame. It's about clarity.

When was the last time you assumed a student's behavior meant disrespect?

Whose voices are missing from your curriculum? Your PLC? Your support plans?

Do you see culture as a problem to be managed—or a resource to be honored?

When you feel defensive, whose experience are you centering—yours, or the student's?

When I shift my lens to see culture as capacity instead of deficit, I begin to recognize
_____ as a strength that can deepen learning and connection in my classroom.

❧ part one reflection ❧
Foundations for a Rooted Practice

You've just explored the foundation of resilience-building education—diving into the science of stress, the power of resilience, the architecture of the brain, and the role of historical and systemic harm.

Before we turn inward in Part Two, take a moment to reflect on how these foundational ideas are beginning to shift your perspective and language.

Use the Part One ROOTED IN HOPE Reflection found in Part Five on page 263 or by scanning the QR code below to organize your thinking and start planting seeds of change in your practice.

katherindaryl.org/book-companion

Visit the book companion site for additional materials related to this chapter.

Book Companion Resources

- **Part One Reflection**

✺ part two ✺
The Inner Work of a Resilient Educator

Just like a thriving garden depends on the condition of its soil, the health of a classroom begins with the inner life of the educator.

Each chapter in this section will invite you to turn inward, toward your own story, your identity as an educator, and the beliefs you bring into the room with you every day. You'll be asked to reflect, to wrestle, and to reconnect with the parts of yourself that might've been buried under stress, expectations, or survival mode.

Before we focus on our students, we must start here, with *you*. Your voice, your hope, and your heart are essential to creating a learning environment where healing and growth are both possible and encouraged.

This part of the book is your invitation to return to yourself. This part of the book differs from the typical professional development book. You might consider it a blend of professional learning and therapy, akin to John Hattie meeting Brené Brown.

We will explore your beliefs, values, and experiences, and how they influence your life as an educator. As we begin this part, let me make you a few promises and a disclaimer.

I promise what you will find on these pages will be different from any other professional learning you've had - well, unless you've worked with me in person, in which case you already know what you're getting into.

I anticipate that there may be times when you feel like throwing the book across the room, but effective learning should prompt reflection that challenges our mindsets and beliefs —a process that can be complex.

Yet, I know you'll pick it back up because you need something different this time, something that genuinely works.

A necessary disclaimer: this is not a substitute for therapy. While I am a Licensed Master Social Worker (LMSW), I am not your therapist. If you find that you need professional support, I strongly encourage you to seek a licensed therapist who can provide the personalized care you deserve.

❧ five ❧
Remember Your Why

WAIT! Don't put the book down.

I know that statement can be triggering to those of us who have been in education for a while. It's synonymous with *"Teachers are in it for the outcome, not the income"* and *"Do what's best for kids,"* which feels more like *"this is going to cause you more work and burnout."* Trust me - this isn't that.

Yes, we will talk about the importance of relationships. Yes, I would like you to reflect on why you chose to become a teacher, but I will not tell you that building a connection with that kid in your class will stop him from throwing chairs at you, because we both know it's not that easy. At the same time, reconnecting with what initially drew you to education can help you navigate the tough days.

In this chapter, we will revisit your purpose, connecting with your core values, and aligning your past experiences with your aspirations. To begin, I invite you to take some time for reflection, considering your educational journey and career to date.

Establishing Your Why[41]

Think back to your own PK-12 experience. Reflect on a memory from school that brings you joy. What do you remember feeling? What comes up for you when you recall the memory today?

How about a memory from your PK-12 experience that was painful or stressful? What do you remember feeling, and why do you think that memory has stuck with you all these years?

As a child, did you have an adult at school who was "your person?" Someone you trusted, someone who was committed to helping you grow, and that made you excited about your future? Who was this person? What did they do to show they cared? What message did you get about yourself from this person?

Think about your career so far as a teacher and reflect on the story of a student that you consider to be one of your success stories.

Now, who is a student that you wish you could go back in time for? What do you know now that you wish you had known then? What did you need that you didn't have at the time?

What hopes do you have for your future students as you become Rooted in Hope?

The memories you carry from your own PK–12 experience, both joyful and painful, shaped the lens through which you view education today. The trusted adults who helped you feel seen, as well as the moments when that didn't happen, have left an imprint that likely informs how you show up for your students. As you think about the students you've taught, the ones you've celebrated, and the ones who still weigh heavily on your heart, hold space for what those stories reveal about your values, your growth, and your hopes for the future.

Let these reflections guide you in writing your mission statement. This isn't about getting the "right" words; it's about honoring your *why*. Why do you teach? Why do you care? Why this work matters enough to keep showing up, even when it's hard.

Use the prompt below to begin crafting your own *Rooted in Hope* mission statement. This will serve as a compass throughout the rest of this book and your journey.

Here's mine...

I am becoming a Rooted in Hope educator because I know that healing doesn't happen in isolation, and transformation isn't a checklist to be completed. It's a daily, intentional practice rooted in connection, compassion, and curiosity. I've lived the cost of disconnection, and I've witnessed the power of safe, consistent relationships to help people reconnect with themselves.

The people I show up for used to be the students who carried invisible weights, those without the language for their pain but deserving of spaces that made them feel seen, known, and safe. While those students will always matter deeply to me, I now find myself showing up for the educators, the ones who are exhausted, who feel alone in systems that weren't built for healing, and who carry their own untold stories while holding space for everyone else.

I want to be the kind of educator who reminds others that they don't have to choose between caring for others and caring for themselves. I want to model what it looks like to hold pain and possibility at the same time, to lead with empathy, act with intention, and make space for humanity in our schools and systems. I want to help others reconnect with their "why," and build lives and classrooms that are rooted in purpose, not just performance.

My mission is to create trauma-informed, neuro-aligned, and equity-rooted frameworks that empower not just students, but the adults who serve them. Through Rooted in Hope, I want to help educators remember that they are not powerless. That change is possible. That hope is not abstract; it's a science, a skill, and a lifeline we can learn, model, and pass on.

❧ reflection ❧

I am becoming a Rooted in Hope educator because...

The students I show up for are...

I want to be the kind of teacher who...

My mission is to...

❧ six ❧
The Pendulum Swing

If you've been in education for more than a minute, you've likely seen it: the pendulum swing.

> *Whole language or Phonics.*
> *Zero Tolerance or Restorative Justice.*
> *Inclusion or Pull-out.*
> *Letter Grades or Standards-Based Reporting.*

One year, we're all-in on social-emotional learning; the next, it's back to "rigor."

Just when you've finally mastered the latest acronym, it gets replaced. For many teachers, especially those who've weathered more than a few curriculum adoptions, leadership turnovers, or initiative rollouts, the word "change" doesn't inspire hope; it sparks exhaustion. We call it pendulum fatigue, the emotional whiplash that occurs when education swings reactively instead of responding intentionally.

You Are Not Imagining It

If you feel like the ground is constantly shifting beneath your feet, you're not wrong. Teachers are expected to be the anchors in their classrooms, even as the system around them changes direction with each new mandate, budget crisis, or political spotlight. The truth is, some swings are necessary. Growth requires movement. However, when that movement lacks consistency, clarity, or care for the people implementing it, it becomes more than disorienting; it becomes demoralizing.

The Emotional Toll

Pendulum fatigue doesn't just live in our calendars and staff meetings; it lives in our nervous systems. It shows up in the deep sigh when someone mentions "one more thing." In the tension that builds when you're asked to abandon something you've poured yourself into. In the quiet disconnection that creeps in when top-down changes fail to account for the lived realities of your classroom.

If you've found yourself feeling skeptical, withdrawn, or even cynical, it's likely not because you've stopped caring, but because you've cared deeply, over and over again, often without the support, consistency, or recognition needed to sustain that care. That exhaustion is not a character flaw. It's a signal.

The Rooted in Hope Response

In a system that swings like a pendulum—new initiatives, shifting mandates, the next big thing—it's easy to lose your footing. So how do we stay grounded? The *Rooted in Hope* framework offers us an anchor. It invites us to hold tight to what truly matters: purpose, trust, and intentionality so that we can stay centered through the chaos of change.

Purpose gives us clarity. When we know why we do what we do, we're better equipped to filter out the noise and stay focused on what matters most. Trust gives us stability. When we trust ourselves, our students, and each other, we build relationships that remain steady, even when the systems around us don't.

Intentionality gives us power. It keeps us from being swept up in a sense of urgency. It reminds us to pause, reflect, and respond with wisdom rather than react out of fatigue. We may not be able to stop the swing, but we *can* choose how we plant our feet. We can choose to root ourselves in what's real, what's right, and what's relational—and we can choose to care for ourselves and each other while we do it.

Connection is Not a Swing

Responding to students in need of connection isn't something that should swing with policy, fads, or political pressure. The trauma-informed movement isn't about swinging from one extreme to the other. The truth is, we've been conditioned to live on the edges, overcorrecting instead of anchoring. Real trauma-responsive practices live in the middle.. They hold boundaries and care. Expectations and empathy. Structure and softness.

We don't build connected classrooms by chasing the next new thing or waiting for the pendulum to land perfectly. We build them by becoming steady. Rooted. Intentional. Discernment tells us when to stretch and when to stay grounded. Openness allows us to see our students and ourselves clearly. Hope reminds us why we started. Purpose keeps us from losing our way.

So if you're tired of the extremes, you're not alone. Let's not confuse fatigue with failure. Being in the middle of the swing might feel unfamiliar, but it's precisely where the real work happens, not swinging wildly and not standing frozen. Finding your rhythm, balanced, neuro-informed, and grounded in relationship. Let's take a breath, because while I'm telling you, we aren't going to swing, that doesn't mean we will stand still.

Rooted in Hope... Growing with Science

When it comes to understanding the brain, especially how it learns, heals, and grows, we are still in the early chapters of a very long book. If brain research were a novel, we've only just finished the prologue.

Think about dyslexia: we've had strong, peer-reviewed science on how to identify and support dyslexic learners since the 1980s.[42] Yet it took decades, and tireless advocacy by parents, researchers, and brave educators, before most schools even began to recognize the word "dyslexia," let alone offer structured, evidence-based interventions. In many places, we're still catching up.

Now imagine applying that same snail's pace to the vast, complex science of the brain, its development, its plasticity, its response to trauma, and its capacity for resilience. We are just beginning to uncover how profoundly experiences shape neural wiring, and even further from seeing that understanding reflected in the average classroom.

So while we know more now than ever before, we are still in the pioneering days. Just as with dyslexia, this knowledge won't translate into better systems unless we advocate, educate, and persist.

The good news? We've learned from the dyslexia journey. We know that research doesn't implement itself; people do—and you, as an educator, are part of the generation helping bridge the gap between what we know and what we do.

The bad news? Things will keep changing. As brain science evolves, so will our understanding of what students need. That means we can't get too comfortable; we have to stay rooted, but not rigid. We must continually return to the *Rooted in Hope* framework, embracing openness to new ideas, engagement in the process, a neuro-informed lens, discernment to identify what suits our learners, trust in our relationships, intentionality in our practice, and empowerment for both students and ourselves.

✒ reflection ✒

Pendulum fatigue is real, and it doesn't mean teachers have failed—it means they've cared deeply through countless shifts and changes. The Rooted in Hope framework reminds us that even when systems swing, we can stay anchored in purpose, trust, and intentionality. True resilience isn't found at the edges of the pendulum but in the steady, relational center where connection and learning take root.

Take a moment to reflect on your career:

What pendulum swings have you taught through?

Which ones felt energizing? Which felt disheartening?

What stayed the same for you, even as the system shifted?

One thing I've learned from the swings in education is...

◄§ seven ≈►
Reimagining the Purpose of Education

I began my teaching career in a kindergarten classroom with a calendar on the wall, tiny chairs, and a closet full of thematic unit boxes. There were ten in total, one for each month of the school year. In August, we did "Back to School." September was apples. October? Pumpkins. November focused on Thanksgiving, December on holidays, January was winter, February brought friendship, March meant leprechauns, April was dinosaurs, and May—well, May was survival. Honestly, it worked.

There was space to build relationships, follow the children's interests, and introduce content in meaningful ways. There were books, songs, shared stories, and genuine joy. That was before the full weight of No Child Left Behind took hold, before the pendulum swung hard toward standardization, and before kindergarten became the new first grade.

Over the years, I watched education shift. The joy was slowly replaced with pacing guides. Play was replaced with testing. The closet of thematic units sat untouched. While academic rigor increased, our students' resilience appeared to decline. They came to us dysregulated, exhausted, and disconnected. As for educators, many of us were equally overwhelmed and left with fewer tools, tighter timelines, and less flexibility to meet them where they were.

The Brain-Aligned Success Journey

We are in an education crisis, not just in achievement scores, but in alignment. The practices embedded in most schools are no longer in sync with what research tells us about how humans learn, how the brain works, how the nervous system responds to stress, and how behavior reflects unmet needs. We're using outdated tools for a world that has fundamentally changed. The system we inherited was designed for efficiency and obedience, not for connection, creativity, or critical thinking. It's failing both our students and ourselves.

Let's examine what education was *intended* to do and what it *must* become. My friend and colleague James Moffett frames the shift this way: in the old model, education moved in predictable stages, early childhood focused on foundational literacy, numeracy, and social interaction; primary education emphasized academic skill-building, rule-following, and peer dynamics; secondary education aimed for subject mastery, identity formation, and responsibility; and post-secondary education was about specialization, independence, and career readiness.[43]

However, in a brain-aligned success journey, the roles shift, not just for students, but for the adults guiding them. The educator becomes a co-regulator, sharing their calm and nervous system with students in moments of stress. Serving as a guide, educators help students understand how their brains influence learning, behavior, and emotion. They are boundary-setters, building the kind of structure that wires the brain for self-control and responsibility. Their actions model ethical influence, helping students internalize important values and character traits. Acting as meaning-makers, educators connect content to real-world purpose and relevance.

In turn, students are no longer passive recipients; they become purpose-driven leaders, open and curious learners, resilient and accountable decision-makers, and thoughtful collaborators, communicators, and critical thinkers. This is what it means to align our educational goals with the science of the developing brain and the humanity of the learner.

Yes, academics still matter; literacy and numeracy are essential, but the curriculum is no longer the destination - it's the vehicle. The destination is a connected, creative, communicative, and curious young adult who understands themselves, their world, and how to make a difference in it. A brain-based understanding becomes the GPS, constantly adjusting course based on real-time feedback related to behavior, stress levels, relational cues, and emotional signals.

What Do You Believe Is the Purpose of Education?

In this chart, you'll reflect on eight core domains that shape every classroom: Academics, Social-Emotional Learning (SEL), Relationships, the Ultimate Goal of Education, Discipline, the Student Role, the Teacher Role, and Equity & Inclusion. Each row presents a continuum of beliefs, ranging from more traditional to more progressive perspectives. Your responses reveal not only your teaching style but also the assumptions and priorities you bring into your classroom.

As you consider each domain, pause to notice your reactions:
Which statements feel most natural or affirming?
Which spark discomfort or resistance?
Where do your current practices align with your circled beliefs?
Where do they conflict?

Remember, this is not about right or wrong answers—it's about uncovering the lens through which you view teaching and learning. That lens shapes how you respond to behavior, structure your lessons, interpret student needs, and build relationships.

Finally, keep in mind that beliefs are not fixed. A trauma-responsive, neuro-informed educator continually revisits these domains, filtering new initiatives, research, and experiences through them. This process ensures that what you believe, what you practice, and what students experience are in alignment—grounded in safety, dignity, and belonging.

Directions: Circle the belief in each row that most reflects your perspective.

Domain	Traditional View	Moderate View	Progressive View
Academics	School is for mastering core content and producing measurable academic outcomes.	School should balance academic rigor with real-world relevance and skill development.	School should nurture curiosity, critical thinking, and lifelong learning through flexible, student-led exploration.
Social - Emotional Learning (SEL)	Social-emotional development is the family's job; school should focus on academics.	SEL is important when it supports learning and behavior.	SEL is foundational—students must feel safe, seen, and regulated before they can learn.
Relationships	Respect is earned and maintained through rules and authority.	Positive relationships help create a supportive learning environment.	Relationships are the heart of learning—connection drives everything.
Ultimate Goal of Education	To prepare students for college and careers by ensuring they meet academic standards.	To develop well-rounded individuals ready for the demands of adulthood.	Empower students to know themselves, contribute to the community, and challenge injustice.
Discipline	Rules are rules. Students must follow them to succeed in life.	Expectations should be clear and consistent, but flexible when needed.	Behavior is communication. Discipline is an opportunity for healing and growth.
Student Role	Students are expected to listen, follow directions, and work hard.	Students should be active participants in their learning, guided within a structured framework.	Students are co-creators of knowledge, bringing valuable lived experiences.
Teacher Role	The teacher is the authority who provides knowledge and maintains order.	The teacher is a guide and facilitator of learning.	The teacher is a partner in growth, learning with and from students.
Equity & Inclusion	All students have the same opportunity. It's up to them to succeed.	Equity and inclusion mean providing extra support where it's needed.	We must actively dismantle barriers and design schools for those most marginalized.

A Neuro-Informed, Resilience-Building School

When we think about a resilience-building, neuro-informed school, we are really talking about a system designed to honor both the science of the brain and the lived realities of students. This means recognizing that learning doesn't happen in isolation from regulation, relationships, or culture. It means understanding that when students are dysregulated, their survival brain is in control—and no amount of academic pressure will move them into their thinking brain without first restoring safety and connection. In this way, literacy, numeracy, and content knowledge remain vital, but they are integrated with practices that expand a student's window of tolerance, strengthen executive function, and nurture resilience.

The chart you just explored offers a mirror for this shift. Each row—whether it's about discipline, relationships, or the role of the teacher—presents a spectrum from traditional to transformational. A trauma-responsive, neuro-informed lens doesn't ask us to simply pick the most "progressive" answer. Instead, it helps us discern where we are, where our students need us to be, and how to align our daily practice with the realities of the developing brain. For example, when we see behavior as communication rather than defiance, we begin to respond with regulation strategies instead of punishment. When we view relationships as central rather than peripheral, we start to see co-regulation as an instructional practice, not just a classroom management tool.

This is where adaptability becomes essential. Teachers who have weathered pendulum swings know the fatigue of constant change. However, neuro-informed practice isn't just another initiative; it's a foundational principle that helps us navigate change with clarity. Trends may come and go, but the science of the brain remains a steady guide. When educators anchor themselves in what we know about regulation, connection, and resilience, they gain the confidence to filter new mandates through a stable framework. The question is no longer,

"How do I survive this new swing?"

but,

"How does this fit with what I know about how students learn and thrive?"

In a resilience-building school, flexibility and consistency live side by side. Teachers adapt their methods without losing their center. They respond to students' nervous systems with intentionality, holding boundaries while honoring dignity. As they model this balance, students begin to internalize it too—learning not only how to master content but also how to navigate stress, build trust, and remain open to growth even in uncertain times. That is the true transformation: not replacing one pendulum swing with another, but rooting education in science, compassion, and purpose so that both teachers and students can flourish.

Closing Thoughts

If understanding the brain helps us respond to individual students with more compassion, then examining our beliefs helps us respond to entire school systems with more intention. The chart you just explored isn't about labeling your answers as right or wrong. It's about uncovering the *assumptions* we've inherited and questioning whether they still serve the students in front of us.

Every belief you hold about discipline, student voice, relationships, and the purpose of education is part of the soil from which your daily practice grows. When those beliefs are rooted in safety, dignity, and a sense of belonging, your classroom becomes something more than just a learning environment. It becomes a healing one.

That's what it means to become a resilience builder. A trauma-aware school understands the science. A trauma-responsive school applies it. It doesn't just know that behavior is communication; it structures time, space, expectations, and relationships around that truth. It doesn't just acknowledge the impact of adversity; it actively works to interrupt it. As we move into the next chapter, keep these reflections close at hand. The transformation of systems begins with the transformation of the people inside them.

❧ reflection ❧

Reimagining the purpose of education means moving beyond content delivery to cultivating whole, resilient, and compassionate humans. When we align our practices with the brain and the nervous system, we shift from compliance to connection, from control to curiosity. True transformation begins when we question our inherited beliefs, root our classrooms in dignity and belonging, and design learning that equips students to thrive with purpose.

Which of your responses surprised you?

Which ones felt hard to choose?

How do your beliefs shape your classroom, discipline practices, and relationships?

How do your values align (or not) with the dominant culture in your school?

❧ eight ❧
Your Professional Quality of Life

In resilience-building education, we often talk about supporting students through stress, adversity, and burnout. Yet we don't always pause to ask: *How are the adults doing?* That's where the Professional Quality of Life Scale, or ProQOL, comes in. The ProQOL is a free, evidence-based self-assessment tool designed to help helping professionals—including educators—measure the impact of their work on their personal well-being.

The ProQOL tool didn't just appear out of nowhere. It's rooted in the research of Dr. Beth Hudnall Stamm, a leading scholar in the fields of compassion fatigue, secondary traumatic stress, and the emotional toll of caregiving professions. Stamm began studying the experiences of those in helping roles—therapists, nurses, teachers, social workers, and first responders—who regularly support others through trauma. What she found was simple but profound: doing meaningful work doesn't just lift us up—it can wear us down. Often, both things are happening at once. To capture that complexity, Stamm developed the Professional Quality of Life Scale, now in its fifth version, which is used worldwide.[44]

In one of the first published studies focused exclusively on educators, Koenig and colleagues (2017) found that over 40% of teachers and support staff experienced significant emotional exhaustion and secondary traumatic stress, with nearly half scoring in the clinical range on compassion fatigue measures. The study also found that burnout and compassion fatigue were tightly linked and that these symptoms occurred regardless of teaching experience. Notably, a brief professional development intervention significantly improved awareness and coping strategies, suggesting that support and reflection can make a difference.[45]

Between 2021 and 2024, I collected Professional Quality of Life (ProQOL) data from 637 educators across various school settings. What I found confirmed what many teachers have quietly known for years. Compassion satisfaction was low for over one-third of educators (34.5%), with only 1.7% reporting high satisfaction. Most landed in the moderate range (63.2%)—not thriving, but not fully depleted either.

Burnout risk was moderate or high for 56% of respondents, with only 3.5% reaching the high-risk category. That may seem small until you remember that these are real people—colleagues—running on fumes. Secondary Traumatic Stress (STS) was moderate or high in more than 56% of participants, meaning over half of educators are absorbing stress, emotion, and trauma in ways that impact their own well-being.[46]

These aren't just numbers. They're stories. They're sighs in parking lots and tears behind closed classroom doors. They are signs that we have a field filled with people who *care deeply*—and who are paying a high cost for that care. Yet, amid that reality, most educators are still showing up, still hoping, and still anchoring themselves to something bigger than survival.

Compassion Satisfaction

In a profession that can so often feel like a constant sprint toward an ever-moving finish line, we need to pause and name the things that keep us going. One of those things is compassion satisfaction, the sense of fulfillment that comes from doing meaningful work rooted in purpose, connection, and care.

Compassion satisfaction refers to the emotional reward or sense of fulfillment that arises from helping others and engaging in meaningful work. Stamm defines compassion satisfaction as "the pleasure derived from being able to do your work well."[47] It includes feelings of connection, purpose, and the belief that your efforts are making a difference.

In the context of education, especially trauma-responsive education, compassion satisfaction is not just a nice-to-have. It's a protective factor against compassion fatigue, which includes burnout and secondary traumatic stress. Compassion satisfaction supports our ability to bounce back after hard days. It increases our longevity in the field and aligns with the values that led us to become educators in the first place. This work exposes us to harm—not just student trauma, but moral injury, emotional labor, and systemic inequity. Without something to fill us up, we run dry. Compassion satisfaction is what keeps us from becoming cynical. It's what sustains the heart, so we don't forget the human side of why we started teaching in the first place.

The importance of compassion satisfaction is easy to overlook. Especially when the to-do list is long, the data is overwhelming, and the behavior plan feels more like a temporary solution than a lasting one. It's that moment when a student who never makes eye contact finally smiles at you. It's hearing from a family that something you said made a difference. It's sitting in your car after a long day and realizing that, despite all the hard work, your work means something. Compassion satisfaction doesn't erase the complex parts; it coexists with them, and it can be cultivated, just like resilience and hope.

Practice: Cultivating Compassion Satisfaction

Compassion satisfaction can be strengthened by intentionally noticing it and naming it.

Try this:

At the end of the day, jot down one moment that mattered.

Name the feeling it brought you.

Connect it to a value.

Give yourself credit. Let that moment be enough.

This is how we build a practice of noticing what's working. Of seeing the good, not in a toxic positivity kind of way, but in a grounded, "this work is hard and still worth doing" sort of way.

✿reflection✿

Take a few quiet minutes for yourself.

Recall a moment recently that filled you up. It could be a tiny interaction or a breakthrough. What happened? What did you feel at that moment?

What things that you value were honored in that experience? Was it a connection? Growth? Equity? Creativity? Consider how this moment affirmed what matters most to you.

What story do you tell yourself about that moment? Did you feel proud, affirmed, inspired, or validated? Did it help you remember why you do what you do?

How did this moment replenish you? Did it shift your energy? Your outlook? Your patience? Your confidence?

When Teaching Hurts

Compassion fatigue is the umbrella term that captures the emotional cost of caring deeply in high-stress, high-stakes environments, especially when you're supporting others through trauma. It has two main components: burnout and secondary traumatic stress (STS).[48]

Burnout shows up gradually through chronic exhaustion, frustration, and emotional depletion. It often stems from primary stressors, such as systemic issues like unmanageable workloads, a lack of support, inadequate resources, or the sense that one's efforts don't make a difference. It builds over time and can lead to a loss of motivation or a sense of disconnection from your work.[49]

Secondary traumatic stress (STS), on the other hand, is the emotional residue that comes from being exposed to others' trauma. It arises from secondary exposure, such as hearing about, witnessing, or supporting someone through their pain and suffering. Symptoms can include fear, intrusive thoughts, anxiety, or helplessness. For educators, this might mean sitting with a child who has experienced abuse, listening to stories of violence, or constantly absorbing students' emotional needs. Sometimes the exposure is indirect, through stories or disclosures, and other times it is direct, such as intervening in a crisis or witnessing harm firsthand.[50]

We live in an incredibly stressful period in human history, and the effects of this extend deeply into the lives of children and youth. However, not just the younger generation feels the weight of these challenges, but they also profoundly affect the adults who support them. Much of the stress children experience originates outside the classroom, yet they inevitably carry it into school. As a result, teachers and school staff often find themselves absorbing some of that burden, without fully realizing its impact. This weight doesn't simply disappear when the school day ends. Instead, educators bring it home, where it seeps into their personal lives, creating a ripple effect that can be difficult to escape.

Over time, this ongoing cycle of stress can have serious consequences. If left unaddressed, it can lead to burnout or even vicarious trauma, where those who care for and support others begin to experience the emotional toll of the suffering they witness. This cycle affects not just individuals but entire communities, underscoring the urgent need for support systems that acknowledge and address the emotional well-being of both students and the adults who guide them.

We've all been told that to take care of others, we first have to take care of ourselves; yet, most of us struggle with this concept. Our hearts bleed for those who need us, but if we aren't careful, the cost of caring may be our health and happiness.

Uprooted and Replanted

Burnout crept in early for me, though I didn't have the words for it at the time. I just knew I was always angry. Tired in a way that sleep couldn't fix. I was cynical, emotionally shut down, and full of self-doubt. I had been working with students who had experienced deep trauma while still carrying my own. It was like trying to pour from a cup that was cracked and empty. Then, one particularly challenging student was placed in my class. He had low academic and social skills, a difficult home life, and anger that showed up daily in harmful ways.

He bit me. He locked me in a closet. He fashioned scissors into weapons. He threatened self-harm and others' safety. Every day, I tried something new. I showed up, I cared, I documented, I cried. Still, it felt like nothing changed. Over time, my body began to tell the story. I was getting chronic migraines, missing work frequently, and avoiding anything that might trigger more stress. I thought, *"If I can't help this student, what kind of teacher am I?"* I didn't realize then that burnout wasn't about a lack of effort. It was about a lack of support, a lack of healing, and a system asking too much of someone who was already running on empty.

Risk Factors

What I didn't understand at the time was that I wasn't just burned out; I was also carrying secondary traumatic stress. I had internalized the pain and chaos my student brought into the classroom. His trauma wasn't mine, but it *felt* like it was. I'd go home and still be on edge, replaying the day in my head. I had nightmares. I flinched at sudden noises. My nervous system was lit up all the time, as if I were the one in danger.

RISK FACTORS

- Type of work
- Dose of exposure
- Inexperience in the field
- Young age
- Female gender
- Prior trauma exposure

Compassion fatigue can affect anyone working closely with people who've experienced trauma. In helping professions, we open our hearts and minds to support others, and sometimes, our brains absorb that distress as if it were our own.
Some professionals replay stories so often that the line between the experience and reality blurs.
While we need bright-eyed eager people in this work, we also need to recognize that inexperience and a lack of support can quickly lead to burnout.
This risk increase in environments where trauma is frequent or severe.
For those with personal trauma histories, especially unprocessed ones, the self-care account may already be in the red.

Secondary Traumatic Stress happens when you hear about, witness, or work closely with trauma over and over again. It doesn't require direct harm to you; it just involves proximity to pain. When you care deeply, you can't stay emotionally detached.

Your empathy becomes a bridge, and sometimes, you end up carrying more than you realize across it.

That year was my breaking point. But it also became a turning point. I learned that healing wasn't just for my students; it had to be for me, too. I realized that we can't be trauma-responsive to others if we're not trauma-responsive to ourselves.

Compassion fatigue can affect anyone who works closely with individuals who've experienced trauma, but some of us are more vulnerable to it than others. I was one of them. Like many who enter the helping professions, I came in bright-eyed and bushy-tailed, determined to make a difference.

However, I also came in carrying years of my unprocessed trauma. That combination — deep empathy, high expectations, and unresolved pain — is a risky cocktail. When you've lived through harm and then spend your days witnessing the pain of others, your nervous system doesn't always know the difference. The stories stick. Sometimes they play on repeat. Over time, your brain stops distinguishing between what happened to them and what's happening to you.

Environments where professionals are constantly engaging with trauma, whether that's a full caseload or one student who carries a storm inside, naturally increase the risk. When we show up without the tools to both offer and receive support, we put ourselves in danger of slowly burning out. When we ignore the emotional toll, we end up overdrafting from an account that was already in the red. That's not a sign of weakness; it's a signal that the work is hard, and the care needs to go both ways.

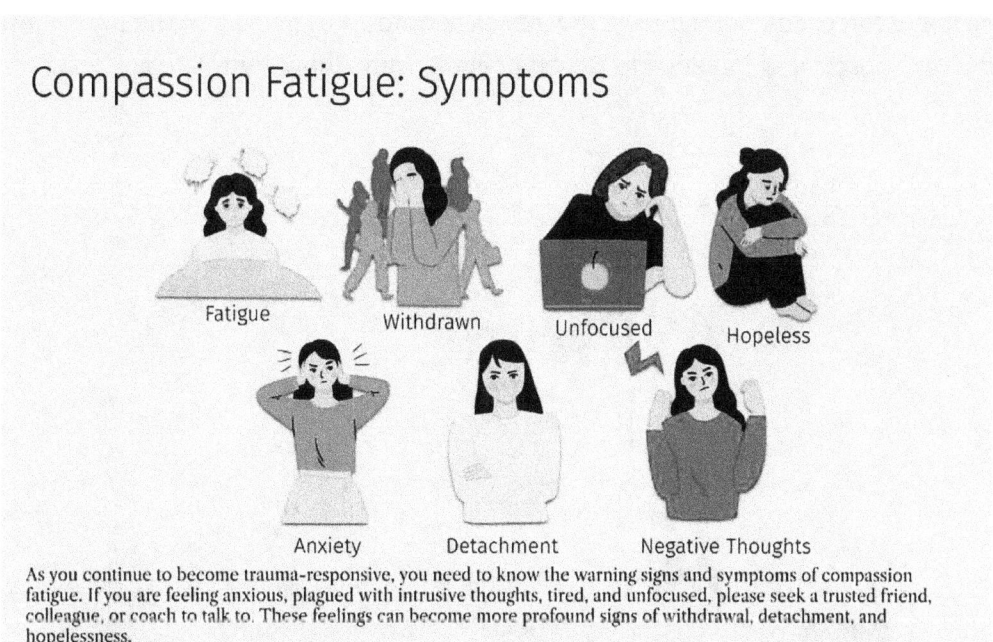

Compassion Fatigue: Symptoms

Fatigue Withdrawn Unfocused Hopeless

Anxiety Detachment Negative Thoughts

As you continue to become trauma-responsive, you need to know the warning signs and symptoms of compassion fatigue. If you are feeling anxious, plagued with intrusive thoughts, tired, and unfocused, please seek a trusted friend, colleague, or coach to talk to. These feelings can become more profound signs of withdrawal, detachment, and hopelessness.

After years of teaching in high-intensity environments, I thought I had finally arrived at a place where I could breathe. I had moved back to my hometown and was now teaching at what many considered the "good school." From the outside, it looked like I had made it. I had strong relationships with students and their families, supportive colleagues, and a professional reputation that led to my winning the district Teacher of the Year award.

Yet, inside, I was unraveling. I was exhausted in a way that no amount of sleep could touch. I started withdrawing from coworkers, friends, and even the students I once connected with so easily. My thoughts became foggy and negative, and I found it harder and harder to focus. I missed meetings, forgot details, and constantly felt behind, no matter how hard I worked.

Looking back, the warning signs were all around me. I was hypervigilant, constantly scanning for what might go wrong. I had poor boundaries, saying yes to everything while silently resenting it. I minimized my stress and ignored what my body was screaming at me. I masked my pain with wine and obsessive workouts, trying to sweat out the pressure I refused to acknowledge. My body began to break down. I developed chronic ailments, some of which led to surgeries. I grew cynical toward my colleagues, the system, and even the profession I once loved.

The worst part was the growing lack of empathy I felt toward students who didn't have "real" trauma. If their pain wasn't visible or intense, I dismissed it, because I had nothing left to give. I was angry, disillusioned, and ashamed. How could I be struggling like this when I was supposed to be at the top of my game? How could I feel so inadequate at the very moment I was being celebrated? This wasn't just burnout. This was compassion fatigue in full force, and I didn't have the language or tools to name it at the time. I just knew I wasn't okay, and I needed to start telling the truth about that.

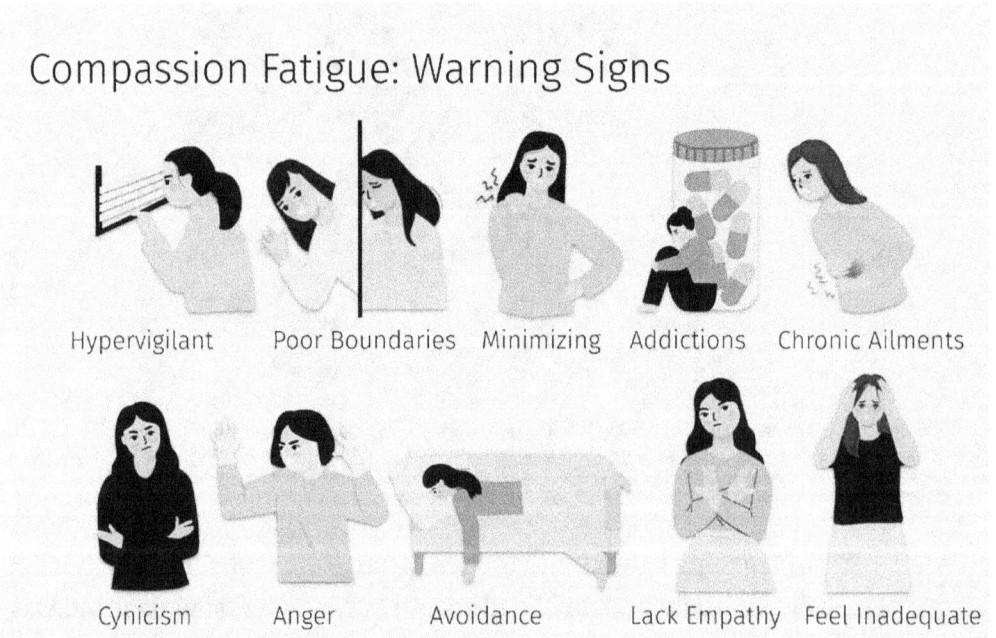

Compassion Fatigue: Warning Signs

Hypervigilant   Poor Boundaries   Minimizing   Addictions   Chronic Ailments

Cynicism   Anger   Avoidance   Lack Empathy   Feel Inadequate

As painful as that season was, it marked the beginning of my actual journey toward becoming a trauma-responsive educator. That same year, while quietly grappling with feelings of inadequacy, disconnection, and exhaustion, I was named one of the eight Kansas Teachers of the Year. It was a surreal moment. Publicly, I was being celebrated. Internally, I was holding on by a thread. That thread, fragile as it seemed, was like the end of a tapestry strand, just enough to pull and begin weaving something new.

As part of the Kansas Teacher of the Year team, I had the opportunity to travel across the state with seven other incredible educators. Together, we utilized our platform to discuss not only best practices and curriculum, but also hope. We leaned into the powerful idea, echoed in the words of Dr. Shane Lopez, that hope is teachable.[52] We grounded our message in the timeless truth captured by Haim Ginott: that the decisive element in the classroom is the adult. That year of speaking, listening, and connecting was transformational. I realized that if I wanted to stay in education, I had to do it differently. I had to prioritize well-being - my students' and my own.

"I've come to a frightening conclusion that I am the decisive element in the classroom. It's my personal approach that creates the climate. It's my daily mood that makes the weather. As a teacher, I possess a tremendous power to make a child's life miserable or joyous. I can be a tool of torture or an instrument of inspiration. I can humiliate or heal. In all situations, it is my response that decides whether a crisis will be escalated or de-escalated and a child humanized or dehumanized."

-Haim Ginott[53]

Two years later, I stepped into full-time consulting. My focus deepened and sharpened. I began speaking, training, and writing about what I now understood firsthand: that professional quality of life, educator wellness, and trauma-responsive practices are inseparable. A system cannot be trauma-informed if its educators are traumatized. That hope isn't just a feel-good concept; it's a framework for resilience and a strategic approach to transformation. Rooted in Hope was born out of that season of both collapse and clarity. It's not just what I teach. It's what I live.

Burnout

Let's just say it out loud: this work is heavy. It's meaningful, but it's also messy. It's sacred, but sometimes it's thankless. Over time, even the most passionate educator can feel the slow erosion of joy, patience, or clarity. That slow drain is what we call burnout, and it doesn't mean you're broken. It means you've been carrying too much, for too long, without enough care poured back in.

Burnout isn't just about being tired. It's about the profound fatigue that comes when purpose runs dry. It's when your empathy feels worn out. When the behaviors you used to meet with compassion now leave you frustrated. When your "why" feels blurry or out of reach.

Here's something else that's important to note: burnout is often circumstantial. It's not usually a sign that you're in the wrong profession; it's a signal that something in your current environment isn't working. A shift in leadership, a mismatch in grade level or content area, taking on too many commitments, or even changes in your personal life can all contribute to this. Sometimes, a change in those circumstances-big or small-can bring clarity, energy, and joy back into your work. You may not need to leave education; you may just need to leave what's not aligned. The truth is: you can love your students and still feel burned out. You can be committed to this work and still need a break. You can be a phenomenal educator and deeply human.

Practice: Honoring the Signal

Burnout isn't a personal failure. It's a message from your body and spirit saying: something has to change. Let's shift the narrative from pushing through to tending to.

Try this:

Write a permission slip for yourself. Something like:

"I have permission to rest. I have permission to care for myself as fiercely as I care for others."

Name one small boundary you can set this week that protects your energy. (Ex: leaving on time twice a week, saying no to extra duty, taking a screen-free lunch.)

Consider what refills your cup, and schedule it like you would a meeting. (Walking, reading, laughing, breathing, not talking about school.)

This isn't about fixing yourself. It's about not forgetting yourself. You are part of the system you're trying to transform, and your well-being matters.

❧reflection❧

Let's take a moment to check in, gently, without judgment.

What signs of burnout have you noticed in yourself lately? (Consider physical, emotional, or mental cues: fatigue, irritability, detachment, brain fog, overwhelm.)

When did you start noticing these signs? Was there a specific event, season, or shift in your workload or life?

How is burnout affecting your connection to your work? Are you finding it more challenging to be present? To feel effective? To care?

What are the current demands you're facing that feel unsustainable? Think broadly about home, school, leadership, and emotional labor.

Are there any internal or external changes that ease this load? A conversation with your administrator? A shift in grade level? Letting go of a committee? More support at home?

What do you need right now that you're not getting? Be bold here. Rest? Boundaries? Validation? A teammate who truly sees you?

Secondary Traumatic Stress

You didn't live it, but somehow, you carry it within you.

That's the essence of secondary traumatic stress. It's what happens when we bear witness to someone else's pain so often and so deeply that it begins to impact our own mental, emotional, and physical health. It's the cost of caring without a release valve. STS doesn't mean something is wrong with you. In fact, it's a signal that your empathy is working. You are showing up, staying connected, and holding space for hard things. However, even empathy has limits. You were never meant to absorb every story, every tear, every hurt. You were meant to care and *also* recover.

Some signs of secondary traumatic stress (STS) can be subtle at first, a lingering heaviness you can't quite name, or a student's story replaying in your mind long after the school day ends. You might find yourself emotionally numb one moment, and unusually irritable the next. Sleep becomes harder. Concentration slips. You notice an undercurrent of anxiety, guilt, or helplessness you didn't use to carry. Sometimes it shows up physically, in headaches, body tension, or a deep fatigue that no weekend can fully fix.

These are not signs of weakness. They are signs that your nervous system has been bearing witness to pain without enough time or space to recover. Sometimes it's not one big story, it's the slow drip of too many small ones. The students you worry about as you drive home. The trauma histories you carry in your mind during lesson planning. The emotional weight makes it harder to enjoy time off or sleep soundly. This is the invisible tax of proximity to pain.

Practice: The Container

Caring doesn't mean carrying everything. Here's a gentle practice to help you acknowledge what you're holding and offer it a safe place.

The Container Practice

> On paper, write down (or draw) what you're carrying emotionally from a recent student interaction. Be specific.
>
> Draw a small container around it. A box, a jar, a crate, whatever feels right. Write "Not mine to hold alone."
>
> Below the container, write one small action:
>
>> A colleague I could talk to
>>
>> A way I could refer or escalate support
>>
>> A moment of self-care I could give myself today.

This isn't about closing our hearts. It's about creating space to breathe, so we can keep showing up with presence, not just proximity. Secondary traumatic stress is real. It's valid, and it's something we must acknowledge if we want to sustain ourselves in this work in the long term. Being Rooted in Hope means holding fierce compassion *and* fierce boundaries. You are not the fixer. You are the guide, the steady presence—and you're allowed to be human, too.

If you'd like to learn more about your professional quality of life, you can use the QR code to take the ProQOL assessment.

Book Companion Resources

- **Professional Quality of Life assessment**

✎ reflection ✎

Is This Mine?

Take a moment to reflect on these questions. Be honest, and be gentle.

Is there a student whose story or pain you carry with you long after the school day ends?
 What part of their experience sticks with you most?

Have you ever felt emotionally depleted after listening to a student or family member share something traumatic?
 What did you do with those feelings afterward?

Are there ways you've started to numb out, distance yourself, or shut down emotionally as a way to protect yourself?
 What impact is that having on your relationships with students or with yourself?

What support systems do you have in place to process the weight you carry?
 Do you feel safe sharing this with a colleague, supervisor, or mental health professional?

Are you treating your emotional well-being with the same urgency and care you give to your students?

◆ nine ◆
Loosen Up Your Buttons

Before we get into specific tools and frameworks for responding to student behavior, we're going to focus inward. Why? How we interpret and experience behavior, especially moments that feel disrespectful or challenging, starts with *us*. In this next activity, we'll begin the first step of the *Transforming Discipline* process. We won't delve into the whole model just yet; you'll revisit this in a later chapter. For now, this is about awareness. It's about noticing how you *feel* when certain behaviors emerge, and what beliefs or values might be underlying those feelings.

Keep what you discover in mind. You'll come back to it with a fresh perspective later in the book, and it may surprise you how much clarity you've gained. To start, take a moment here and pause to consider: How do your values show up in the way you respond to students? When are they honored in your work? When are they challenged? What do you notice in yourself when someone else, perhaps a student, family member, or colleague, seems to be operating from a different value set?

One of the most important shifts we aim to make in a resilience-building school is learning to recognize when our own beliefs, values, and perceptions interfere with our ability to assess student behavior objectively. Our values are powerful; they shape how we interpret the world, how we make decisions, and often, how we judge the behavior of others, even unconsciously.

What are Your Guiding Values?

In this exercise, you'll begin by identifying your top three personal or professional values. If you're wondering which lens to use — personal or professional — know that for many of us, those lines are blurred. If they feel distinct to you, choose to reflect through your professional lens for this activity's purposes.

Directions:

1. Quickly scan the list and highlight 20 words that are important to you.

2. Narrow your list of 20 down to 10 words by putting a star next to the word.

3. Reduce from 10 to 5 words that you aspire to live by.

4. Finally, from those five words, identify your top 3 values that subconsciously guide your decisions, judgments, and relationships.

Accountability	Creativity	Home	Order	Simplicity
Achievement	Curiosity	Honesty	Parenting	Spirituality
Adaptability	Dignity	Hope	Patience	Sportsmanship
Adventure	Diversity	Humility	Patriotism	Stewardship
Altruism	Environment	Humor	Peace	Success
Ambition	Efficiency	Inclusion	Perseverance	Teamwork
Authenticity	Equality	Independence	Personal	Thrift
Balance	Fairness	Initiative	fulfillment	Time
Beauty	Faith	Integrity	Power	Tradition
Being the best	Family	Intuition	Pride	Travel
Belonging	Financial stability	Job security	Recognition	Trust
Caring	Forgiveness	Joy	Reliability	Truth
Collaboration	Freedom	Justice	Resourcefulness	Understanding
Commitment	Friendship	Kindness	Respect	Uniqueness
Community	Fun	Knowledge	Responsibility	Usefulness
Compassion	Future	Leadership	Risk-taking	Vision
Competence	Generosity	Legacy	Safety	Vulnerability
Confidence	Giving back	Leisure	Security	Wealth
Connection	Grace	Love	Self-discipline	Well-being
Contentment	Gratitude	Loyalty	Self-expression	Wholeheartedness
Contribution	Growth	Nature	Self-respect	Wisdom
Cooperation	Harmony	Openness	Serenity	Youth
Courage	Health	Optimism	Service	Zeal

My top three values are:

1.

2.

3.

In the many times I've led this exercise with hundreds of educators in person, I've yet to encounter two people in the same room who selected the same three values in the same order. That uniqueness is important. It reminds us that we each filter the world through our internal compass, and that what feels "disrespectful," "irresponsible," or "unmotivated" to us may look entirely different through someone else's lens.

Understanding your values is a crucial first step in transitioning from a reactive to a reflective mindset. When we don't pause to examine our beliefs, we tend to default to habits, many of which were shaped by systems that prioritized compliance over connection. Yet, when we clarify what matters most to us, we begin to respond from a place of intention, not instinct.

When Behavior Pushes Your Buttons

The purpose of this activity is to notice how your values, beliefs, and emotional responses shape the way you perceive behavior. This is the first step toward transforming discipline from a reactive act into a relational and restorative one. This matters because this kind of self-awareness is a primary tenet of a resilience-building school.

When we understand our internal landscape, we're more equipped to stay grounded in moments of challenge, to respond with curiosity instead of control, and to create environments where all students, especially those carrying trauma, can feel safe, seen, and supported.

Before we dive in, a gentle reminder: this activity isn't about judgment. It's about awareness. You're not doing anything wrong if student behavior frustrates or confuses you; it's a natural response.

Step 1: Identify Common Behaviors

Consider your own classroom or school environment. List 3–6 student behaviors that are common and tend to be disruptive or challenging (e.g., blurting out, refusing to work, tardiness, off-task, making excuses).

Now, for each behavior, write down:

- What do you believe the student's intention might be (without your trauma-informed lens, just your gut reaction)?
- What is the usual consequence, either from you or from school policy?

Example:

> *Behavior: Blurting out*
> *Perceived Intention: Just trying to get attention*
> *Usual Consequence: Moved to the back of the room or have to sit on the bench at recess*

Behavior	Perceived Intention	Usual Consequence

Step 2: Identify What Pushes *Your* Buttons

Now think about three student behaviors that personally push your buttons, the ones that bother you more than others.

For me, three behaviors that personally push my buttons are

1. *Denying responsibility*
2. *Making up excuses*
   And this one is going to seem ridiculous...
3. *Rustling papers while I'm talking.*
   I can't explain it, but that sound just hurts my ears deep in my stomach.

Write them here:

1.

2.

3.

Now, pick one that hits you the hardest. Write it below:

Step 3: Reflect on the Emotional Impact

How do you feel *in the moment* when this behavior shows up?

☐ Mad

☐ Sad

☐ Afraid

☐ All three

☐ Something else: _____

Now dig a little deeper. If you feel mad, are there any hidden layers? Sometimes anger is just the surface, and underneath we may feel hurt, helpless, overwhelmed, or afraid. Write down the *deeper feeling* you think might be present.

Example:

"I'll never forget one particular day. I was prepping my class for a group from the State Department of Education to come in and film a lesson. I was up for an award, and I wanted to showcase our best effort. As I ran through the lesson with my class, all I could hear was the shuffling of papers. Looking back, it seems silly, but in the moment, I was beyond irritated. I felt annoyed and overwhelmed. These feelings led me to lose my cool and shout at them to drop their papers and put their hands in their laps."

Step 4: Connect It to Your Values

Now flip back to your values list. Which ones are being "stepped on" when that student behavior shows up?

Example:

> "Two of my top values are contribution and competence. At that moment, both were being crushed. I wanted to look good for the film crew. Not just because I was up for an award, I was proud of my students and excited to show off their hard work as much as my own. I just needed them to contribute a little effort, and all I was asking was that their papers be still."

Step 5: What Message Are You Receiving?

Think about the *unconscious message* you might be receiving from the student's behavior. Not what they're intending, but what *you* are interpreting.

When this happens, I'm telling myself:

Example:

> "I was telling myself that if my students were unwilling to help me out, I would look incompetent...and if I looked incompetent, I didn't deserve to be nominated for an award... in fact, it would actually mean I was terrible at my job, because what teacher can't get their students to keep their papers still? A bad one. So the message is, I am a bad teacher."

Here's the truth: these aren't conscious thoughts. These are *shadow messages*—quiet, underlying beliefs we carry about ourselves that get activated in moments of stress or vulnerability.[54] They often stem from early experiences or internalized expectations and may sound like, "I'm not good enough," "I have to fix this," or "I'm failing." In the classroom, these messages can quietly hijack our nervous systems, pulling us into reactive cycles. We may think we're responding to a student's behavior, but in truth, we're often reacting to the fear or shame that has been stirred up within us.

This isn't a flaw. It's part of being human. When we become aware of our shadow messages, we gain the power to pause, reflect, and choose a different response—one rooted in regulation rather than reactivity.

In resilience-building work, awareness is everything. When we start recognizing the *underlying reasons* behind our emotional reactions, we can begin to show up differently, both for ourselves *and* for our students. Here's where it gets real. Take a moment to consider the shadow message you uncovered, for example,

> *"I'm not a good enough teacher"* or
> *"They don't respect me."*

Step 6: Permission to React

Sometimes, when we feel hurt, helpless, or disrespected, that shadow message gives us unspoken permission to shut down, overreact, become rigid, give up, take it personally, or even emotionally distance ourselves from a student.

This is not about judgment or shame. This is about awareness.

Example:

"The shadow message that I'm a bad teacher gave me permission not only to snap at my class, but also led me to attempt to shame them into compliance. Later that day, I set up my Flip camera during a math lesson to catch them rustling their papers, proving how loud and distracting it was. During specials, I uploaded the video to my computer with plans to watch it with them afterward, only to find that the camera hadn't picked up any sound at all. My insecurities amplified the noise. My shadow message was hijacking my stress response. My buttons were pushed, and I reacted."

What did that belief, even if it was unconscious, give me permission to do in response?

You've just completed the first part of the Transforming Discipline process, the part that starts with you.[55] You've explored the internal landscape that shapes how you perceive behavior, including your emotional responses, values, shadow messages, and instinctive reactions.

Later in the book, we'll return to this exact moment. We'll explore how to disrupt that default reaction and shift toward responding with intention, grounded in regulation, connection, and repair.

So go ahead: flag this page, highlight it, stick a sticky note on it, fold the corner, or draw a doodle in the margin. Whatever works. *Don't lose this reflection*, it's a critical piece of the puzzle. For now, just hold this new insight with curiosity. You're doing the work already.

❧ ten ❧
The Cover Story

Though we may not think of it often, part of what makes us human is our capacity for emotion. Our feelings aren't just internal experiences; they're deeply social. Emotions shape our culture, drive our relationships, and fundamentally guide how we learn and interact with one another. From infancy, we're wired to seek connection. Those early bonds form the blueprint for how we interact with others and how we perceive ourselves.

Yet, somewhere along the way, especially in spaces like teaching, where performance is prized, we begin to believe that not all emotions are safe. We categorize parts of ourselves as "good" or "bad," acceptable or shameful. We start to believe that vulnerability is a liability, and we create cover stories —polished versions of ourselves — that we can present safely to the world.

As educators, we are especially prone to this.

We craft a version of ourselves that looks composed, confident, and compassionate. We want our students, colleagues, and communities to see us as steady and strong, balancing data meetings, recess duty, and dinner with ease. That our kids are thriving, our relationships are solid, and our practices are rooted in purpose and resilience. We want to be seen as hopeful people. Yet, behind that carefully constructed narrative, many of us are carrying a different story.

If I'm honest, there are moments I've feared I don't deserve to be writing this book. I've questioned whether I failed students by focusing too much on connection and not enough on content. I've lost sleep over the relationships I missed, the needs I overlooked, the mistakes I couldn't undo. I've come home too many times with nothing left to give the people I love most. That fear and self-doubt reached a breaking point last year.

I was working as a consultant, doing work I once felt called to. However, over time, the organization I served shifted. What began as a mission-driven endeavor evolved into something entirely different. Leadership changed. A scarcity mindset took hold. The culture turned toxic. We preached trauma-responsive practices, but inside our system, we weren't living them. Meetings became minefields, filled with tears, shame, and fear. The work I loved had become a source of dread.

Then my dad got sick.

In the earliest days of his hospitalization, I asked for a pause, a moment to be present with my family. Instead, I received an email laced with disappointment and accusation. I was told I was failing to communicate. That email was a catalyst. In the space created by the crisis, my clarity returned. I saw that I was no longer aligned with the system I was working in. I was burned out, becoming jaded by trying to continue leading with hope in a system that had begun leading with fear.

Faced with the possible loss of my father, my priorities shifted. My sense of calling came back into focus. I made a choice I never thought I was brave enough to make:

I walked away.

I began again, this time not with performance or approval as the goal, but with a sense of rootedness, not with a cover story, but with a commitment to wholeness. In *A Hidden Wholeness*, Parker Palmer writes, "We arrive in this world with birthright gifts... Sadly, we often abandon those gifts... as we are drawn into conformity with cultural values."[56] He speaks of the split between our inner truth and our outer life, and the pain that results when we live in a divided state.

That division is where shame thrives. Shame, as Dr. Brené Brown defines it, is the intensely painful belief that we are flawed and unworthy of love and belonging. Shame makes us small. It tells us we are impostors. It feeds the whisper that we are not enough.[57]

I'll be honest, as soon as I hit send on the email containing my resignation letter, I spiraled. I questioned everything. I replayed conversations. I ruminated over mistakes. I shut down. I let shame take the driver's seat. And like before in that silence, something else rose to the surface:

Hope.

Hope found me in the wreckage and reminded me who I am.

You and I walk around every day with imagined thought bubbles over other people's heads, guessing what they think of us. If we believe we're affirmed, we stand taller. If we believe we're judged, we shrink. We may not call it shame, but that's what it is. We rename it: awkwardness, low self-esteem, stress. We bury it in busyness. We pretend it's not there, but it is.

The only way through it... is through it.

So here I am, with no stage, no mic, no PowerPoint clicker. Just a page, and a voice, and a truth I want to share with you:

You do not have to be perfect to be powerful.
You do not have to hide your heartbreak to lead with hope.
You do not have to curate a cover story.
You just have to show up.

Take a second look at your own story. Yes, there may be pain. Yes, there may be shame. Look again. There is hope, and where hope takes root, healing begins.

Let's go forward, not with performance, but with presence. Not with illusion, but with integrity. Let's do this work with our whole selves, because wholeness, not perfection, is what our students need most.

❧ reflection ❧

Listening to the Teacher Within
Parker Palmer reminds us that "we teach who we are."

Who are you, beneath the titles, roles, and expectations?
Take 10–15 minutes to write from the voice of your inner teacher. Don't overthink, just let the words come.

What I want people to believe to be true about me is...

What I fear may be more true about me is...

I feel most like myself when I...

I've been sacrificing _____ in the name of success, and I'm ready to reclaim it.

When you're finished, read it back, gently. What stands out? What surprises you? What does this inner voice need more of in your current season?

❧ eleven ❧
The River of Harm in Education

The Cruelty We Don't Name

When we speak about trauma in schools, we often think of what students carry in with them: poverty, neglect, family conflict, or community violence. But there is another kind of trauma that quietly lives inside the school walls—cruelty that is passed from teacher to student, teacher to teacher, and administrator to teacher. It doesn't always leave visible marks, but it does leave deep imprints on nervous systems, relationships, and the culture of learning.

Abuse: Imposing One's Will

Abuse in schools is often invisible because it hides in the ordinary. It's not always an outburst; sometimes it's a calculated act of control. Abuse happens when one person imposes their will over another in ways that diminish dignity.

A teacher shames a child for reading below grade level.

A colleague bullies another teacher in a team meeting.

An administrator isolates a staff member by excluding them from decision-making.

Even the use of student data can become a tool of abuse when numbers are weaponized to label, embarrass, or coerce rather than to support. Abuse is less about what is done and more about the imbalance of power and the harm caused when that power is used to strip another person of agency.

Violence: Behavior Designed to Create Fear

Violence in schools is often subtle. It doesn't require physical contact—it only requires fear. A look across the room, a voice raised in anger, the closing in of proximity until the body tenses—these are forms of violence that activate the survival brain. Gossip works in a similar way, spreading a fog of uncertainty and threat.

Fear becomes the currency of control. Students comply not out of respect but out of survival. Teachers silence themselves in staff meetings, not because they lack ideas but because they fear the repercussions of speaking up. Violence in this sense erodes trust, and when trust collapses, so does authentic engagement.

Physical Violence: Fear Through Contact

Physical violence in schools can look small, almost trivial, but the nervous system doesn't distinguish between "minor" and "serious" when safety is at stake.

A teacher flicks a student's ear to get attention.

A colleague taps another's chest in an argument.

An eraser is thrown across the room.

A teacher yanks the backpack or hoodie of a student as they walk down the hall.

A computer lid is slammed shut in anger.

Even "trained" uses of physical restraint, though sometimes justified by policy, carry with them an undeniable truth: the body has been overpowered. Physical violence always communicates fear, even if the adult insists it was necessary or harmless.

The Cycle of Cruelty

Cruelty is contagious. What is done to teachers often trickles down to students. An administrator who uses shame to manage staff creates teachers who use shame to manage students. A teacher who feels bullied by colleagues may, without intending to, pass that same bullying down to children. What we do to each other does not stay contained in professional silos—it becomes the hidden curriculum our students learn every day.

To see this more clearly, pause for a moment and reflect on what you have personally witnessed in your school community. Consider each of the three categories—abuse, violence, and physical violence.

Abuse (imposing one's will over another): What moments of shaming, exclusion, isolation, or misuse of data have you seen?

Violence (behavior designed to create fear): What non-physical acts—like looks, yelling, gossip, or proximity—have you noticed being used to control others?

Physical Violence (fear through contact): What "small" or "normalized" physical acts—like yanking a hoodie, slamming a computer shut, or unnecessary restraint—have you observed in classrooms or staff interactions?

Take a few minutes to generate your own list. Write down specific examples, even if they seem minor. Naming them is the first step to breaking the cycle. You don't have to share this list with anyone else—it is for your own awareness.

Abuse	Violence	Physical Violence

When we create these lists, the patterns begin to emerge. We see how cruelty, in its many forms, shows up in the daily life of a school. We also see the ways we may have participated—by acting, by tolerating, or by remaining silent. These are not easy truths, but they are necessary ones if we hope to redirect the current of harm.

The Work of Hope

Naming these cruelties is uncomfortable, but silence only allows them to persist. Abuse, violence, and physical violence in schools are not just policy violations; they are betrayals of the very trust education requires. To be trauma-responsive, we must start by telling the truth about the harm we sometimes cause inside our own walls. Only then can we root our practices in hope, dignity, and safety—for students, for teachers, and for every adult who steps into a school.

And this is where the river of harm begins. Each unaddressed act of abuse, each subtle form of violence, each moment of physical domination becomes a stone tossed into the current. One stone may seem insignificant, but over time, the river swells, carving deep channels of mistrust, shame, and fear.

Unless we step back to name and interrupt the cruelty, the river carries students, teachers, and leaders downstream—often toward burnout, disengagement, or despair. Recognizing cruelty is not the end of the work, but it is the entry point to understanding how the river of harm is formed and how it can be redirected.

Educators are often positioned as helpers, protectors, and changemakers, but we are too rarely invited to explore the harm that *we ourselves* have experienced within the system. Whether that harm is systemic (e.g., lack of resources, unsupportive leadership, or policy pressure), relational (e.g., public criticism, isolation, or betrayal by colleagues), or personal (e.g., vicarious trauma, burnout, or loss of purpose), it shapes how we show up. It also shapes how we see ourselves.

The River of Harm

This reflective process is adapted from the River of Cruelty model, which is typically used to understand the cycle of interpersonal and intergenerational harm. The River of Cruelty is a concept originating from the work of Alice Miller, a renowned Swiss psychoanalyst and author. Her insights continue to inform trauma-informed care, attachment theory, and inner child work today and illustrate how unhealed pain, especially from childhood trauma, often flows downstream, passed from adults to children, generation to generation.[58]

When those who were once powerless do not process or repair their suffering, they may unconsciously reenact it on others, continuing cycles of harm. Breaking this cycle requires conscious reflection, compassion, and the courage to stop the flow.

Here, Miller's River of Cruelty work is reimagined as a way for educators to identify and examine how harm within their professional lives flows downstream into beliefs and behaviors that affect them, their relationships, and their ability to sustain this work with purpose and care.[59]

As you read through the following pages, you are invited to walk through the River of Harm in Education—a metaphorical space where we can pause and reflect on our shared humanity in schools. This river represents the flow of harm that moves between students, educators, and systems. At different points in our lives, we may find ourselves in very different roles:

sometimes in the river, experiencing harm ourselves,
sometimes pushing others in, whether intentionally or unintentionally,
and sometimes pulling others out, offering support, care, or repair.

Archbishop Desmond Tutu once reminded us,

"There comes a point where we need to stop just pulling people out of the river. We need to go upstream and find out why they're falling in."

In the context of education, this means looking beyond the immediate crisis or visible harm to examine the sources and conditions that keep the river flowing. That upstream work often begins by honestly examining our own experiences—both the times we have been harmed and the times we have contributed to harm, knowingly or unknowingly. Engaging with the River of Harm reflection means taking responsibility in two ways:

Healing what happened to us. Recognizing and tending to the wounds we carry, whether they came from school, relationships, or systemic forces, so that our pain doesn't spill into the lives of others.

Being accountable for what we have done. Owning the moments we may have caused harm, whether through silence, compliance, or action, and considering what repair or change might look like.

This reflection is not about blame or shame. It is about awareness, honesty, and responsibility—necessary steps if we are to move forward as educators and leaders who create spaces of safety, dignity, and hope.

Sources of Harm

Teachers carry not only the daily stressors of the classroom but also the echoes of deeper patterns that Alice Miller so powerfully named. Harm in education often mirrors the same wounds children experience: silencing, scapegoating, perfectionism, and abandonment. Many of us have been treated as though our voices and expertise do not matter, forced into compliance with rigid systems that deny autonomy.

Others have been singled out and shamed publicly, absorbing the blame for problems rooted in structures beyond our control. Bearing witness to student trauma without space to process or support can feel like what Miller called "emotional desertion"—being left alone with unbearable realities. For teachers from marginalized identities, racism, sexism, ableism, and other inequities compound these injuries, embedding messages of "less than" into the profession itself.

The pressure to perform without adequate resources often repeats the "gifted child" dynamic Miller described: striving endlessly to prove worth while slowly erasing oneself. And perhaps most devastating is moral injury—the moment when we are asked to enforce policies that conflict with our values, splitting us from our integrity.

These harms, unspoken and unacknowledged, shape how we show up in classrooms, just as they shaped us in our families and early lives. Naming them is not weakness; it is the first step toward reclaiming authenticity, connection, and hope.

Sources of Harm

What stands out as a formative hurts you've carried in this work?

Often, we consider some of these things to be an unavoidable reality of the work, but that doesn't mean they aren't harmful.

Generate a list of your experiences, and then focus on one to expand on in greater detail.
Example:
- Comparative use of data between teachers
- Culture of gossip
- Being let go due to a reduction in force
- Lack of quality professional learning
- Unrealistic workloads

As a fourth-grade teacher, 90% of my students had failed the state math assessment the previous year. I had asked repeatedly for resources and additional support to help them catch up, but my requests were dismissed. In February, after new formative assessments, my principal announced in a staff meeting that she was assigning a math coach to my classroom "because Katie is struggling to teach."

Adverse Feelings

When we think back on difficult experiences, it's tempting to focus only on what happened—the event itself—while overlooking what it left behind inside of us. However, the feelings associated with those moments matter deeply. They don't just disappear with time. When unacknowledged, they often settle in our bodies, classrooms, and relationships, manifesting in ways we may not recognize.

We sometimes minimize or suppress these feelings, either because they seem "too much" or because we've been taught to push through. Yet they are signals—clues to what those experiences meant to us. Left unattended, they can quietly shape the way we teach, respond to students, or even see ourselves. Naming them doesn't make us weak; it makes us honest. And honesty is a big part of getting out of the River of Harm.

Adverse Feelings

What feelings arose in response to these experiences? Which feelings did you experience most strongly? Which ones are hardest to name or express?

Example:

- Anger, grief, guilt, shame
- Inadequacy or self-doubt
- Bitterness or resentment
- Numbness or disengagement

The comment landed like a punch in the gut. I felt embarrassed, angry, dismissed, and overwhelmed. Instead of feeling recognized for the progress my students had made, I felt shamed in front of my colleagues.

Protective Systems

When feelings become too heavy to carry, we naturally develop ways to protect ourselves. These coping mechanisms often emerge without our awareness and, in the moment, they serve an important purpose: survival. They help us get through the day, shield us from pain, and allow us to keep showing up.

The challenge is that over time, what once protected us can begin to isolate us. Armor may keep us safe, but it can also keep us disconnected—from our students, colleagues, and even from our own sense of self. Becoming aware of these protective systems is not about judgment, but about noticing how they've shaped us. Only then can we choose what to keep, what to release, and what to replace with healthier patterns.

Protective Systems

How did you cope or defend yourself against those feelings? What "armor" did you develop to cope? What was it protecting you from?

Example:

- Sarcasm or emotional detachment
- Perfectionism or over-functioning
- Control, rigidity, or rule-enforcement
- Withdrawal from relationships
- Avoiding students who trigger discomfort

In that moment, I shut down. I didn't advocate for myself and instead retreated into frustration-venting with my teammates about how unfair and unsupportive the leadership felt.

Unintended Consequences

At first, our protective systems feel like solutions. They shield us, help us survive, and create a sense of control in overwhelming situations. However, over time, defenses that once seemed helpful can begin to reshape how we perceive ourselves, our students, and our work. What once kept us afloat can start to weigh us down.

These unintended consequences often creep in slowly. The armor we built for safety can distance us from connection. The habits that once helped us cope can turn into barriers that keep us stuck. We may find ourselves less patient, less creative, or less hopeful—without fully realizing how we got there.

Unintended Consequences

What unintended consequences begin to shape your teaching, relationships, or self-image? What impact did your protective systems have on you and others?

Example:

- Feeling alone or misunderstood
- Difficulty trusting administrators or colleagues
- Disconnect from students or a lack of empathy
- Chronic fatigue, migraines, illness
- Decreased passion or creativity

Because I didn't clarify the full context, my principal's perception of me as a "struggling teacher" remained unchallenged. I fully lost trust in my administrator. I also didn't trust the math coach that was assigned to my room, assuming she also felt like I was not capable.

Internalized Beliefs

Over time, repeated harm or discouragement doesn't just shape our feelings or our defenses—it starts to write a story about who we are. These stories become internalized beliefs, often buried beneath the surface, quietly shaping how we present ourselves in our classrooms, schools, and lives.

The hard part? We don't usually recognize them as beliefs. They feel like truth. And when left unchallenged, they can become powerful forces that limit our growth, connection, and joy.

Internalized Beliefs

What messages or beliefs did these experiences reinforce?

Which beliefs feel familiar?

Which ones still influence how you show up?

These beliefs are often unconscious but deeply rooted.

Example:

"I'm not good enough."

"Nothing I do matters."

"If I don't control everything, it will all fall apart."

"I have to do this alone."

Over time, I began to internalize pieces of that narrative, carrying an unnecessary weight of failure.

Reclaiming the Current

This process is not about blame or shame; it's about understanding how you've been shaped, so you can choose how you want to grow forward. Harm in the system is real—and healing is possible. You get to interrupt the current and build something new.

Reclaiming the Current

Think of one belief you've carried about yourself, your students, or your work that no longer serves you. What is the belief?

What evidence do you have that this belief is true?

    Based on that, what might you need to change, learn, or seek support for?

What evidence do you have that this belief is false?

    What would your students say about you?

    What would your teacher bestie say?

    What would a trusted leader or mentor say?

What belief or value do you want to root deeper into instead?

Example:

My students had already made remarkable progress on the third-grade standards. If they'd been tested on those, most of them would have passed. Expecting two years of growth in one year was an uphill battle, but I was doing the right work-and my colleagues and mentor would have vouched for it. The addition of the math coach could have been seen as a win, a long-overdue resource, if not for the way it was framed publicly.

The truth is, I do have what it takes. Instead of carrying the shadow message of "I'm failing" or "I don't have what it takes," the deeper truth is this: I was resourceful, effective, and committed. The harm was not in my ability, but in how leadership chose to frame support.

This is your chance to rewire. To choose the story you carry forward, grounded in truth, not trauma.

↝ twelve ↜
You Matter: Sustainable Self-Care Practices

Being in education is hard on the body, mind, and spirit. We often say, "Take care of yourself so you can care for others," but how often do we *actually* live by this principle? The truth is: we can't pour from an empty cup. Maybe more importantly, we weren't meant to do this alone. Just as we practice co-regulation with our students, we need to practice co-care with our colleagues. Whether you're navigating burnout, compassion fatigue, or just the normal wear and tear of showing up day after day, care is not optional. It's essential. It's not just for people on the brink, it's for all of us, all the time.

In this chapter, we'll explore practical ways to invest in both self-care tools for building real, lasting resilience. We'll reflect, plan, and commit because the well-being of every adult in the building directly shapes the well-being of every student in our care.

If the pandemic taught us anything, it's that school communities thrive when educators are supported. And since 2020, the challenges haven't stopped. Educators are navigating physical exhaustion, emotional labor, and mental overload. It's time to stop treating wellness like an optional add-on. Wellness is the foundation of a sustainable, trauma-informed school culture.

Our Collective Commitment

We believe resilient staff build resilient kids.

This doesn't mean giving everyone what they want or pretending the work isn't hard. It means building a collective will, a shared commitment to meet students and families where they are, supported by systems that serve *everyone*. That starts with caring for our most valuable resource: our educators. Let's commit to caring for the whole self — body, mind, and spirit — and to doing that care together.

The Self-Care Wheel

True self-care isn't just about bubble baths or yoga classes. It's a deliberate practice across six core areas, some personal, some professional, all essential. These habits can be private or shared with others in a relationship. Together, they form the foundation for emotional regulation, clarity, and stamina.

Physical self-care is about listening to your body. It includes getting enough sleep, staying hydrated, exercising regularly, and nourishing yourself with a balanced diet, adequate rest, and routine medical care. It's the quiet decision to pay attention when your body whispers, before it has to scream.

Psychological self-care means tending to your inner world. That might mean going to therapy, journaling, setting screen-time limits, or simply allowing yourself to disconnect from the noise and mental clutter that clouds your clarity.

Emotional self-care asks us to feel instead of freeze. It's crying when you need to, laughing hard when you get the chance, venting to someone safe, or just making room for whatever's real, without stuffing it down or toughing it out.

Spiritual self-care is about anchoring in something bigger than yourself, whether that's faith, nature, ritual, silence, or a sense of meaning. This is what reminds you who you are and why you're here.

Personal self-care invites you to reconnect with the parts of yourself that extend beyond the classroom. It's hobbies, boundaries, joy, and play. It's remembering who you were before the job, and honoring who you're becoming because of it.

Professional self-care is what keeps the work from swallowing you. It's using your personal days, setting limits, advocating for your needs, investing in growth, and protecting your energy. This isn't quitting the mission; it's sustaining your ability to live it.

Coping vs. Soothing

When we talk about self-care, it's important to distinguish between coping strategies and self-soothing practices. Both matter. Both are necessary. Both serve different purposes, and confusing them can leave us wondering why we still feel stuck. Coping is active. It addresses the root of the stress. It's setting a boundary, debriefing with a teammate, changing a harmful policy, or processing with a therapist. Self-soothing, on the other hand, helps us regulate in the moment. It's lighting a candle, listening to music, sipping tea, or going for a walk. One helps us heal. The other helps us breathe. Resilience-building educators need both. We don't just need to calm our nervous systems; we need to create conditions that reduce the overload in the first place.

Here's the key:

Coping helps you resolve what's happening.

Soothing helps you survive what's happening.

We need both, but if we only soothe, without ever coping, we end up burned out and emotionally numb. A bubble bath won't fix toxic systems, but it might give you the energy to face them. Sometimes, that's where the work begins.

Let's put this into practice.

Self-Care Wheel Activity[60]

Consider the six areas of self-care listed below.

What coping strategies and self-soothing habits do you already practice? Which ones would you add?

Physical	Psychological	Emotional	Spiritual	Professional	Personal

Using the Self-Care Wheel, shade in each section from the center (0) to the edge (10) based on how intentionally you're caring for that area in your life.

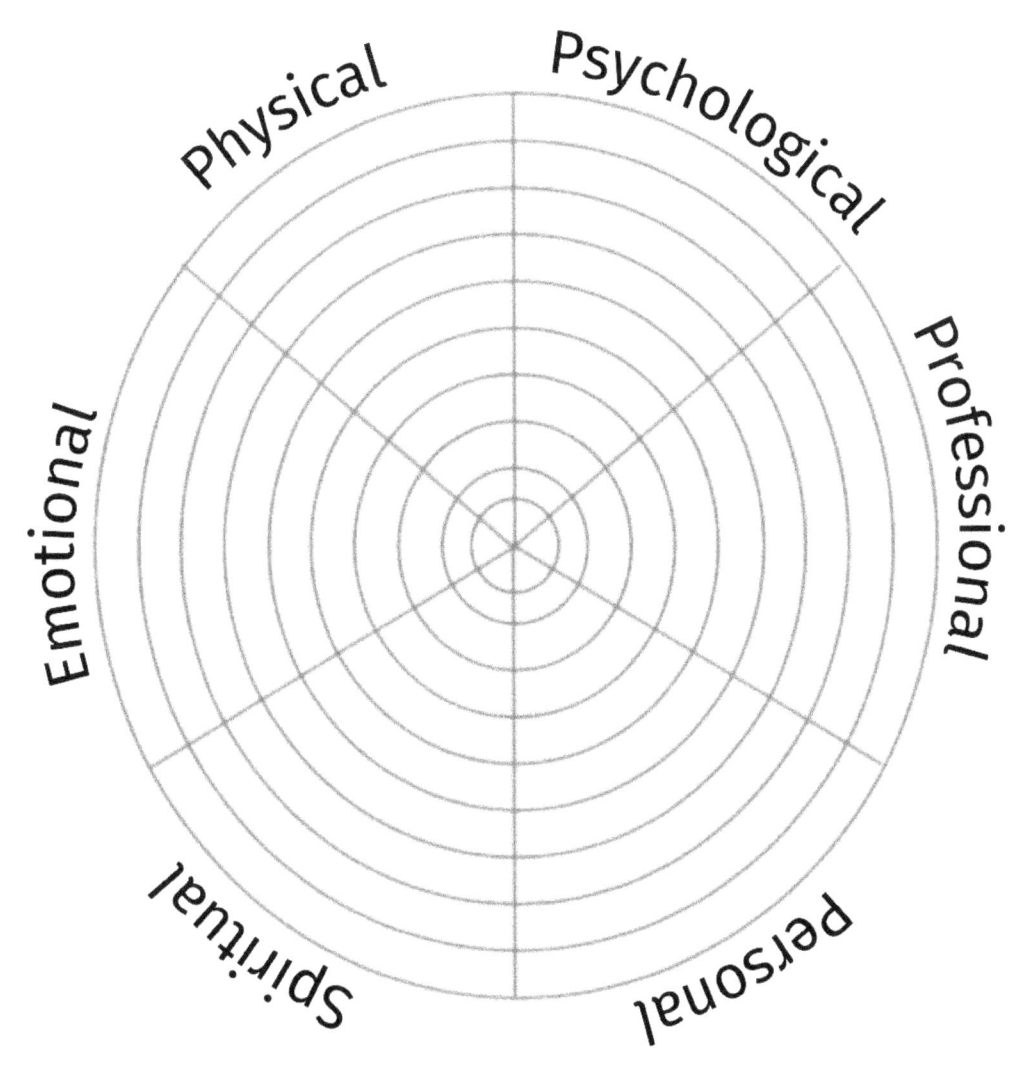

Wheel Check

Visualize pushing this wheel down a road:

- Would it roll slowly, with many rotations, because everything is underdeveloped?

- Would it roll smoothly because you're balanced?

- Would it wobble and halt because some areas are strong while others are struggling?

Make a Move

Choose one area to focus on this week. Write down one action you'll take in the next seven days.

Tell someone. Ask them to check in. Hold yourself accountable.

The Bigger Picture

Resilience isn't built by accident. It's built by small, intentional steps, one habit, one relationship, one boundary at a time. When we do that work together, we don't just care for ourselves; we help carry each other forward. Let's be the kind of educators who live the message we want our students to learn: You matter. You are worth the care it takes to keep growing.

❧ part two reflection ❧
The Inner Work of a Resilient Educator

Before we can lead, teach, or care for others in a trauma-informed manner, we must first understand our roots, where we come from, what has shaped us, and how we respond to challenges, differences, and disconnection.

Use the Part Two ROOTED IN HOPE Reflection found in Part Five on page 270 or by scanning the QR code below to organize your thinking to organize your thinking and start planting seeds of change in your practice.

Take a few deep breaths. Settle into stillness, or take a walk with these questions in mind.

Visit the book companion
site for additional
materials related to this
chapter.

Book Companion Resources

- **Part Two Reflection**

❧ part three ☙
The ROOTED IN HOPE Framework

If Part One grounded us in the science, and Part Two called us inward, then Part Three turns our gaze outward, toward the students we serve. This is not a leap. It's a natural extension of the work you've already begun.

The inner work you've done, learning to identify your nervous system's cues, revisiting your values, and unpacking burnout, shame, and survival patterns, isn't separate from your work with students. It *is* the work. The clarity and compassion you've cultivated in yourself become the foundation for how you interpret, respond to, and support students who show up in pain, disconnection, or defiance.

We can't model regulation if we don't practice it. We can't offer belonging if we're hustling for our worth. We can't hold space for others' stories if we haven't made peace with our own. Most importantly, we can't demand change from students until we're willing to change how we show up.

This next section walks you through how to apply everything you've learned about trauma, the brain, and yourself to real student experiences, especially those who push your buttons or break your heart. This section doesn't offer a checklist. It offers a new way of seeing.

Through the lens of the ROOTED IN HOPE framework, we'll explore how to support a *Student in Need of Connection* facet by facet. Starting with Resilience, we will move through each of the following elements: Origin, Openness, Trust, Engagement, Discernment, Intentionality, Neuro-Informed, Hope, Ownership, Purpose, and Empowerment.

Each chapter is grounded in a story. Each story leads to reflection. Each reflection brings you closer to practicing connection not just as a strategy, but as a daily commitment. These are the shifts that matter, subtle, human, and profound. The work continues, but now, you don't carry it alone. You've met yourself more fully. From that place, you're ready to meet your students again, too.

❧ thirteen ❧
Students in Need of Connection

Connection isn't a reward students earn. It's the foundation they need to grow.

Every classroom has at least one student who is struggling. Some show it loudly, with defiance, disruption, or withdrawal. Others hide it behind high grades and perfectionism, going unnoticed until they crash. Nearly every educator has a moment when they wonder, *'What do I do next?'*

The Student in Need of Connection (SiNoC) Process was created to help answer that question, not with a script, but with a lens.[61]

A way of seeing students not as problems to be fixed, but as people to be understood. This process evolved from real schools, honest coaching conversations, and genuine heartbreak. It was built from listening to the stories of students who were missed or misunderstood and from standing beside educators who cared deeply but weren't sure how to help. It was shaped by my journey as a teacher, coach, and parent, especially the times when my daughter needed to be seen differently and wasn't.

What Is the Student in Need of Connection Process?

At its heart, the SiNoC Process is about slowing down, noticing what's beneath the behavior, and choosing to connect rather than correct. It's about asking better questions, not about what's wrong with the student, but what's going on *within* them.

What are they trying to communicate through their behavior or silence? What do they need that they may not yet have the skills or safety to ask for? Where might they be under-supported, not just academically, but emotionally, socially, or developmentally? What strengths are waiting just beneath the surface, hidden behind survival strategies or misunderstood signals?

Perhaps most importantly: Who are they becoming, and how do we walk alongside them, not to control their path, but to support their growth into that fuller version of themselves?

This process can be easily integrated into the existing structures your school already uses, such as MTSS, RTI, student support teams, behavior intervention plans, or IEP planning. Rather than replacing those systems, the SiNoC process enhances them by offering a more holistic, neuro-informed, and relationally grounded understanding of the student.

The student intervention plans built through the SiNoC Process are just as focused on the adult's response as they are on the student's behavior. Most importantly, it's about returning to what matters most: relationships that restore, not rupture. It brings depth, humanity, and context to the decision-making process. It centers on one essential truth: students don't need better compliance strategies; they need better connection.

Part Three shares this process through the story of students and their teachers, but in Part Four, you'll find the SiNoC Process laid out in a clear, linear structure. It includes step-by-step guidance, reflection tools, and interview protocols to help schools implement connection-based supports at both the individual and system levels. Think of Part Four as your roadmap for action. However, before we get there, we need to walk through the why, and that's what Part Three offers.

A Way to Return to Hope

We live in a world that teaches educators to survive, but this framework invites you to remember that you didn't choose this work to survive. You chose it to make a difference, and making a difference begins with seeing differently.

That's what this part of the book is about. Each story you read, each reflection you take, and each shift you make in your practice is part of this larger journey, from managing behavior to meeting needs, from isolation to inclusion, from shame to hope. You will be invited to lean into the discomfort and beauty of noticing what we might have missed. Because no child is too far gone, and no adult is too late to change how they respond.

Let's Meet Our Students

As you move through this chapter and the rest of Part Three, you'll meet five students: Jayden, Malik, Marisol, Isaiah, and Meredith—each uniquely shaped by their life experiences, attachment patterns, and nervous system responses. These profiles are not fictional composites. They are deeply rooted in the real experiences of children I've taught, coached educators through, and parented. Their names have been changed, but their truths remain.

Jayden – Securely Attached, Steady, and Growing

From Jayden's teacher:

"Jayden's one of those kids who just brings calm into the room. He has a stable home and two parents who are highly involved, and he comes to school ready to learn. He's kind to other kids, helps out without being asked, and if he's having a hard time, he usually just needs a minute to regroup. That said, I've noticed he hesitates to take risks academically. He'll sometimes hold back if he's not sure he'll get it right, and he can be a little too focused on 'doing it perfectly.' I think he trusts me and the classroom space, but I'd like to push him to be more confident in himself. He has the foundation; we just need to stretch him gently, give him more leadership opportunities, and keep encouraging that ownership piece. He's doing great, but I don't want to miss the chance to help him grow."

Malik – Avoidantly Attached, Guarded, and Disconnected

From Malik's teacher:

"Malik's tough to connect with. He barely looks at me, shrugs off any help, and kind of floats through the day like nothing matters. When he does engage, such as when he's sketching or building something, I can see that there's more going on. He lives with his grandma, and from what I understand, it's been a pretty unstable few years. There's been a lot of back and forth between caregivers, and I think he's learned not to rely on adults. He acts like he doesn't care, but I don't buy it. I think he's protecting himself. Academically, he's behind in reading and writing, and I see him give up before he even starts. He's got the potential, but the wall is up. He needs consistency, predictability, and an adult he can count on, someone who doesn't take it personally when he pushes back. Right now, he's completely disconnected, and I don't think he trusts anyone here."

Marisol – Ambivalently Attached, Performing and Protecting

From Marisol's teacher:

"Marisol's the kind of student who makes teaching feel easy on the surface. She turns in her work early, volunteers to help, and never causes a disruption, but something's off. She's constantly checking in for reassurance, is overly apologetic, and melts down at home, according to her mom, which doesn't match the image she maintains here.

I know there's trauma in her background; she lost her older brother last year, and the family went through a really tough time before that with domestic violence. She now lives with her mom, and they seem close, but she's carrying a lot of emotional weight. I worry that her success is her shield. She tries to control everything, and when she can't, it sends her into a tailspin. I don't want to miss the pain because her grades look good. She needs space to feel seen without having to earn it. I think if we don't create that space, she'll crash later."

Isaiah – Chronically Dysregulated, Brilliant but Unreachable

From Isaiah's teacher:

"Isaiah's one of the most intelligent students I've ever worked with, but he can't stay in the classroom long enough to show it. He's constantly in fight-or-flight, yelling, refusing, and sometimes just walking out. Honestly, it's exhausting. I know he's had a rough go. He's been through foster care, his mom's rights were terminated a few years ago, and he's bounced around since. Right now, he's with a relative who's doing their best, but it's not always consistent. His nervous system is always in overdrive.

I've tried to build a relationship with him, but I don't think he trusts me, or anyone. When he's calm, he's insightful, funny, and honestly kind of brilliant, but that window is so small. I need help. I don't want to give up on him, but he needs something different than what I can do in a traditional setting. He needs a team, a plan, and a space where he doesn't feel like he's always in trouble for just existing."

Meredith – Anxiously Attached, Insightful, and Underestimated

Meredith is my daughter.

Meredith is fiercely intelligent and deeply perceptive, the kind of kid who sees through people and systems more clearly than most adults, but school has never quite known how to handle her.

She's been labeled disrespectful for asking questions, removed from class for pushing back, and overlooked as she quietly fell apart. After going through a painful divorce in our family, she started showing signs of anxiety and emotional exhaustion.

At home, she has strong opinions and a sharp sense of humor, but at school, she's often guarded, unsure when it's safe to speak. She needs to know that her voice won't be used against her. She needs teachers who won't confuse curiosity for defiance.

When she finds adults who believe in her, not just her performance, but in her as a person, she thrives. She's a leader, an advocate, and a creator. However, when she's dismissed or misunderstood, she shuts down. Her power has always been there. She just needs a place where she's safe enough to use it.

As you read, you're invited to do more than observe these students; you're invited to think of your own.

Who in your classroom reminds you of Malik's defensiveness or Marisol's hidden pain?

Who, like Meredith or Isaiah, might be misunderstood because their nervous system is in survival mode?

Who, like Jayden, is flourishing now, and what helped make that possible?

❧ fourteen ❧
Resilience

Resilience isn't about never falling. It's about building the safety to rise again.

Seeing Strength Beneath the Struggle

We talk a lot about "negative" student behavior. Disruptions. Avoidance. Attention-seeking. Defiance. Rarely do we pause and ask:

What if what I'm seeing is resilience in disguise?

For many students, especially those with trauma histories, showing up at all is a massive act of resilience. The student who yells instead of asking for help may have learned that vulnerability isn't safe. The child who shuts down may be doing the only thing their nervous system knows how to do to stay protected. We must widen our lens to see these actions not as defiance, but as a testament to endurance.

The Challenge: From Frustration to Recognition

Malik is a student with a sharp mind, a sly sense of humor, and a talent for sketching superheroes during math class. He's also a kid who keeps his distance. He rarely initiates conversation, avoids group work like the plague, and shrugs off praise with a smirk or sarcastic "whatever." When things get tough, especially when reading aloud, he tends to act out or check out. When you try to connect, he might crack a joke or just stare past you like you don't exist.

To a casual observer, Malik is a classic case of oppositional behavior, but look closer. What if Malik's aloofness isn't defiance, it's protection? What if his silence isn't disinterest, but fear that the connection will cost him more than he can afford?

Malik's teacher used to take his indifference personally. She'd try to praise him, and he'd dodge it. She'd offer support, and he'd push back. However, something changed when she started asking herself,

"What has this kid had to do to survive?"

instead of,

"What's wrong with this kid?"

Rooted in Hope Focus: Resilience

Resilience is not about bouncing back. It's about growing forward. It's the capacity to endure, to adapt, and to stay in the struggle long enough to find the way through. For teachers, resilience begins with what you choose to see. If you only look for compliance, you'll miss courage. If you're measuring success by calm and quiet, you might miss the student who used every ounce of energy to show up at all. Seeing resilience means looking for small wins and strength signals, understanding behavior in the context of adversity, and honoring what it takes to keep going, even when it's messy.

Although trauma has adverse effects, the human brain has an incredible ability to heal. Individuals experiencing behavioral, social-emotional, or other adverse effects of toxic stress can overcome their challenges. However, this transformation requires time, intentionality, and the unwavering presence of supportive and caring adults.

Dr. Karen Purvis of the TCU Child Development Center reminds us that it can take up to three years to rewire a brain impacted by toxic stress when consistent adult support is available.[62] This journey can be seemingly impossible if the child remains in a toxic environment, whether at home or school, emphasizing the need for safe, nurturing spaces in educational settings.

The Harvard Center on the Developing Child reinforces this truth: One stable and committed relationship with a supportive adult is the most critical factor in fostering resilience.[63]

Think about the time students spend in your school. A typical elementary school has students for six years, middle school for three years, and high school for four years; that's enough time to make a crucial difference, if we all pull together. Our commitment must be intentional and consistent. Resilience grows in relationships, and teachers are the roots that hold so many students steady. This underscores the critical role of educators and caregivers in shaping a child's ability to adapt and grow.

Teacher Practice Shift: Resilience Builders

Take a moment to flip back to chapter four, where you reflected on your own experiences in school. I am guessing that the profound impact of adult support on your life was either deeply present, leading to your decision to become a teacher, or it was severely lacking, influencing the type of teacher you sought to become. Reflecting on these moments reminds us that the key to resilience lies in the relationships we have with others, particularly the people who walked beside us during difficult times, the mentors who encouraged us, and the teachers who believed in our potential.

These experiences serve as a call to action for educators and caregivers. Just as someone once believed in us, we can become that trusted adult for the students in our care. Through intentional co-care, we support their journey toward healing and equip them with the resilience they need to face life's challenges and succeed.

Resilience begins with co-care, which is the active and intentional support that adults provide to children. Co-care is about offering help *with*, not just *to*, students as they navigate challenges. Supportive adults in this process are known as Resilience Builders.

Resilience Builders offer an empathetic presence, ensuring students feel seen, heard, and understood. This helps validate the students' experiences, normalize their feelings, and foster a sense of safety.

Ultimately, they provide hope and encouragement, nurturing a belief in the possibility of healing and growth. This lays the foundation for long-term resilience, empowering students to face future adversities with courage and optimism.

Actions of Resilience Builders

Qualities	*Strategies*
Empathetic	Uses restorative practices
Listener	Teach accountability
Supportive	React vs Respond
Trusting and trustworthy	Ask vs Tell
Loves unconditionally	Listen to understand
Practice healthy relationships	Comfort and collaboration
Compassionately detached	Celebrate and honor

Children's time in school represents a crucial window for healing and growth, especially for those who have navigated adverse experiences. For children whose home environments are marked by instability or neglect, their schools are often the closest support systems.[64] As educators, we are morally obligated to provide these children with the protective factors they need to thrive and flourish. This responsibility reflects the deeply rooted belief that "it takes a village to raise a child."

Being the village might mean acting as surrogate family members who provide structure, predictability, and unconditional positive regard in schools. It requires fostering a non-judgmental attitude and avoiding assumptions. It requires seeing behavior as a signal of need, not a measure of worth.

Building Relationships in Schools

Research underscores the value of meaningful relationships between students and educators. Gallup Poll data reveal that students who agree with the following statements are 30 times more likely to be engaged in school:

"My school is committed to building the strengths of each student."

"I have at least one teacher who excites me about the future."[65]

While schools may feel they provide a safe and caring environment, students may perceive the situation differently, particularly in cases involving unresolved bullying or exclusion. These gaps underscore the need for deliberate efforts to cultivate positive and trusting relationships in the classroom.

Intentional Relationship-Building Practices

Malik's teacher intentionally began to work on her relationship with him. Instead of demanding connection, she offered presence. A quiet chair near her desk where he could sit during independent work. Casual check-ins during transitions. No forced eye contact. No big emotional talks. Just a calm, predictable, low-pressure connection.

She noticed the patterns: Malik was triggered by criticism, unpredictable changes, and moments when he felt on display. So, she adjusted her feedback style, offered choices, and gave him time to draw when he was dysregulated.

Over time, something shifted. He started lingering after class. He offered to help organize the Chromebook cart. One day, he left a doodle of her as a cartoon superhero on her desk, with a tiny word bubble that said, *"You're not the worst."* It was the start of something.

External and Internal Protective Factors

Protective factors are crucial elements that help reduce the negative impact of trauma and stress on individuals, serving as a buffer against risk factors.[66] These factors can be external, such as supportive relationships and safe environments, or internal, including personal resilience and effective coping mechanisms. While protective factors are especially vital for children experiencing trauma, they are foundational for the success and well-being of all children.

External protective factors encompass resources and relationships within a child's environment that offer support, guidance, and stability. Examples include a caring teacher, a positive school culture, and community programs. These external supports act as a bridge for students who lack internal protective factors, such as emotional regulation or problem-solving skills, which are often underdeveloped in children exposed to chaotic or unpredictable home environments.[67]

Protective Factors That Promote Resilience

External Factors	*Internal Factors*
Strong, safe relationships	Sense of Purpose
Opportunities to contribute to the community	Good health
Safe and stable environment	Hope
Clear expectations for success	Autonomy
Sense of belonging	Impulse control
Access to mental and physical care	Self-regulatory Skills

It's essential to recognize that external factors do not impede the development of internal factors. Instead, they create the conditions necessary for internal factors to emerge. Many children who face adverse experiences, including those with high ACE scores, may not have had the opportunity to develop internal tools due to their age, developmental stage, or lack of stable and supportive relationships in their primary caregiving environment.

Building Resilience Through Protective Factors

The school setting provides a unique opportunity for students to "redo" and "catch up" on the social and emotional skills they have not yet developed. Schools can become a space where resilience flourishes through consistent, compassionate relationships and exposure to a supportive environment. Helping students develop the tools to handle stress and adversity empowers them to move toward a future of hope, healing, and growth.

Skills Related to Protective Factors[68]

Internal Skills:	*Relationship Skills:*
Self-regulation	Attach to caring adults and peers
Self-esteem	Develop trust in others
Trust in oneself	Maintain healthy relationships
Self-advocacy	Work as a cooperative team member
Ability to recognize success	Show appreciation for others
Cognitive Skills:	*Emotional Skills:*
Develop decision-making capabilities	Identify triggers that create reactivity
Develop problem-solving skills	Show empathy
Make appropriate choices	Express feelings
Communication Skills:	*Behavioral Skills:*
Listening skills	Acknowledge mistakes
Speak logical	Take personal responsibility
Ask for and accept help	Accept consequences

A Closing Thought

Malik's teacher didn't "fix" these things. However, she helped create the conditions that allowed them to begin growing. Through relationship building and compassionate presence, she began to meet his core need: emotional safety without pressure. She became a Resilience Builder, not because she had the perfect plan, but because she chose to keep showing up. Not with force. Not with pity. With steadiness. And Malik? He started to believe that maybe, just maybe, connection didn't always come with strings.

✺ reflection ❧

Think of a student that you struggle to connect with, who is frequently dysregulated, or has other challenges making school difficult.

What behaviors might be resilience in disguise?

What protective factors might they be missing—internal or external?

How could you shift your response from reaction to co-care?

What's one small, consistent way you could show up for that student this week, without pressure, but with presence?

What would it mean for you to become a "Resilience Builder" in your classroom, not just in theory, but in your daily presence?

Becoming a Resilience Builder in my classroom means I will consistently show up with _____, even when _____.

❧ fifteen ❧
Trust

Trust isn't built by being perfect. It's built by being predictable, present, and willing to repair.

A Band-Aid and a Broken Bridge

It was Meredith's first day of first grade.

She sat at her desk, tiny legs swinging, trying to balance her pencil perfectly upright on the flat, pink eraser. The kind of task that first graders find wildly entertaining. It's not as easy as it looks; balance is tricky, and at some point, the pencil slipped. The point of graphite was just sharp enough to poke her hand and produce a single, perfect droplet of blood. She raised her hand and asked her teacher for a Band-Aid. The teacher, likely overwhelmed with first-day logistics and twenty-something tiny humans, told her she'd get one later. Later never came.

When I picked her up from school, she climbed into the car, threw her backpack down, and said with dramatic first-grader certainty:

"I'm not going back. My teacher hates me. She said she'd give me a Band-Aid, and she never did. I don't trust her."

As a mom, my heart clenched when she shared this story with me. As a teacher, I understood. She didn't need a Band-Aid. I've said it myself: "Put a wet paper towel on it."

That moment wasn't about the band-aid. It was about trust. This teacher didn't know Meredith yet, and she didn't know this teacher. What she knew, in her six-year-old brain, was that she had been told she would get a Band-Aid, and she didn't. That one small promise, however insignificant it might seem to an adult, mattered deeply to a little girl trying to figure out whether this new adult was safe, kind, and worthy of trust. Of course, she went back the next day, and the day after that. However, something significant occurred in that initial interaction, and it never fully recovered.
Trust was never built.

The truth is, young people with developing brains aren't just learning math and reading. They're learning whether the adults around them can be believed. Whether we mean what we say. Whether we see them. Whether we care. They are watching us, listening to our tone, and measuring our follow-through. While we may not remember the moment we didn't get the Band-Aid, they do. Our words and actions, even the smallest ones, carry weight. Especially on Day One. Especially when trust is still being offered like a fragile gift.

In the classroom, we don't just teach content. We teach whether we are safe. Ultimately, that may be the most important lesson of all.

"Consistency builds trust - but so does repair."

Most teachers want their students to trust them. It's easy to believe we've earned that trust by being kind, fair, or well-intentioned, but trauma doesn't respond to intentions. It responds to patterns, especially the ones that break and rebuild with care.

Trust is fragile for students who adults have let down. It's not built by telling them we're safe. It's built by *showing* them, again and again, that we will not use our power to harm or abandon them, even when they mess up.

Especially then.

The Challenge: When You're the Trigger

You raise your voice to get the class's attention. Most students quiet down. Meredith flinches, lowers her head, and won't meet your gaze for the rest of the morning. She's shut down. You didn't yell at *her*. You were redirecting the class. It wasn't personal, but for Meredith, it was.

For students with trauma histories, even neutral or helpful authority can feel threatening. Tone, posture, and proximity are cues that tell their nervous systems what's coming next. In that moment, the question isn't, *'Did I mean to hurt him?'* It's, *'What can I do now to rebuild trust?'*

Rooted in Hope Focus: Trust

Trust is a felt experience, not a declared one. For many students, it isn't built through words; it's built through presence. It's the quiet knowledge that someone is reliable, safe, and steady, even in the storm. For students who've learned that adults are inconsistent, punitive, or unavailable, trust isn't automatic. It's earned, through consistency, regulation, and repair. We build trust by holding boundaries without punishing, by returning after ruptures, and by choosing co-regulation over control. You don't have to be perfect. You just have to keep coming back, with honesty, with steadiness, and with the willingness to try again.

Authenticity and Assumptions

Authenticity is the foundation of any meaningful relationship, especially in a school setting where trust is critical to student success. The key to building authentic relationships with students is to be yourself; don't alter your personality or adopt a false sense of relatability, especially when working with students from different backgrounds.

Students are incredibly perceptive, and any attempt to be someone you're not will likely come across as insincere. Instead, approach each student with an open mind. Avoid making assumptions about who they are, where they come from, or what they have experienced. Every student has a unique story, and we are responsible for listening and understanding rather than judging or categorizing them based on preconceived notions.

Assumptions are often rooted in stereotypes, personal bias, and misinformation, all of which can create barriers to connection. Building authentic relationships requires patience. For students who have experienced trauma, trust is not freely given; it must be earned, sometimes over a long time. If there are cultural differences, whether real or perceived, trust may take even longer to develop. Connection does not require mimicking a student's language, style, or interests. It is built through consistent, genuine care and effort. Above all, be persistent.

The students who seem the most resistant to connection are often the ones who need it the most. Keep showing up for them. Keep trying new strategies. Continue to demonstrate that you see, hear, and believe in them.

Authentic relationships take time, but they are worth the effort. Trust is not built overnight. However, when it is established, it creates a foundation for learning, growth, and resilience that can profoundly impact a student's life.

The Neurobiology of Trust and Safety

Trust begins in the nervous system. It's not just emotional; it's biological. The amygdala constantly scans for cues: *Am I safe? Will this person hurt me? Can I let my guard down?* Raised voices, sarcasm, and unpredictability? Those say "danger," but a calm, regulated, and responsive adult says, "Safety." That re-engages the prefrontal cortex, the part of the brain responsible for reasoning and learning. That's when students come back online, not just for the content, but for connection.[69]

Teacher Practice Shift: From Control to Co-Regulation

Instead of:
"They need to trust me more."
Try:
"How do I show them I am safe, especially when they're not?"
Start by asking yourself:
What does my tone, posture, and pacing communicate when I'm under stress?
Do I offer predictability, or do I unintentionally add to the chaos?
When a rupture happens, when trust is broken, do I move toward repair,
or do I move on and hope it fades?

These aren't questions of perfection; they're questions of presence. To shift your practice, focus on what your nervous system is broadcasting. Use consistent routines and visual cues to reduce uncertainty. When you make a mistake, own it:
"I raised my voice. That probably didn't feel good. I'm sorry."
Lead with presence before correction. Let the student settle. Then reflect together. This is how safety is built, one choice, one moment, one repair at a time. Trust doesn't mean lowering expectations. It means raising relational safety to meet expectations with dignity and respect.

Understanding Trust in Relationships

What I learned from my daughter's first-grade experience was something I hadn't truly considered before: at the beginning of the school year, I am a stranger to my students. For years, I had eagerly awaited the arrival of my class list, filled with anticipation about the relationships we would build. I would spend hours setting up my classroom to make it feel warm and welcoming, sure that a connection would come naturally.

However, Meredith's story, that moment when she needed a simple Band-Aid and was met with dismissal, made me realize that while I saw the year as the start of something special, my students may have felt uncertain, unsteady, even unsafe. They didn't know me yet. I hadn't earned their trust. That changed me.

I began to think differently about those early days, wondering how many times I might have missed small opportunities to build trust, or worse, how many tiny missteps I made throughout the year that unknowingly chipped away at it. Her story made the invisible visible and reminded me that trust isn't assumed just because we care. It has to be built, offered, and protected from the very first day forward.

When considering trust in the classroom, it is helpful to think about three general types: organic trust, contractual trust, and relational trust. Organic trust is unconditional; it's the kind we extend naturally to people we've always felt safe with. Contractual trust is based on roles and expectations. *"You're the teacher, so I'm supposed to trust you."* The third, and the kind of trust that most often defines student–teacher relationships, is relational trust. It's built slowly, through consistent, observable behavior.

Students learn to trust us not because of our title, but because we consistently demonstrate calmness, honesty, fairness, and presence, day after day. Especially for students who carry histories of broken trust, this kind of relationship becomes the bridge to safety, regulation, and meaningful learning.

Megan Tschannen-Moran, education leadership professor at the College of William and Mary, defines trust as

---

"an individual's or group's willingness to be vulnerable to another party based on confidence that the latter is benevolent, reliable, competent, honest, and open."[70]

This definition emphasizes the importance of authenticity and reliability in fostering trust between educators and students. Let's break down each facet of trust with an example and its importance in a teacher-student relationship:

Benevolence means showing care and good intentions. It might look like a teacher noticing a student seems withdrawn and quietly asking if they're okay, offering a safe space to talk. It's acknowledging effort, not just outcomes. Students who experience trauma often expect adults to be punitive or dismissive, so for some students, benevolence is disarming.. When a teacher consistently shows kindness and support, the student begins to believe the teacher genuinely cares about their well-being, not just their academic performance, laying the foundation for emotional safety and engagement.

Honesty is being transparent and genuine. It's admitting when you've made a mistake, like misgrading an assignment or jumping to a conclusion. It's giving feedback that is both truthful and compassionate: "I can see you worked hard on this, but let's work together to figure out how to improve it." Students respect and trust truthful adults, even when the truth is complicated to accept. Honesty models integrity, encouraging students to be authentic and take responsibility for their actions.

Openness is about sharing both information and power. It involves students in conversations about classroom norms or explaining the "why" behind a decision or policy. When students are included in decisions, they feel respected and valued. Students are less likely to resist when they understand the rationale behind certain practices. Involving them in decision-making fosters ownership and empowerment, which is crucial for students who may feel powerless in other areas of their lives.

Reliability means being consistent and predictable. If you say you'll check in, you do. If you respond to conflict calmly and fairly, students learn they can count on you. For trauma-impacted students, unpredictability often equals danger. A reliable teacher becomes a source of stability, helping students feel more secure and less on edge, which allows them to focus on learning.

Competence is demonstrated by both skill and flexibility. It's the ability to take a concept that isn't landing and find a new way to reach the student, through visuals, stories, movement, or a shift in pacing. A competent teacher doesn't just repeat the same strategy louder; they adapt. They say, *"Let's try something different,"* and they mean it. This communicates to the student: *"I'm not giving up on you. We'll figure it out together."* And students notice.

Teacher Credibility

According to John Hattie's research, teacher credibility, which encompasses students' perceptions of a teacher's competence, has one of the highest impacts on student achievement.[71] When students believe their teacher knows what they're doing, they engage more deeply, trust the process, and persist through challenges. Competence, then, isn't just about content knowledge; it's about being the kind of steady, responsive presence that makes learning feel possible.

When all these facets come together, trust forms, and trust is the bridge to accountability, motivation, and emotional resilience. A student who feels safe, valued, and supported by their teacher is far more likely to take academic risks, engage in learning, and work through challenges.

Consistency and High Expectations: A Path to Trust

Trust isn't just built through warmth; it's also built through consistency. One of the most powerful ways we demonstrate to students that they can trust us is by holding them to high expectations and following through with support and structure. A trauma-informed lens doesn't ask us to lower the bar. It asks us to change how we support students in reaching it.

Maintaining high expectations for every student, regardless of their background, behaviors, or story, sends a clear message: *I believe in you.* When we apply expectations consistently across people and situations, we communicate fairness and predictability. This steadiness signals safety to the nervous system. It helps students know they don't have to guess whether today's teacher will show up tired, reactive, or checked out. The rules don't change based on our mood or who's in the room. They change when students grow and the context requires it, and when they do, we name it. This kind of consistency builds trust.

However, consistency doesn't mean rigidity. It's not about handing out the same consequence every time or ignoring context. It's about showing up with the same belief: that students are capable, worthy, and able to succeed, and that when they struggle, we won't give up on them. High expectations in a trauma-informed classroom mean more than academic standards. They include behavioral expectations, emotional safety, and relational accountability. They're grounded in mutual respect and centered around repair, not rejection. We don't enforce limits to control students; we hold them to create a safe environment. Predictable boundaries and follow-through help students feel anchored in a world that often feels chaotic or hostile.

Importantly, equity isn't about giving every student the same thing; it's about giving each student what they need to reach the same goal. Some students need scaffolds, others need space. What matters is that we never confuse support with pity or lower our standards in the name of compassion. It's not compassionate to tell a student they don't have to try. It's not trauma-informed to assume they can't handle a challenge.

When we maintain high expectations while offering flexible, targeted support, we affirm a deeper truth: that success is not a one-size-fits-all journey. It's a shared belief that the student has what it takes, and that we'll walk alongside them until they see it too.

Using Student Voice to Reflect on Trust

As we follow the stories of Jayden, Malik, Marisol, and Isaiah, a thread quickly becomes visible: trust isn't just an abstract idea; it's a felt experience. Some students instinctively trust the adults around them. Others hesitate. Some have learned to keep their walls up. Others may appear connected but are internally guarded.

To understand and respond to this spectrum of relational safety, we must do something both radical and simple: ask students how they feel. The Student Trust Scale used in this section is adapted from the Student Trust in Faculty Scale (STF-Scale), a research-based tool developed by Dr. Curt Adams and Dr. Patrick Forsyth at the University of Oklahoma.[72] Their work defines trust as a student's willingness to be vulnerable to school adults based on the belief that those adults are benevolent, reliable, competent, honest, and open.

The original STF-Scale includes 13 Likert-style items, each rated on a scale from 1 (strongly disagree) to 4 (strongly agree). It has been validated through extensive research and demonstrates high reliability, confirming its effectiveness in measuring students' perceptions of trust within school relationships. This tool invites teachers to hear directly from students about their perceptions of school relationships. The statements are designed to surface how students experience trust, care, dependability, and support within the classroom and school community. These aren't just data points. They're insights into a child's nervous system, belief system, and capacity to connect.

In this book, the scale has been adapted and simplified to support trauma-responsive reflection and integration within the ROOTED IN HOPE framework. It is not intended for formal evaluation or comparison. Instead, it serves as a tool for noticing, an invitation to center student voice, reflect on classroom culture, and identify areas where trust can be strengthened. At its heart, it's about deepening relationships through curiosity and care. When we ask students how they perceive the adults around them, we are not just collecting data. We are honoring their lived experience. We are signaling that their perspective matters, and we are creating space for growth, not just for them, but for us as well.

This kind of reflection matters. It helps us recognize which students are quietly disconnected and where relational safety is thriving, or missing. It sheds light on how students experience us, not just as instructors, but as people. It helps us determine whether our classroom culture is genuinely rooted in the kind of safety and consistency that supports healing.

This is not just a student survey. It's a mirror. A chance to reflect on questions that often go unspoken: Are my students experiencing me as someone safe and consistent? Do I listen in a way that communicates care? Who in my classroom might feel invisible, and how would I know? Perhaps most importantly, now that I know how they think, how will I respond? When we see students' answers, especially those that surprise us, it's not about guilt or blame. It's about alignment. It's about bringing our intentions and their experience closer together.

As you work through the next section, consider how students, Jayden, Malik, Marisol, Meredith, and Isaiah, might respond to this survey. Even more importantly, consider your students. Whose answers would surprise you? Whose might break your heart? Whom do you still have time to rebuild trust with? We can't change every story, but we can be the chapter where trust is restored.

Statement	Malik	Jayden	Marisol	Isaiah	Meredith
My teachers are always ready to help	2	4	3	1	2
My teachers are easy to talk to	1	4	2	1	1
I am well cared for at this school	2	4	3	1	3
My teachers do what they are supposed to	2	3	4	1	2
My teachers really listen to students	2	4	2	1	2
My teachers are honest with me	2	4	2	2	2
My teachers do a terrific job	2	4	4	2	2
My teachers are good at teaching	3	4	4	3	2
My teachers have high expectations	3	4	4	2	2
My teachers do NOT care (reverse scored)	2	1	2	3	3
I can believe what my teachers say	2	4	2	2	2
I learn a lot from my teachers	3	4	4	2	2
I can depend on my teachers for help	2	4	3	1	2

Sample Teacher Reflection: What the Students Showed Me

When I first reviewed the student survey results, I thought I had a fairly good sense of how my students would respond. Jayden's answers didn't surprise me; he trusts easily and engages openly. His responses affirmed what I already felt: we've built something safe together. But the other results gave me pause.

Malik rated most of the statements about trust and care with twos, and even a few ones. At first, I felt defensive. I've tried to reach him. I've given him space, options, and check-ins. But then I remembered: connection for Malik doesn't start with what I think I've done. It starts with how he experiences it. He's learned not to rely on adults. His low scores aren't rejection-they're protection. And that shifts how I show up.

Marisol's answers were the most unexpected. She agreed that teachers work hard and have high expectations, but she disagreed when asked if she feels listened to or emotionally supported. That hurt a little. She's my "easy" student. She always performs, always complies, but her responses reminded me that compliance isn't the same as connection. She needs emotional safety, not just academic affirmation. I need to slow down, look beneath the surface, and be curious, not just grateful that she's "doing fine."

And then there's Isaiah. His scores were low across the board. He doesn't believe teachers care. He doesn't feel safe. He doesn't feel heard. Reading his answers was hard, not because I didn't expect them, but because they confirmed what I already feared: he doesn't trust any of us. That realization left me sitting in silence for a while. Not in shame, but in grief. Grief for the ways the system has failed him and for the walls he's had to build just to get through the day. I keep thinking: now that I know, I can't look away.

Meredith seems to be just flying beneath my radar. Clearly, there is more going on with her than I am noticing.

These responses aren't just data. They're messages. Invitations. Redirections. They don't demand perfection from me, but they ask for presence. They remind me that what I say and how I respond matter, especially in the moments when students are at their most guarded.

This tool didn't tell me who was "good" or "bad." It showed me who feels safe, who feels seen, and who still doesn't. And that's where I begin again, with compassion, humility, and a renewed commitment to rooting every interaction in hope.

A Closing Thought

Trust isn't a program, a strategy, or a checkbox on a relationship plan. It's a posture, a choice we make every day to be steady, safe, and seen. It's built slowly, in small moments that signal: *You matter here.* For students who have learned that adults can't be counted on, our calm presence is more powerful than any perfect lesson. We don't earn trust by demanding it. We earn it by showing up, especially when it would be easier not to. If we get it right, we won't just open the door to learning; we will also unlock the potential for growth. We'll open the door to healing.

tutoring.cherisheliving.org/book-companion

Visit the book companion
site for additional
materials related to this
chapter.

Book Companion Resources

- **Student Trust in Faculty Scale**

❧ reflection ❧

Trust is built not through one grand act, but through the repeated signals we send about our benevolence (I care about your well-being), our honesty (I will be clear and fair), our openness (I will listen and not judge), and our reliability (I will keep showing up, even when it's hard).

Think of a student who may not yet trust you. What signals have you sent, intentionally or not, about who you are?

How do your words and actions reflect reliability and honesty, even in discipline?

In what ways are you creating space for openness, especially for students who don't yet know how to trust adults?

A moment I missed where I could have shown benevolence was _____.

A moment I honored trust through reliability was _____.

One way I can embody openness and honesty with my students this week is _____.

❧ sixteen ❧
Origin

You cannot understand a student's behavior without understanding their story.

Honoring the Story Beneath the Surface

When we step into a classroom, we don't meet blank slates. We meet biographies. Every child carries a story, their lived experiences, culture, relationships, fears, and dreams. Some wear it openly. Others hide it so well, it's easy to forget it's there. Here's the truth: behavior doesn't happen in a vacuum. It's a mirror, a message, and a map. To teach well, we must be willing to look back before moving forward.

The Challenge: When the Past Is Present

Some students announce their pain. Others whisper it.

Marisol is the kind of student who makes teaching feel easy, on the surface. She's always prepared, turns in her work early, offers to help clean up, and never causes a disruption. She's polite, quiet, and attentive. The kind of student who flies under the radar because she gives adults no reason to worry. Marisol checks in constantly, "Is this okay? Are you sure?" and apologizes even when she hasn't done anything wrong. According to her mom, she often melts down at home, sobbing after school or shutting down over small mistakes. That's not the version of her seen in class. There, she's polished. In control. Safe. Perhaps, though, her success is a shield.

Marisol lost her older brother last year. Before that, her family endured years of instability and domestic violence. She now lives with her mom in what seems like a more stable environment, but the scars haven't healed just because the chaos has ended. She's carrying a lot of emotional weight that's hard to see when you're only looking at behavior or grades.

You're teaching a mini-lesson one day when something shifts. Marisol, usually eager and engaged, is suddenly gone, not physically, but emotionally. She's staring out the window, unmoving. Not disruptive. Not oppositional. Just unreachable. You ask her a question and get no response. Later, she doesn't turn in her work. You start to feel frustrated. She knows the expectation. You've gone over it. You consider reissuing the same consequence you always use for missing work.

Then something in you pauses. What if this moment isn't about effort at all? What if something happened last night, raised voices, a loud door slam, a reminder of everything she's trying to keep at bay? What if she didn't turn in the work because she was afraid it wasn't perfect, and turning in something imperfect feels like exposure? What if her silence is her survival skill, the way she disappears when things feel unsafe?

Marisol's story reminds us that behavior is never just behavior. It's communication, adaptation, and origin. The quieter the pain, the more attuned we have to be.

Rooted in Hope Focus: Origin

Origin asks us to consider the whole narrative, ours and theirs. It's not just about trauma histories or ACE scores; it's about honoring each student's identity, culture, and context. It means staying curious about what shaped them, without assuming we know the answer.

The Adverse Childhood Experiences (ACE) study provides valuable insights into how early adversity can increase a child's risk of adverse outcomes across emotional, behavioral, and academic domains.[73] Teachers are not expected to identify every ACE a student may have experienced, nor should they administer ACE assessments to students or families. Instead, educators can use the study as a framework to build awareness around common risk factors that may already be evident in the school setting.

Factors such as parental divorce, poverty, incarceration of a caregiver, or the death of a parent may already be known through educational records or shared naturally within the teacher-student relationship. Recognizing the presence of these factors is not about assuming harm has occurred; it is about understanding that they may increase the student's vulnerability and influence how they engage, learn, and regulate in the classroom.

Importantly, not all ACEs result in trauma, and every child responds differently. Teachers should not attempt to diagnose or label students based on this information. Instead, this awareness can help guide compassionate, trauma-informed responses that prioritize safety, trust, and connection. It's about increasing protective factors, not defining a student by their risk.

When we discuss a student's origin, we are asking: *What experiences have shaped how this child navigates the world?* Rather than focusing on what's *"wrong,"* we focus on what happened, biologically, relationally, and environmentally, that may explain the behaviors we see.

How Biology and Beginnings Shape the Child

While the ACE study helps us build awareness of adversity, it's only one part of the story. A child's origin is shaped not just by what has happened in their home or family, but also by what has happened in their body, their environment, and even their biology long before they enter a classroom. Understanding origin requires us to go deeper than external events. It invites us to explore how a student's early development, from birth history to sensory processing, may influence their ability to regulate, relate, and learn.

These factors are often invisible, but they are real. When we begin to see these patterns, not as problems to fix, but as adaptations to understand, we expand our ability to respond with compassion, creativity, and care. What follows are some common early influences that may shape a student's nervous system and how we interpret their behavior.

Maternal Stress and the Story Before Birth

Not all origin stories begin *after* birth. Increasing research in the field of epigenetics, the study of how the environment influences gene expression, has shown that stress experienced during pregnancy can impact a developing baby's nervous system before they are even born.

When a pregnant person experiences chronic stress, trauma, poverty, violence, or emotional isolation, their body's stress chemistry, including the hormone cortisol, can cross the placenta. This doesn't just affect physical growth; it can shape how the baby's nervous system develops, particularly their sensitivity to threat, ability to regulate, and even their threshold for stress.[74]

This doesn't mean a child is "damaged" before they're born. It means their body learned early that the world might not be a safe place. They may arrive more easily dysregulated, with heightened sensitivity or difficulty calming, not because of anything they did, but because their earliest environment was already asking them to adapt.

When we understand this, we stop asking, *"What's wrong with this child?"* and start asking, *"What story were they born into?"* That question alone can shift how we respond, with softness instead of suspicion.

Prenatal Exposure to Substances

Prenatal exposure to substances can have a lasting impact on a child's brain development, especially in areas related to regulation, attention, sensory processing, and executive function. When a fetus is exposed to alcohol, nicotine, opioids, or other drugs, it can alter how the brain wires itself in utero, disrupting the development of key systems involved in stress response and learning.[75] These children may later struggle with impulsivity, emotional control, sensory sensitivities, or difficulty adapting to routine classroom expectations. These challenges are often misunderstood as "behavior problems," but they are rooted in early neurodevelopmental disruption, not intentional defiance.

Premature Birth / Low Birth Weight

Babies born prematurely or at low birth weight often miss crucial developmental time in the womb. They may spend time in the NICU, where touch, sound, and routine differ from those experienced in utero. These early disruptions can affect attachment, sensory processing, and emotional regulation. Many of these students may show hypervigilance, anxiety, or difficulty transitioning, not because they are difficult, but because their nervous system started its story under stress.[76]

Traumatic Birth

Birth is the first major transition in a human's life. Suppose a student experienced a traumatic birth, such as an emergency C-section, oxygen deprivation, or maternal distress. In that case, it can impact their physiological stress responses, attachment wiring, and even their relationship to safety and separation. These students may exhibit a heightened startle reflex, difficulty with transitions, or struggle to settle into routines.[77] Recognizing this as part of their origin allows educators to meet them with regulation and rhythm, not rigidity.

Frequent Ear Infections or Ear Tubes

Chronic ear infections, particularly in early childhood, can affect a child's ability to hear and process sound during critical developmental periods. Inconsistent or muffled auditory input can affect language development, listening comprehension, and sensory integration. What is often less understood is that the area around the ear is rich in neural pathways, including a branch of the vagus nerve, which plays a crucial role in regulating the nervous system.[78]

When this area is frequently inflamed or disrupted, it may contribute to chronic dysregulation, not just in how the child hears, but in how they feel and respond to stress. These students may seem inattentive, emotionally reactive, or sensitive to sound, not because they are misbehaving, but because their system has been working hard to compensate. Understanding this piece of origin invites patience and targeted support.

Understanding Attachment: Patterns, Not Pathology

When we begin to understand the biological and environmental influences that shape a child's nervous system from the very beginning, we can't ignore what comes next: relationships. The earliest relational experiences, how a child is held, responded to, soothed, or left alone, form the blueprint for how they connect with others and interpret the world around them. This is the heart of attachment. Whether secure or strained, those early bonds teach the brain what to expect from others: *Am I safe? Am I seen? Am I worth coming back for?* Attachment isn't just a psychological concept; it's a physiological process that wires the brain for trust, regulation, and connection.

In the classroom, the effects of attachment patterns are evident in the way students seek proximity, respond to correction, handle transitions, and form relationships with both us and their peers.[79] Understanding attachment helps us move beyond behavior and begin to meet students where their story began: in a relationship.

Understanding attachment is not about diagnosing disorders. It's about recognizing patterns in our students, and just as importantly, in ourselves. When we become aware of these patterns, we can respond more effectively. We stop taking behavior personally, start seeing more clearly where the connection is needed, and we begin to shift from reaction to reflection.

What the Research Says: We Respond to Familiar Patterns

In *"The Verdict Is In"*, researchers Alan Sroufe and Dan Siegel explored the unconscious ways that attachment patterns shape relationships in school settings.[80] One of their key findings was that educators are more likely to respond positively and empathetically to students whose attachment styles mirror their own. In other words, if a student's way of relating, seeking help, handling emotions, and expressing needs feels familiar to us, we are more likely to feel comfortable with them, to offer support, and to give them the benefit of the doubt.

However, if a student's attachment behaviors feel foreign or uncomfortable to us, if they shut down when we expect them to speak up, or lash out when we offer guidance, we may misinterpret their behavior. We may become frustrated or pull away, even unintentionally. This doesn't make us bad educators. It makes us human. It also calls us to do better. We can't support every student the same way, but we can learn to meet students where they are, and that starts by understanding where we are coming from, too.

The Role of Self-Awareness in Attachment-Informed Teaching

Attachment-informed teaching requires that we examine both student behaviors and our internal responses to those behaviors. Ask yourself:

Which students do I feel naturally connected to?
Who do I find myself withdrawing from or misreading?
What assumptions am I making about what their behavior means?
What does their behavior activate in me,
        and what does that reveal about my attachment lens?

This reflection isn't easy, but it's powerful. When we name our patterns, we gain the ability to *interrupt* them. We can choose connection, even when it's hard. We can offer what a student needs, not just what's most comfortable for us to give.

Attachment Patterns as a Guide to Protective Interventions

Again, this is not about labeling students with an attachment "type" or implying that they have a disorder. Instead, it's about using observable relational patterns to inform how we build trust and what kinds of support a student might need.[81]

Secure Attachment: "You show up for me."

Children with a secure attachment have experienced consistent and responsive care throughout their lives. The early messages they received were clear: *You matter. I will meet your needs. It's safe to be you.* Over time, this security becomes internalized, forming a steady foundation for how they engage with the world. Their view of self sounds like: *"I am seen, heard, and valued. Others will show up for me."*

In the classroom, these students tend to be emotionally regulated, academically engaged, and open to relational feedback. They aren't easily pulled into drama or dysregulation just because it's happening around them. If another student earns a reward or throws a chair, it doesn't shake them. They have a strong internal compass. They know how to get their needs met in appropriate ways and tend to see adults as safe, caring, and helpful.

For securely attached students, your role is to keep building trust while stretching their growth. Honor their autonomy. Offer meaningful challenges. Reinforce their value as contributors and leaders within the classroom community.

Insecure-Ambivalent Attachment: "I have to earn love."

When care is inconsistent, sometimes nurturing, other times withdrawn, children learn to hyperfocus on relationships as a source of safety. Connection becomes a moving target, and the child begins to believe that love is conditional. The internal message becomes: *"I have to work hard to be loved. If I mess up or let go, I'll be left behind."*

In the classroom, these students often appear clingy and need frequent reassurance. They may seek constant proximity to adults, often choosing to spend time with teachers over peers. While their desire for connection is deep and sincere, it can sometimes come across as intrusive or overly needy, making it challenging for them to maintain healthy peer relationships. Their fear of abandonment can create a push-pull dynamic: they draw close, then act out when the connection feels too strong or too uncertain. This pattern often intensifies around transitions or breaks, when the fear of being left is at its highest.

Students exhibiting anxious attachment behaviors require predictable routines, gentle boundaries, and frequent reminders that they are valued beyond their actions. Name their efforts rather than just their outcomes. Reassure them that they are safe, cared for, and remembered, even when they're not in direct contact with you. Your consistent presence helps interrupt the message that connection must be earned or performed for. Instead, you're offering a new narrative: *you are already enough.*

Insecure-Avoidant Attachment: "I don't need anyone."

In avoidant attachment, emotional needs were often dismissed, minimized, or met with discomfort. In response, children learn to suppress those needs. They become overly self-reliant, emotionally guarded, and appear remarkably independent, but that independence is often armor, not confidence. The internal message sounds like: *"I'm safer not needing anyone. My needs aren't going to be met anyway."*

In the classroom, these students may resist connection, avoid eye contact, or tightly control their emotions. Even when they're struggling, they rarely seek help and may appear indifferent to praise, support, or constructive criticism.

Beneath the surface, there is often deep loneliness and fear, but vulnerability feels like a dangerous thing. When trust begins to form, they may suddenly disrupt the relationship, especially during transitions such as holidays or the end of the school year. Leaving first feels safer than being left.

Don't chase closeness, but don't retreat either. Be consistent. Stay present. Gently invite emotional expression without pressure or public attention. If a student seems withdrawn or emotionally distant, it may be an avoidant strategy learned through early experiences where expressing needs didn't lead to comfort. Private check-ins, non-intrusive support, and quiet signals of care go a long way. Remember: emotional distance isn't rejection, it's protection. Your steady presence is the beginning of repair.

Disorganized Attachment: "Love and danger are the same."

Disorganized attachment emerges when caregivers are both a source of comfort and a source of fear. In homes marked by trauma, chaos, or abuse, children learn that connection isn't just uncertain, it can be dangerous. This creates internal confusion and chronic dysregulation. The message they carry is: *"I don't know if I'm safe. I might be too much or not enough."*

In the classroom, these students are often the most challenging to support, not because they don't want connection, but because they've learned not to trust it. You'll have a plan that works, until it doesn't. You'll see progress, then suddenly face withdrawal, aggression, or a complete unraveling of the routine. It's not sabotage. It's survival. These students reject connection even when it's offered with care, because comfort has been unpredictable or short-lived in the past. Their nervous systems expect the good to fall apart, so they push it away first. What they need most is for us to return to the drawing board, not just once, but repeatedly. Every time we do, we send a powerful message: *I won't give up on you.* Prioritize regulation over correction. Your calm presence, consistent boundaries, and steady compassion help rewire what relationships can feel like: not threatening, not fleeting, but safe. A student who appears both overly dependent and resistant may be showing signs of disorganized attachment, shaped by complex trauma. They are not unreachable, but they do need intentional, relational strategies, trauma-informed support, and often, close collaboration with caregivers and mental health professionals. What they need more than a perfect plan is a person who stays.

A Rooted Reminder

Attachment is not fixed; it evolves in relationships. Every child, regardless of their story, can experience healing and repair. You, dear teacher, are often the first safe adult to help rewrite that story.

Trauma-informed education is not about fixing students; it's about supporting them. It's about creating spaces where students don't have to armor up to survive. It's about rooting them in safety so they can grow toward connection, learning, and hope.

"When students experience secure attachment in the classroom, they don't just learn math or reading, they learn that they matter."

The Potential for Change

Attachment styles are not fixed and can evolve throughout life. Consistent, positive relationships with supportive adults, whether teachers, coaches, or community members, can reshape insecure attachments and foster growth. This process takes time, but with stability and emotional attunement, individuals learn to trust, regulate their emotions, and build healthier connections.

For example, a child with anxious attachment benefits from consistent care and reassurance, reducing fears of abandonment. A child with avoidant attachment may learn to open up and trust through gentle encouragement and opportunities for safe connection.

No two children are the same, but every child is asking, "Can I trust you?" "Will you stay with me when I make it hard to love me?" We can support the development of secure attachment if we turn the mirror on ourselves, reflecting on how our attachment patterns may influence the way we build (or avoid) relationships with students. Healing happens in relationships, and in schools, we are the relationship.

Teacher Practice Shift: From Judgment to Curiosity

As educators, we must remember that we step into a student's life mid-chapter. We didn't write the beginning, and we don't know how the story ends, but how we respond in the middle can change everything.

For Marisol, support doesn't look like pushing harder or rewarding compliance. It seems like safety without conditions. Predictability without pressure. Being seen without having to earn it.

We support students like Marisol by:

Asking, What story might this behavior be rooted in?

Recognizing that perfectionism is often a trauma response.

Creating space where students can be human, not just successful.

Offering compassion without requiring explanation.

Sometimes, the strongest students are the ones most at risk, because they've learned to survive by hiding the parts that hurt. Instead of: *"They should know better by now."*

Try: *"What has this child experienced that makes this behavior make sense?"*

Ask yourself:

What do I know about this student's story?

What might I not know?

Then shift your practice by leaning into curiosity. Try using an Empathy Map to step into a student's world—asking yourself, *What might this student be feeling, thinking, saying, or doing?* Notice when labels like "attention-seeking" or "lazy" creep in, and instead pause to wonder, *What is the unmet need?* And whenever it's safe and developmentally appropriate, invite students into the process by asking, *What do you want me to know about you that would help me teach you better?*

A Closing Thought

Every student enters our classroom carrying a story. Some stories are spoken aloud. Others live in silence, tucked behind good grades, polite smiles, or disruptive outbursts. When we only respond to what we see on the surface, we miss the meaning beneath the behavior, and we risk retraumatizing students who are doing their best to survive.

To honor a student's origin is not to excuse harmful behavior. It's to understand what shaped it. It's to meet students where they are, without assuming we know where they've been. When we slow down long enough to ask, *"What might this student's behavior be protecting them from?"* We move from managing to connecting. From correcting to understanding. From reacting to responding. Our job isn't to write over a student's story; it's to become a trustworthy part of the chapter they're in now.

Visit the book companion site for additional materials related to this chapter.

Book Companion Resources

- Empathy Maps
- Attachment Resources

ᔏ reflection ᔐ

Think of a student you've struggled to connect with.

Ask yourself:

How do they typically respond to support or correction?

Could their behavior be shaped by a pattern of protection rather than defiance?

What part of my own story might be shaping the way I respond?

How does your origin influence your teaching?

What parts of your story shaped how you respond to student emotion or behavior?

Who were you as a child? What did you need from your teachers?

I used to assume _____ about students like _____, but I'm starting to see _____.

✦ seventeen ❧
Neuro-Informed Practices

It's not defiance. It's the nervous system doing its job.

Teaching the Brain in Front of You

A student refuses to sit still. Another zones out in the middle of a sentence. Someone else goes from zero to explosion in five seconds flat. These moments frustrate us, but they aren't mysteries. They're messages from the nervous system. To understand students effectively, we need to be trauma-informed; however, to respond wisely, we must be neuro-informed, able to view behavior through the lens of brain development, regulation, and survival.

The Brain and the Body Remember

Neuroscience confirms what students already know: the body keeps score.[82] Early experiences shape the nervous system. Repeated threats, whether physical or emotional, wire the brain for survival. Until that wiring is disrupted through relationship and safety, we react to the world as if it's still dangerous, even when it's not.

When Meredith was about six years old, I took her to the dentist for what I thought would be a routine visit. She had been to the dentist many times before for cleanings. She loved going. She loved picking a prize from the treasure chest, sitting in the big chair, and smiling with her freshly polished teeth. So much so that we'd often schedule our cleanings at the same time, I'd be in one chair, she'd be in the next. She never needed me to go back with her. She felt confident, comfortable, and safe. But this time was different. This time, she was getting her first filling.

As we walked into the office, she casually mentioned she was feeling "a little nervous." I acknowledged it, but didn't give it much weight. I mean, it was just a small cavity, and she had always done so well at the dentist. I figured it was normal nerves. However, the moment the dentist began preparing to numb her mouth, that "little nervous" feeling exploded. Her eyes widened, her lips clamped shut, and her body stiffened. She refused to open her mouth.

At first, I tried what I knew: logic. "These people are nice," I reminded her. "You've been here before, and it's always been okay." No response. I tried to employ empathy. "You're a big, brave kid. Let's show the little one in the room next door how to be brave, too." Still nothing.

I could feel my frustration rising. I could also feel the eyes of the hygienist and dentist on me. I felt like I was failing some invisible "good mom" test. I gritted my teeth and leaned in. "Open your mouth. This is taking too long, and they have a job to do. Let's go." Silence. Frozen body. Locked jaw.

Eventually, the dentist offered to try a little laughing gas to help her calm down. We agreed. She took a couple of deep breaths under the mask, then suddenly sat up and told us she needed to use the restroom. Without thinking, we said okay. Big mistake. She didn't go to the bathroom. She bolted. She ran right out the front door, high on nitrous oxide, sprinting across the parking lot, yelling, "I'm going to get my daddy!" Her dad's workplace was across the street, and she was headed straight for a busy road. Thankfully, we caught her before she made it off the sidewalk. We brought her back inside, shaken and tear-streaked. The dentist kindly looked at me and said, "We're not going to do the fillings today. Let's reschedule."

I was humiliated. Angry. Frustrated. I felt judged. Truthfully, I was furious at her. I snapped at her all the way home. My nervous system was shot, and at that moment, I wasn't thinking like a regulated adult. I was thinking like a parent whose fear, embarrassment, and shame had collided. When we got home, we both took some time apart. After a little while, she walked up to me with red eyes and said softly, *"Mommy, I was so scared. It felt like the time they lied and took my blood at the doctor's office."* That's when it hit me like a freight train.

Her reaction had nothing to do with dental tools. It had everything to do with memory, safety, and survival. Her brain was doing precisely what it was designed to do. Through the lens of Dr. Bruce Perry's brain map[83], she wasn't functioning from the top of her brain (the cortex, where thinking and reasoning happen). She was stuck in the lower parts, her brainstem and midbrain, where regulation, fear, and reflexes live.

Her amygdala was firing off danger signals like a five-alarm fire. Her hippocampus had retrieved the memory of a previous traumatic moment, a blood draw where a well-meaning phlebotomist told her, *"I'm just looking,"* and then jabbed her arm with a needle. Her insula distorted her sense of time and space, making her feel like she was back in that betrayal.

Her anterior cingulate cortex, the brain's relay station, stopped sending reliable data to her prefrontal cortex, the part of the brain that makes logical, calm decisions. That part of her wasn't online anymore. Her brainstem, responsible for basic survival instincts, said the only thing it could in that moment: "Run."

She *literally* could not access her reasoning brain. And what did I do?

I tried to reason with her cortex using logic, pressure, and even shame, but she wasn't even in her thinking brain. I skipped past her need for regulation and went straight to expectation.

Bruce Perry teaches that connection is a sequential process.[84] First, we must regulate, then relate, then reason.

I skipped regulation (helping her feel calm and safe).
I missed relating (empathizing and co-regulating with her fear).
I went straight to reasoning ("be brave," "they're nice," "open your mouth"), and it didn't land because it couldn't.

Her whole system was trying to protect her, but it was operating on faulty information. There was no betrayal of trust today, no hidden agenda. Just a dentist trying to numb her mouth. Yet, her nervous system didn't know that. It remembered the betrayal. It remembered the fear. At that moment, logic didn't matter.

I think about that day often. Not because of what she did, but because of what I did. I responded with frustration instead of curiosity. In the language of trauma-responsive care, I went "top-down" when her brain needed me to go "bottom-up." She didn't need a lecture. She needed connection. She needed safety cues. She needed co-regulation.

That day wasn't a parenting failure; it was a nervous system failure for both of us. It was also a turning point. A moment that reminded me how powerful memory, emotion, and survival instincts are. How easily a calm child can tip into dysregulation. How trauma, big or small, doesn't have to make sense to us to feel real to them. How we, as adults, have the sacred responsibility to pause, breathe, and choose connection. Even when we are angry. Even when we're embarrassed. Even when we're scared. Especially then.

The Challenge: When Logic Doesn't Work

I know the previous story didn't happen in the classroom. Sometimes I think it's easier for us to understand a non-classroom example and accept the idea that behavior is a form of communication. I'm guessing some of you can empathize with the mom side of me. Now, let's bring it back to the classroom. Can you still hold onto the truth that the brain can get stuck in survival mode, even when the setting looks more structured and the stakes feel different?

Imagine this:

You're trying to explain directions. Isaiah starts to escalate. You stay calm and restate the expectation. He interrupts. You offer him a choice. He yells. You try again. He throws a pencil. In your mind, you think: *But I stayed calm. I followed the plan.* And you did.

However, Isaiah's brain wasn't available for logic. He wasn't choosing defiance. He was stuck in survival. Being neuro-informed doesn't just help us stay calm; it helps us see differently. It provides us with a lens to interpret behavior through the lens of safety and connection, rather than judgment. It helps us respond with clarity and compassion, not compliance and shame. Once we understand the brain, we stop taking behavior personally and start responding intentionally.

Diagnoses Through a Neuro-Informed Lens

In trauma-responsive, brain-aligned classrooms, we don't view diagnoses as labels that define a student; we see them as clues. A neuro-informed perspective invites us to understand that behaviors often attributed to disorders like ADHD, Autism Spectrum Disorder (ASD), Oppositional Defiant Disorder (ODD), Generalized Anxiety Disorder, Conduct Disorder, or Adjustment Disorder are not willful disruptions but expressions of how a student's brain and nervous system have developed in response to their biology and environment.

These diagnoses point us toward unique patterns in regulation, perception, executive function, and relational safety. Instead of asking, *"How do I control this behavior?"*, we begin to ask, *"What does this brain need to feel safe, regulated, and engaged?"* This shift enables us to teach from a place of understanding, rather than urgency, creating space for every student to succeed in a way that aligns with their unique system, rather than against it. To help establish a definition for these disorders, the following summaries come from the American Psychiatric Association's Diagnostic and Statistical Manual of Mental Disoders.[85]

ADD/ADHD

Attention-Deficit/Hyperactivity Disorder isn't a discipline issue or a motivation problem; it's a brain-based difference in how attention, impulse control, and executive functioning develop. Students with ADHD often have faster, more reactive nervous systems and may struggle with staying still, waiting, or following multistep directions, not because they're defiant, but because their brain is wired for movement and novelty. Understanding ADHD as part of a student's origin helps shift the response from frustration to support, using strategies that match their neurotype rather than punishing their behavior.

Generalized Anxiety Disorder (GAD)

Anxiety isn't just worry; it's a nervous system stuck in hyper-alert mode. Students with GAD often experience constant internal tension, even when nothing appears wrong. Their brains are wired to scan for danger and anticipate worst-case scenarios, which can show up as perfectionism, avoidance, irritability, or trouble concentrating. They may appear withdrawn or controlling, not because they're defiant, but because their system is doing everything it can to stay safe. A neuro-informed lens helps us see that calming these students down doesn't start with logic; it begins with co-regulation and safety.

Depression

Depression in children can look different from how it does in adults. Instead of sadness alone, it may show up as irritability, apathy, low energy, disconnection, or even anger. These students may seem like they've "checked out," but inside, they may be experiencing deep hopelessness, shame, or emotional numbness. From a neuro-informed perspective, we understand that their reward system and emotional regulation circuits may be underactive or overwhelmed.

Autism Spectrum Disorder (ASD)

Autism is a neurodevelopmental difference that impacts communication, sensory processing, and social interaction. Students on the spectrum may interpret the world differently, and their responses often reflect overstimulation, confusion, or an intense need for predictability, not disrespect. When we understand Autism as part of origin, we stop trying to "normalize" behavior and instead learn how to connect, co-regulate, and communicate in a way that honors the student's brain and body.

Pathological Demand Avoidance (PDA)

PDA is a profile within autism that looks like extreme resistance to everyday demands, but underneath is a nervous system flooded by anxiety and a deep need for control. Students with PDA aren't refusing out of spite; their avoidance is a survival strategy to protect themselves from feeling overwhelmed. A simple request— *"please open your book"* or *"line up for lunch"*—can trigger panic, leading to withdrawal, distraction, or even explosive reactions. When we understand PDA as part of origin, we stop labeling these students as manipulative or oppositional and instead see their behaviors as signals of fear. Connection, choice, and collaboration—not compliance—are the keys to helping these students engage. By reducing pressure and honoring their need for autonomy, we create safety that allows trust, learning, and growth to emerge.

Adjustment Disorder

Adjustment Disorder is a diagnosis that reflects difficulty coping with a significant change or stressor, such as a divorce, loss, move, or school transition. These students are not inherently disordered; they are simply reacting to change with more intensity or duration than expected. Their behavior may look like anxiety, depression, defiance, or withdrawal, depending on how their nervous system processes stress. Understanding this through a neuro-informed lens means we don't rush them through the adjustment. Instead, we give them time, regulation tools, and the message: It's okay to struggle, we're here to walk through it with you.

Oppositional Defiant Disorder (ODD)

ODD often shows up as chronic defiance, argumentativeness, or resistance to authority. Beneath the surface, it can be a response to environments that felt unsafe, chaotic, or overly controlling. Many students diagnosed with ODD have histories of trauma, inconsistent caregiving, or unmet needs for autonomy. What appears to be opposition is often a protective strategy, an attempt to regain control in a world that has felt out of control. It is essential to look at ODD through the lens of a student's origin story, asking, *"What is this behavior protecting them from?"*

Conduct Disorder (CD)

Conduct Disorder is often misunderstood as simply "bad behavior," but a neuro-informed perspective reveals something deeper: a nervous system adapted for protection over connection. Students with CD may engage in aggression, destruction, rule-breaking, or deceit, not because they lack morality, but because trust, empathy, and safety have never been consistent or reliable in their world. Many have experienced chronic trauma, neglect, or environments that rewarded power and survival over vulnerability. These students need firm, consistent boundaries and relational repair. They won't respond to traditional reward systems, but they may slowly begin to trust us when they see that we won't give up on them, even when their behavior suggests otherwise.

Teacher Practice Shift: Executive Function & Regulation Lagging Skills

Through the lens of Dr. Ross Greene's work, I began to understand that what appeared to be defiance was actually a signal, an unsolved problem waiting to be understood. Greene's radical yet straightforward premise —that *kids do well if they can* —challenged everything I thought I knew about student behavior.[86] Collaborative Problem Solving (CPS), developed by Dr. Greene, is a compassionate and practical approach to addressing challenging behavior by recognizing it as the result of lagging skills rather than deliberate defiance.[87]

Instead of relying on rewards or consequences, CPS invites educators and students to engage in structured conversations that identify specific unsolved problems and work together to develop mutually satisfying solutions. The lists below are adapted and expanded from CPS, reflecting the real-world skill gaps often observed in students.

These are not willful behaviors; they are lagging skills that require co-regulation, scaffolding, and support. This list is not a diagnostic tool; it serves as a lens for understanding behavior through the lens of brain development, nervous system functioning, and unmet needs. When we assume skill gaps rather than bad intentions, we can stop reacting and start responding.

Cognitive Flexibility & Perspective-Taking

Some kids struggle to shift their thinking. They get stuck on their original idea, belief, or plan, and can't easily see that something else might also be true or possible. These students may seem oppositional, but often they're overwhelmed by the demand to adapt. Their rigidity isn't defiance; it's a lagging skill in cognitive flexibility. They need models, not ultimatums. Scaffolding, not shame.
Here are some common ways difficulties with cognitive flexibility and perspective-taking may show up in students' behavior:

> *Difficulty shifting from original ideas, plans, or expected outcomes*
> *Difficulty understanding or considering other points of view*
> *Difficulty recognizing how their behavior is affecting others*
> *Difficulty considering alternative solutions or strategies*
> *Difficulty taking into account the situational context when making decisions*
> *Difficulty with inflexible or distorted thinking (e.g., "Everyone's out to get me," "Nobody likes me")*

Impulse Control & Future Thinking

Impulse control is often expected before it's developed. Students who struggle here often act impulsively, not because they don't care about consequences, but because their brains haven't yet developed the ability to pause and consider the consequences. They often know the rule *after* they break it. What they need isn't more punishment; it's co-regulation, clear structure, and plenty of opportunities to practice pausing with support.

Here are some common ways difficulties with impulse control and future-thinking may show up in students' behavior:

> *Difficulty considering potential outcomes or consequences before acting*
> *Difficulty slowing down in the moment to think before responding*
> *Difficulty adjusting behavior when a previous strategy didn't work*
> *Difficulty persisting through frustrating, boring, or non-preferred tasks*

Communication & Self-Expression

Not all students have the words they need when they need them. Some have big feelings with no outlet, or needs they've never been taught how to name. Others misread tone, timing, or intent in social interactions. When a student "shuts down," "blurts out," or "won't talk," it's worth asking: *Have we taught them how? Have we made it safe to try?* Expression is a skill, one that many students are still learning.

Here are some common ways difficulties with communication and self-expression may show up in students' behavior:

> *Difficulty identifying and expressing emotions or needs with words*
> *Difficulty initiating conversations, entering peer groups, or sustaining interactions*
> *Difficulty asking for help or clarification*
> *Difficulty using appropriate tone, timing, or social cues in communication*

Emotional Regulation & Stress Tolerance

Regulation is not automatic. It's built over time, in relationships, and through repeated experiences of feeling safe. When students escalate quickly or seem to fall apart over "little things," they're often telling us: *My nervous system is already at capacity.* These students don't need to toughen up. They need adults who can help them return to baseline, again and again, until they learn how to do it on their own.

Here are some common ways difficulties with emotional regulation and stress tolerance may show up in students' behavior:

> *Difficulty managing emotional responses in the face of frustration*
> *Difficulty returning to baseline after failure, correction, or peer conflict*
> *Difficulty tolerating unpredictability, ambiguity, or novelty*

Attention & Social Perception

Some students miss things that seem obvious to us, such as social cues, peer reactions, and classroom norms, because their attention is either scattered or so narrowly focused that everything else fades. Others misinterpret social signals entirely. These aren't "rude" kids or "space cadets"; they're students who need direct teaching, gentle reminders, and adults who don't assume they're doing it intentionally.

Here are some common ways difficulties with attention and social perception may show up in students' behavior:

Difficulty maintaining focus and following multi-step directions
Difficulty attending to or accurately reading social cues and nuances
Difficulty noticing others' emotions, reactions, or boundaries
Difficulty differentiating between safe and unsafe situations or people

Sensory Processing & Regulation

Students with sensory processing differences aren't just "overreacting" or "acting out." They're trying to survive in an environment that may feel overwhelming or physically uncomfortable. Noise, light, texture, and even the movement of others can create distress or distraction. Sensory-based needs often hide beneath behaviors that appear to be avoidance, refusal, or hyperactivity. We must look deeper.

Here are some common ways difficulties with sensory processing and regulation may show up in students' behavior:

Difficulty with sensory and/or motor challenges that interfere with participation, attention, or regulation
Difficulty filtering sensory input (e.g., overwhelmed by noise, texture, visual clutter)
Difficulty with movement-seeking or movement-avoiding behaviors that mask underlying sensory needs

Lagging Skill or Just Being Human

Executive function skill deficits must always be considered in light of developmentally appropriate standards. In other words, we are not comparing students to an impossible ideal, but to what is typical for their age and stage of growth. Too often, school expectations go beyond that baseline, treating normal human behavior as "deficits."

Think about it: how many of you have had a side conversation during a staff meeting or professional learning session? Was it because you were being disrespectful? Because you were lagging in impulse control? Or was it simply human nature to be social when sitting next to colleagues? The same is true for students—side conversations aren't always evidence of a broken skill; they're often evidence of being human. Consider other examples:

Walking in line, single file—where else in life do we do that? At the airport? The grocery store? Even then, people spread out, pause, or talk.

Blurting out an idea in a meeting—outside of school, this is often called brainstorming, not a deficit.

Forgetting your pencil—how many of us have shown up to a meeting without a pen, laptop, or charger?

Struggling to sit still for long periods—when adults do this, we stand, stretch, or grab coffee; we don't get written up.

The point is that executive function challenges should be understood within a realistic developmental and human framework. If we confuse everyday behaviors with deficits, we risk labeling kids for being what they are: people still learning how to navigate both the expectations of school and the wider world.

A Closing Thought

That day at the dentist wasn't about a filling; it was about fear. What I saw as defiance was a flood of unresolved memory and nervous system activation. Her body locked down, not because she wouldn't cooperate, but because she couldn't. At the time, I thought I was helping her regulate her emotions.

In reality, I was missing what her nervous system was trying to tell me: *"I'm scared, I don't feel safe, and I can't find my words."* She wasn't lacking obedience; she was lacking skills. Skills such as emotional expression, fear identification, and self-advocacy. That day taught me that what appears to be a refusal may actually be a missing capacity. When we name the skill instead of labeling the child, we can finally begin to support growth.

Isaiah's teacher felt like she'd done everything "right" with clear expectations, a calm voice, and gentle redirections, yet Isaiah's behavior still escalated. It would've been easy to see it as a student choosing defiance. When she slowed down and applied a neuro-informed lens, she saw something else: Isaiah wasn't resisting the rules; he was struggling to manage his internal state. His nervous system was dysregulated. His thinking brain wasn't online. His behaviors were signals of lagging skills in self-regulation, impulse control, and emotional expression. By identifying those gaps, she could stop asking, *"How do I stop this behavior?"* and start asking, *"What does this student need to learn, and how can I help him get there?"*

In both stories, the adults stopped reacting to behavior and started interpreting it. They stopped trying to fix the child and started identifying the *lagging skills* the nervous system couldn't access in the moment. A neuro-informed mindset shifts the goal:

From compliance to co-regulation. From control to skill-building.

✑ reflection ✑

How do you respond when students are dysregulated, and what does your nervous system bring into that moment?

Where have you tried reasoning before regulation? What happened?
For a frequent behavior, which lagging skills might be underneath (e.g., flexibility, impulse control, emotional expression)?

What 1–2 micro-skills could you teach explicitly this month (e.g., "how to ask for a pause," "how to repair after a rupture")?

Which student taught you the most about the nervous system this year, and what did you change because of them?

When I see behavior through a neuro-informed lens, I shift from _____ to _____.

⋆ eighteen ⋆
Discernment

Behavior is communication. My job is to listen, not label.

Shift From Judgment to Discernment Through Curiosity

You've seen it. A student rolls their eyes. Another slams a book shut. Someone mutters under their breath. Your pulse jumps, your instinct fires. Your voice tightens. Just like that, you're not teaching anymore. You're defending, correcting, and asserting. But what if you paused?

Discernment is that pause. It's the space between what just happened and what I choose to do next. It's not soft or passive. It's the power of self-awareness in action. It's one of the greatest gifts we can bring into a trauma-informed classroom. Discernment isn't about fixing students. It's about learning to see them more clearly. In resilience-building classrooms, discernment means looking beyond the surface of a student's actions to ask: What might be going on beneath this behavior?

The Challenge: When You Want to Prove a Point

Isaiah's teacher noticed he was sleeping in the middle of her math class, again. She went over to his desk and tapped on his shoulder, telling him he needed to wake up. He scoffed, "Whatever," and put his head back down on his desk. She felt it instantly: the heat of being challenged, the weight of every eye in the room. She wanted to act. She wanted to reassert control. She wanted to prove that you're the adult in charge. What if not reacting is the most powerful move in this moment?

Rooted in Hope Focus: Discernment

Discernment invites us to pause before responding. It helps us notice our nervous system signals, such as tight shoulders, a rising tone, and a clenched jaw, and ask: *What's driving this moment? The student's behavior, or my need to win?* Discernment shifts us from reactivity to intentional leadership. From "What just happened?" to "What's actually happening here, and why?"

Discernment is clarity under pressure. It's the ability to slow down, observe what's really going on (in the student and yourself), and choose a response that aligns with your values. Discernment says:

"I can notice without judging."

"I don't need to win this moment, I need to understand it."

"I can hold boundaries without losing my peace."

It's not about avoiding hard things. It's about meeting them with wisdom instead of reactivity.

It's a Brain Issue, Not a Behavior Issue

One essential truth guides discernment: *"It's a brain issue, not a behavior issue."*[88] Many challenging behaviors, outbursts, defiance, and avoidance aren't intentional disobedience. They're the result of dysregulation in the nervous system, especially for students who've experienced trauma.

Students who can't yet regulate themselves need support, not punishment. Our job is not to demand compliance; it's to guide them toward regulation, just as we teach other essential skills, such as reading or math.

My job isn't to make this student behave.

My job is to help them regulate.

This simple shift reframes how we see behavior, not as something to "fix," but as something to understand.

Behavior Is Communication

Every behavior communicates something. Discernment means learning to "listen" to what students are telling us, through both their words and their actions. When a student's behavior feels frustrating or confusing, ask:

What unmet need might this behavior be expressing?

What is this student's nervous system experiencing right now?

What skill might this student be missing or struggling to use?

This mindset enables you to respond with compassion rather than control.

Teacher Practice Shift: Transforming Discipline

In trauma-informed schools, we don't abandon discipline; we redefine it. A common misconception is that being trauma-responsive means avoiding consequences. Real trauma-informed practice doesn't remove accountability; it *roots* it in relationship, context, and care. That's where discernment comes in. Discernment is the practice of slowing down and asking deeper questions before reacting. It means we pause to wonder *why* a behavior is happening instead of rushing to manage or punish it. It allows us to move beyond what's visible and examine the *story beneath the surface.* Take Isaiah, for example.

Brilliant yet chronically dysregulated, Isaiah regularly falls asleep in class. His teacher wakes him up. He walks out. He yells. He avoids. His behavior can easily trigger a teacher's fight-or-flight response. The temptation is strong: issue a consequence, call the office, make it clear who's in charge—but what if those actions reinforce the very things we're trying to heal?

What Isaiah needs is not less structure, but a different kind of structure —one rooted in discernment: high expectations paired with high support. The Social Discipline Window illustrates this powerfully. Without support, high expectations become punitive. Without expectations, support becomes permissive. True trauma-responsive discipline lives in the top-right quadrant: WITH students, not *to* or *for* them.

Social Discipline Window

Let's consider the ways that Isaiah's teacher could choose to respond by looking through the Social Discipline Window.[89] This is the final step of the Transforming Discipline process.[90]

Each quadrant of the window offers a different approach, but only one truly balances both care and accountability. Teachers who lean toward *TO* or *FOR* may have good intentions, but their responses often erode trust and diminish student growth. The *NOT* approach leaves students adrift, unsure of where the boundaries lie or how to move forward. Only the *WITH* stance—high expectations paired with high support—creates the conditions where discipline becomes transformational rather than transactional.

Social Discipline Window

TO: Punitive	**WITH: Restorative**
• Maintains high expectations but lacks individualized support. • Relies on strict consequences without addressing underlying needs. • Creates power struggles and an adversarial dynamic. • Students may feel discouraged rather than motivated to improve.	• Maintains high expectations while providing individualized support. • Encourages problem-solving, collaboration, and accountability. • Recognizes that while expectations remain high, the path to success may look different for each student. • Build relationships to help students grow and succeed.
NOT: Neglectful	**FOR: Permissive**
• Lacks both high expectations and necessary support. • Fails to provide structure, guidance, or encouragement. • Students may feel ignored or unmotivated, leading to disengagement. • Can result in classroom management issues on a larger scale due to unclear expectations	• Provides support but does not uphold high expectations. • May over-accommodate students, preventing them from developing resilience. • Avoids accountability, leading to missed learning opportunities. • Students may feel cared for but not challenged to grow.

Support (vertical axis, pointing up and down)

←←←←←←←←←←←←←**Expectation** →→→→→→→→→→→→→→

When Isaiah disengages, refuses work, puts his head down, or walks out, his teacher faces a choice. How she interprets his behavior determines her response. Here are four possible perspectives she might take:

The Punitive Perspective: "He's being disrespectful."

Assumed intention: Isaiah is trying to avoid responsibility or challenge authority.

Response: Engage in a power struggle, issue a referral, or assign ISS.

Impact: Isaiah's behavior may pause temporarily, but the root cause goes unaddressed—trust fractures. Shame increases. The nervous system remains activated.

>**Behavior change?** No.
>
>**Connection built?** No.

The Permissive Perspective: "He's tired. Life is hard."

Assumed intention: Isaiah is overwhelmed, and it's understandable given his life circumstances.

Response: Allow him to disengage without follow-up. Remove demands to avoid escalation.

Impact: While well-intentioned, this response lowers expectations and removes structure. Isaiah remains unregulated. His sense of competency erodes.

>**Behavior change?** No.
>
>**Connection built?** Momentary relief, but not sustainable trust.

The Neglectful Perspective: "Maybe he's just lazy."

Assumed intention: Unclear. Teacher detaches, perhaps due to burnout or frustration.

Response: Ignores the behavior, doesn't intervene. Assumes the student will "figure it out."

Impact: Isaiah internalizes the message that no one cares. Disconnection grows. Protective factors shrink.

>**Behavior change?** No.
>
>**Connection built?** No, and possibly further harm caused.

The Discerning Perspective: "What's this behavior trying to protect?"

Assumed intention: Isaiah's behavior is communication. He may be overwhelmed, dysregulated, or unable to access learning in this moment.

Response: The teacher pauses. She gently checks in, affirms his emotional state, and seeks to understand his feelings. She collaborates with Isaiah and a support team to create a proactive plan for safety, regulation, and participation.

Impact: Isaiah feels seen, not shamed. His behavior becomes a doorway, not a dead-end. Trust begins to grow—slowly, but steadily.

>**Behavior change?** Yes, over time.
>
>**Connection built?** Yes, with intention and support.

Discernment doesn't excuse behavior. It explains it. When we understand, we can respond with strategy, not shame. This is the heart of discernment: seeing beneath behavior and responding in a way that fosters trust rather than fear. It's not about removing consequences—it's about ensuring our response doesn't become *another trauma.* In resilience-building schools, discipline is no longer about compliance—it's about connection. We don't respond to behavior to prove authority. We respond to teach accountability, build self-awareness, and restore safety.

Punishment isolates and shames.

Discipline teaches and restores.

Discernment determines which path we're on.

Isaiah and students like him don't need us to lower expectations. They need us to raise our ability to hold expectations with empathy. They need us to show that they are not too much, not too broken, not beyond reach. However, they will only believe that if we stop reacting to their dysregulation and start discerning the unmet needs that drive it.

When we shift from reacting to discerning, from power to partnership, we create what all students, especially those with trauma histories, need most: a place of safety, belonging, and dignity.

The TEA Strategy: A Tool for Discernment

It's one thing to read an example of transforming discipline, and a completely different thing to put it into action in the moment. The TEA Strategy offers a straightforward and practical approach for transitioning from a reactive to a discerning mindset.[91]

Identify Your Initial Thoughts, Emotions, and Actions

Example:
When Isaiah walked into class late again, my first thought was, "He always comes in tardy and rudely interrupts my directions." That thought immediately stirred up feelings of annoyance and frustration, and I caught myself taking his behavior personally.

Thoughts: What am I telling myself about this student or situation?

Emotions: What am I feeling right now? Why?

Actions: How do I want to respond? Is this helpful or harmful?

Pause and Reframe

> *Example:*
> *But when I paused to reconsider, a new thought surfaced: "Isaiah's previous class is all the way on the other side of the building. If he needs to stop by the restroom or his locker, that could easily make him late." With that shift in perspective, my emotions also shifted. Instead of frustration, I felt more compassion and even some optimism. I found myself releasing judgment and seeing him with a little more understanding. Originally, I was ready to call him out in front of the class—remarking on how he was tardy again and making it clear his behavior wouldn't be tolerated. But with a calmer outlook, I chose a different action. I decided to talk with Isaiah after class, not to scold him, but to develop a plan together. We discussed how he might use his passing period more efficiently so that he could get to class on time without feeling rushed.*

Thoughts: What else could be true about this situation?

Emotions: What might the student be feeling? What unmet needs might be driving this behavior?

Actions: What response would promote safety, dignity, and belonging for everyone involved?

This process empowers you to shift from judgment to discernment through curiosity, without dismissing accountability, but with greater clarity and compassion.

A Closing Thought

Discernment is not weakness; it is wisdom. It's the quiet strength of an educator who chooses curiosity over control, relationship over reaction, and understanding over urgency. In a trauma-informed classroom, discernment isn't a delay in discipline; it *is* the discipline. It teaches us to see the story behind the behavior, the nervous system behind the disruption, the child behind the coping strategy. When we lead with discernment, we don't lower our expectations—we elevate our humanity. In doing so, we offer our students the one thing they've always needed: a safe place to be seen, to belong, and to begin again.

◦⟋ reflection ⟍◦

Discernment isn't about doing nothing. It's about doing the right thing—intentionally, not impulsively. As you reflect on Isaiah's story and your practice, consider:

When do you feel most tempted to react quickly in the classroom? What sensations show up in your body?

What kinds of behaviors push you into judgment? What stories do you tend to create in those moments?

How often do you pause to ask, What might this behavior be trying to protect?

How can you practice noticing without labeling?

Where are you already showing discernment? How can you build on that strength?

When I feel challenged by a student, my first instinct is to _____.

When I pause and practice discernment, I begin to see that _____.

One way I will respond differently next time is by _____.

ᵔ nineteen ᵔ
Engagement

Students don't disengage because they don't care.
They disengage because they no longer feel seen.

The Challenge: When Students Check Out

Meredith's sixth-grade year is one I won't soon forget, and neither will she, though for all the wrong reasons. It was a challenging year for both of us. We were adjusting to life after divorce, which, while necessary for our safety and well-being, had shaken both of our nervous systems. My daughter, always bright and perceptive, was carrying the weight of that transition in ways that weren't always obvious to others. She'd been diagnosed with generalized anxiety and adjustment disorder. She was also a gifted student, intensely curious, deeply sensitive, and frequently bored in school. That's not always a good combination. Bored, bright kids often find their ways to create engagement... and sometimes that comes in the form of disruption.

Meredith was wary of adults by then, unsure who to trust or what their motives were. She already questioned the point of school, especially in classes where the work felt too easy or disconnected from anything meaningful.

One day, her teacher assigned a journal prompt that probably seemed harmless enough: "Who do you miss the most right now, and what would you do if they were here?" But for a child still reeling from the aftershocks of divorce, anxiety, and upheaval, it wasn't harmless. It was intrusive. The prompt brought big feelings that she wasn't ready, or willing, to share.

Rather than shut down, she got creative. She wrote about how she was "engaged to Shrek," but he had ghosted her, leaving her stuck with nonrefundable wedding deposits. She noted, with a perfectly dry wit, that she would be accepting donations —cash, Venmo, or gift cards — at lunch to help recoup the losses. And if Shrek were here? She'd ignore him. Her classmates giggled at the absurdity. Her teacher, however, didn't find it amusing.

"Is this a joke?" the teacher asked.

"Yes," Meredith replied flatly.

"Do you even know anyone named Shrek?"

"No. He's a cartoon. We also weren't engaged. I'm twelve."

She was immediately sent out of the room.

What her teacher saw that day was disrespect. What was really happening was avoidance, a clever, protective attempt to sidestep vulnerability in a space that didn't feel safe. Meredith wasn't ready to answer that prompt because the honest answer wasn't something she could say aloud in that room. She did what so many kids do: she used humor as armor. Instead of inviting conversation or seeing the moment for what it was—a child signaling discomfort—the teacher shut her down. From that moment on, the relationship didn't just struggle; it ceased to exist altogether.

By the time parent-teacher conferences rolled around that fall, I already knew my daughter's sixth-grade year wasn't going well. Every story I heard from her was about getting in trouble, feeling bored, or being misunderstood, but what I wasn't prepared for was how her teacher had written her off entirely. I sat across from this teacher, hoping for a conversation about how we could get back on track. Instead, she began by describing a student I didn't even recognize, a version of Meredith who sounded lazy, disrespectful, and disinterested in anything related to learning. I asked her to share some of Meredith's *strengths*, hoping we could build from there.

Her response? "She might be smart, but she doesn't bother to show it."

I remember the sting of those words. Not just the dismissal of Meredith's intelligence, but the absolute disinterest in understanding *why* she wasn't showing it.

I took a deep breath and did what many parents in my position try to do: I offered more context, hoping it would help her see the bigger picture. I shared openly about the trauma our family had been through during the past year, including the divorce that had, while necessary, upended our lives. I explained that Meredith had undergone a complete mental health evaluation, where she'd been diagnosed with generalized anxiety disorder and adjustment disorder..

I asked if we could talk about *repair*. I wanted to know what we could do together to mend the broken relationship between my daughter and her teacher. What could we try to rebuild trust and engagement? Her response stopped me cold: "How long do you think she'll *have* an adjustment disorder?" It wasn't just the words; it was the tone, thick with dismissal and skepticism, as though I had shown up asking for excuses instead of solutions.

I left that conference feeling heartbroken, but I also had a clear understanding that no one in that room was going to fight for Meredith's engagement in sixth grade. She would have to get through the year unseen, with her strengths unrecognized, her humor misunderstood, and her emotional needs ignored. I realized that what Meredith was learning about teachers, from not receiving a Band-Aid for a tiny cut to being overlooked when she needed care for a wound on the inside, echoed the same lessons I had learned in my school years: teachers don't always see the kids without visible bruises.

Here I was, back in the same cycle, but this time, I wasn't the kid, nor was I even just a parent; I was also an educator, and my students were other educators. It was *literally my job* to help provide teachers with strategies to prevent this kind of harm. Yet, I couldn't stop it from happening to my child.

Rooted in Hope Focus: Engagement

This story isn't just about my daughter. It's about how easily we, as adults, can miss the fulcrum tipping. That year wasn't about behavior or defiance; it was about a child whose engagement was out of balance.

"Students engage when they feel seen, safe, and significant."

Engagement isn't about flashy lessons or entertaining performances. It's about resonance, making learning feel deeply connected to a student's life, identity, and sense of purpose. I've learned that when we invite students into the process, giving them voice, choice, and a say in what and how they learn, we shift from delivering content to co-creating meaning. Authentic engagement happens when we design with co-regulation, creativity, and connection in mind. It's in the small moments: a student seeing themselves in a story, being trusted to lead a discussion, or being met with curiosity instead of control. When students feel seen, safe, and significant, they lean in. Not because they have to, but because they want to.

If we're honest, student disengagement isn't just about disrespect, laziness, or distraction. It's often about disconnection from the content, the teacher, the community, or oneself. Engagement isn't about entertainment. It's about belonging, relevance, and voice. Engagement doesn't happen in isolation. It depends on a child's ability to stay regulated throughout the day, and regulation itself sits on a fulcrum. Four balancing components help determine whether a student can remain engaged, regulated, and ready to learn: Relationship, Responsibility, Rigor, and Relevance.

The Regulation Fulcrum

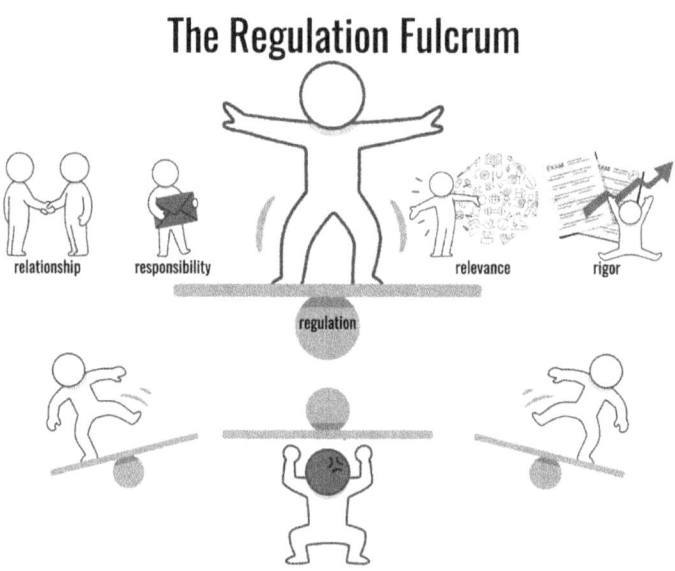

Relationship always comes first, because before a student can learn, they need to feel safe, seen, and supported. We must ask ourselves, *Does this child have someone in the building they trust? Someone who knows their story, believes in their future, and shows up consistently?* This connection is not about compliance or behavior management; it's about belonging. From that foundation, students can begin to develop a sense of personal responsibility, not only in their behavior but also in their learning and contributions to the school community.

Responsibility doesn't grow in isolation; it grows through inclusion. We must ask: *Are we giving this student genuine opportunities to participate, or have we quietly removed them because of their past?* Students who are always viewed as problems rarely feel empowered to show up as partners. Finally, regulation is essential; without it, engagement is out of reach. Regulation isn't demanded; it's nurtured. Through co-regulation, calm environments, and explicitly taught strategies, we help students build the skills they need to stay grounded enough to learn.

This model closely aligns with Deci and Ryan's Self-Determination Theory, which identifies three essential psychological needs for motivation and engagement: autonomy, competence, and connectedness.[92] Trauma-informed learning environments recognize that students require more than just rules and routines; they also need relational safety and psychological nourishment. Self-Determination Theory provides a powerful lens for understanding what motivates students and what they need to re-engage, especially after adversity.

Autonomy is the need to feel in control of one's actions and choices. This includes having a sense of agency, voice, and choice in how, when, and where learning happens. Trauma strips away control. When students feel powerless in their lives, they may resist control in the classroom. Trauma-informed teaching honors their need to reclaim agency. Autonomy supports motivation because people are more engaged when they feel a sense of ownership over their goals and tasks. In the classroom, offer voice, choice, and meaningful participation in their learning journey. Create environments where students feel safe to express themselves without fear of retribution or punishment.

Competence is the need to feel capable and effective. People need opportunities to build skills, gain mastery, and experience success in ways that feel meaningful. Support and encouragement help learners believe they can improve and grow. Students impacted by trauma often internalize beliefs that they are "bad," "broken," or incapable. Trauma-informed educators restore the belief that they can by providing scaffolding, celebrating small wins, and offering feedback that emphasizes progress over perfection.

Connectedness is the need to feel a sense of belonging and connection to others. Trauma often damages a student's sense of belonging. Relationships can feel unsafe, conditional, or unpredictable. A trauma-informed educator becomes a steady presence who says, You matter. You belong. People thrive when they feel seen, valued, and cared for, and when they can offer care and connection in return. Relationships are foundational to motivation and well-being when they prioritize connection before correction, build rituals of care, co-regulation, and community, and show students they are not alone. When we talk about engagement in a trauma-informed, neuro-informed classroom, we're asking:

Does this student feel connected and safe?

Do they have a meaningful role and responsibility in this context?

Is the work challenging enough, but not too challenging, to promote growth?

Can they see why this learning matters to their current life or future?

Teacher Practice Shift:

Relationship

Ask yourself, "Does this child feel connected to others in school?"

I know, bringing up relationships again might feel like we're trying to steer a ship that's already circled the harbor a hundred times. However, we cannot expect engagement, academic, social, or emotional, without first establishing a foundation of trust, safety, and connection. Regulation and engagement aren't independent skills; they're relational experiences. A student's ability to participate, take risks, or persevere through challenges is directly tied to their sense of belonging and their belief that at least one adult sees them, values them, and *likes* them for who they are, not just for how they behave or perform.

We've already explored how the nervous system scans for safety before it can learn. The same is true for engagement. Students need to know:

I'm safe here.

I matter here.

Someone here knows me beyond my grades or behavior.

In classrooms where that's missing, even the most academically capable students can become disengaged. Too often, when we see disengagement, we immediately jump to changing the task, modifying behavior plans, or increasing consequences. The first, most essential question we should ask is: Does this student have a meaningful relationship with an adult here?

The Small Strategy That Changes Everything: The 2x10 Approach

One of the most powerful tools for building connection, especially with students who seem the hardest to reach, is something deceptively simple: the 2x10 strategy.[93]

The concept is straightforward:

Spend 2 minutes a day for 10 consecutive school days talking with a student about anything *other than academics or behavior.*

Let *them* lead the conversation.

No fixing. No correcting. Just *listening* and *connecting.*

That's it. Two minutes a day of authentic, no-strings-attached conversation.

Research has shown that the 2x10 strategy can significantly improve student behavior, engagement, and teacher-student relationships, especially for students who are struggling the most. However, beyond the research, here's what it does: it tells a student, *You matter to me even when you're not in trouble and even when you're not doing schoolwork.*

In trauma-informed, neuro-informed classrooms, we aren't just teaching content; we're repairing broken relational patterns. The students who push us away the hardest are often the ones who need connection the most, but who also fear it the most. The 2x10 strategy is one way we gently rebuild those bridges.

Responsibility

Ask yourself: *Does this student have meaningful opportunities to contribute or take ownership?*

Responsibility isn't just about chores or tasks; it's about belonging. Having a job, a role, and a reason to contribute to the school community helps students feel capable, trusted, and connected to their school community. Responsibility can be regulating. Some of the most powerful student jobs I've seen weren't really about the job at all; they were about relationships, focus, and regulation.

Take, for example, the student who proudly walked the therapy dog every morning. No one else wanted the job because, well, someone had to pick up the poop, and this student didn't mind. It got him outside, moving, and regulating, giving him a meaningful reason to show up. Or the student who had "Old Man Coffee Time" with the school janitor. Every morning, they'd wander the halls, coffee cup in hand, casually chatting as they looked for scuffed walls, loose screws, or bulletin boards needing attention. He wasn't just fixing things; he was learning how to notice his environment and building a relationship that anchored him to the building.

Some students will naturally seek out these types of jobs. Others may need us to *strategically assign* them, because the student who seems the least ready to lead may need it most. In my classroom, I had two highly coveted jobs that were only assigned to a few select students: my Shoe Keeper and my CCC Keeper (for coffee, clickers, and cell phones).

I am one of those people who hardly even have shoes on my feet. It's just who I am. I needed someone to know where they were at all times, just in case someone *"important-looking"* popped in or there was a drill. This student's job was to keep track of my shoes and discreetly get them on my feet if needed.

My CCC Keeper had to stay attuned to me throughout the day to ensure I had my coffee, remote clicker, and phone, three things I notoriously lost multiple times daily. This wasn't about convenience; it was about *connection*. These jobs were reserved for students who needed a reason to stay focused on me and who needed a strong adult tether throughout the day. These weren't random tasks; they were strategic. They gave students *purpose* and a *regulated relationship* to lean on.

Responsibility isn't about keeping kids busy; it's about giving them a reason to show up, a role to play, and a person to rely on. Too often, the very students who most need opportunities to contribute are the first to have those chances taken away because of behavior. It can seem logical to ask why we would grant extra privileges to a student with challenging behavior. Contribution isn't just a reward; it's a *need*.

When we remove opportunities to participate, we take away a key ingredient for developing self-determination, connection, and a sense of belonging. According to Deci and Ryan's self-determination theory, students thrive when they experience autonomy, competence, and relatedness.

Being trusted with responsibility, even after mistakes, can support regulation, build protective factors, and help students practice the very skills they are struggling with. Instead of withholding meaningful roles as punishment, we must reframe these opportunities as interventions that foster growth and resilience. For many students, contributing to the school community isn't a privilege to be earned; it's a pathway to healing and hope.

Rigor

Ask yourself: *Is this student's academic work appropriately challenging, neither too hard nor too easy?*

Once students feel safe and connected, they become more receptive to challenge — but the challenge must be the right kind. In trauma-informed and neuro-informed classrooms, rigor doesn't mean piling on more work, more complex texts, or faster pacing to see who can survive it.

That traditional view equates rigor with compliance, memorization, and endurance, rather than meaningful growth. In contrast, the *Rooted in Hope* view of rigor emphasizes creating purposeful challenges that invite students to think critically, explore multiple perspectives, and apply learning in authentic ways — all within a safe, supportive environment that balances high expectations with relational safety and regulation. True rigor asks:

Is this student being challenged in a way that promotes growth, not shutdown?
Are we providing the right scaffolding so that the student can experience success, even when the task feels challenging?
Are we considering the whole child's readiness, both emotionally and cognitively, before increasing demands?

Many disengaged students aren't disinterested in learning; they're either overwhelmed by tasks that are beyond their current capabilities or bored by tasks that don't require their best thinking. Rigor that exceeds a student's current ability without support triggers dysregulation. It floods the nervous system with feelings of failure, fear, or helplessness.

Likewise, a lack of rigor can also dysregulate, especially for students who are bright or curious but chronically under-challenged. This is especially true for gifted students with trauma histories, who may mask their frustration until it bursts out in disruptive ways. Rigor isn't about making the work easier or more complicated; it's about making the challenge meaningful and within reach.

Relevance

Ask yourself: *"Does this student see the connection between what they're learning and their personal goals, identity, or future?"*

Even with connection and the right level of challenge, relevance remains a critical component of engagement. Students are far more likely to persist, regulate, and engage when they see that what they're learning matters to their lives, identities, or futures. Relevance is more than just tying content to real-life scenarios. It's about answering the question every student silently asks: Why does this matter to me?

Trauma-impacted students, in particular, often struggle to engage in abstract learning. Their brains have been wired for survival, not long-term planning. They need help connecting learning to immediate interests, personal goals, or lived experiences.

Relevance emerges when students are given voice and choice in their assignments, and when they're invited to co-create learning goals and see their interests reflected in the work. It's found in lessons that connect to their communities, cultures, and passions, not as an afterthought, but as a central part of the design. It's strengthened when we pause to have honest conversations about why the content matters, not just for a test, but for life beyond the classroom.

Relevance doesn't mean every lesson must be about their favorite hobby, but it does mean that learning should feel purposeful, empowering, and connected to their world in some way.

A Closing Thought

When regulation starts to slip, returning to this fulcrum helps us pinpoint where the imbalance lies. By identifying the root, we can adjust our approach, not to rescue students from challenges, but to restore the balance they need to stay engaged and regulated.

About a year after the Shrek journal entry incident, I found myself sitting in the car, listening to Meredith talk about her day at school. This time, it wasn't a story about feeling misunderstood or another project that felt like a waste of time. Her face lit up as she told me about choir, about how her teacher, Ms. Haas, had selected her for Singer of the Month. This teacher had not only recognized her talent but had nurtured it. She didn't just teach music; she taught belonging.

At one point, Meredith hesitantly asked Ms. Haas whether she had a good chance of being chosen for the honor choir again next year. Meredith said that she reassured her that her chances were high, but then quietly added, "I had to fight for you to get in this year." That sentence landed like a stone in my chest, knowing that teachers from the previous year provided character recommendations for the group.

Thankfully, what Ms. Haas saw wasn't just a kid who could sing; it was a kid who could lead. She saw a kid who wanted to belong. A kid who had something to say. She didn't wait for Meredith to prove she was worth fighting for; she just fought for her. I still have the voicemail that her choir teacher left me a few days after this conversation, saved on my phone, and she still has the certificate hanging on her mirror.

"Hey Katie, this is Ms. Haas. I was just calling to make sure you knew Meredith was selected as the Singer of the Month for January. She has received a certificate, her photo is hanging autographed on my wall, and she gets a positive phone call home. I wanted to share some observations I've made about her throughout this year. I love that she's been stepping up as a leader.

She sings out beautifully with that great voice, and I appreciate that. She's also just easy to work with. She's a kid I can depend on to do what she needs to be doing and not be distracting or talking a bunch when we're working with another section. She's just a really good teammate, and I've been super proud to watch her grow this year.

I just want to encourage her to continue and join the eighth-grade choir and all that good stuff. I hope you guys have a great weekend. I'm super proud of her."

Ms. Haas didn't just hand her a spot in the honor choir. She handed her back a narrative where she was more than the sum of her mistakes. She gave her what every student needs to stay engaged: A place to matter. A person to believe. A reason to show up.

Engagement doesn't begin with content; it begins with connection. It starts when a student feels seen, not just managed; challenged, not overwhelmed; included, not merely tolerated. Sometimes, it begins when one adult decides to see the kid behind the coping strategy, the humor, or the silence, and chooses to fight for them anyway. As trauma-informed, neuro-informed educators, our job isn't to entertain students into attention. It's about building spaces that say, "You belong here." Your voice matters. I won't stop trying to reach you. When learning feels alive again, for them and us, we don't just change test scores. We change stories.

❧ reflection ❧

Consider a student who appears disengaged.

What might they be trying to communicate through their withdrawal, distraction, or disruption?

Which part of the engagement fulcrum—relationship, responsibility, rigor, or relevance—might be out of balance for that student?

Are there students in your room who show up every day but still feel invisible? How do you know?

When was the last time a student lit up because they felt seen or successful? What conditions made that possible?

How often do your students have the chance to feel ownership over their learning, not just compliance with expectations?

What systems or habits in your classroom might unintentionally send the message: You only matter when you behave, perform, or comply?

When I see disengagement, I respond with _____, because I believe _____.

I can restore engagement by offering more _____, adjusting _____, or inviting _____.

❧ twenty ❧
Openness

Trust grows in the presence of openness, in what is shared, explained, and co-created.

Inviting Voice, Sharing Power

In trauma-informed spaces, we talk a lot about student voice, yet we don't always listen with more than an intent to respond. Openness isn't just about allowing someone to speak before we respond; it's also about being receptive to their thoughts and ideas. It's about what we do with what we hear. Openness is about how we listen, communicate, and involve students and families in the decisions that impact their daily lives. It's about stepping back just enough to make room for perspectives we didn't anticipate, for truths that might make us uncomfortable, and for ideas that weren't ours.

We often associate openness with vulnerability, and that's part of it; however, in a trauma-informed classroom, openness also encompasses transparency, collaboration, and shared power. It asks us to move from "Here's the plan" to "Let's shape this together." It challenges us to stop assuming what's best and start asking what's needed. Openness doesn't diminish our role as educators. It deepens it.

The Challenge: When the Plan Was Made Without the Student

Let's return to Malik. Avoidantly attached. Hilarious, brilliant when regulated, and chronically under the radar. He was the kind of student who could flip a classroom energy with one joke, sometimes in the best way, and sometimes in the most frustrating way.

In an earlier chapter, we learned that his teacher was able to use the 2x10 strategy to improve her connection with him; however, it wasn't a magic wand that immediately resolved everything.

By mid-year, Malik had a behavior plan. There were tiered supports, daily points, and weekly meetings. On paper, it looked solid, but something wasn't working as expected. He was still shutting down. Still blurting, still disengaged, and, if we were honest, the plan felt like something we were doing to Malik rather than with him.

At a student support meeting, his grandmother sat at the table. She had a quiet strength, protective but kind. She listened carefully to the data, the updates, and the interventions. Then, when the team finished presenting, she looked around and asked:

"Did anyone ask Malik what he thinks about all this?"

There was silence. Not resistance. Just a realization. We'd talked around Malik, about his behaviors, his needs, his goals—but we hadn't talked with him. Not in any meaningful way. We had created a plan meant to support him, but we never checked if he felt supported. In that moment, her question did more than nudge us toward student voice. It confronted our cultural lens. Malik's voice hadn't just been overlooked; it had been unintentionally filtered through dominant systems that prioritize compliance over context. We hadn't stopped to ask: *What does support look like to him? How does his family define respect? How do his lived experiences, his identity as a young Black boy navigating systems that often misread him, shape the way he receives our "support"?*

The next day, we sat down with Malik for a Student in Need of Connection (SiNoC) interview. At first, he offered the usual answers, accompanied by shrugs, vague nods, and minimal eye contact. However, eventually, one question opened the door:

"What's something you wish adults at school understood about you?"

He paused. Looked up. Then said, "That I'm not stupid. I just get tired of always being in trouble before I even try."

The plan didn't vanish, our support didn't dissolve, but the posture changed. We didn't defend the plan. We opened it. We made space for his voice, his culture, his dignity. This doesn't mean we stop setting boundaries. It means we stop writing scripts that ignore the storyteller.

Rooted in Hope Focus: Openness

Openness is the work of replacing assumptions with inquiry. It asks:

Do students understand why we do things, or just what we expect of them?

Do families feel like partners or like recipients of pre-written plans?

Do we leave space to listen, or just pause long enough to keep talking?

In resilience-building classrooms, openness is a form of regulation. It offers students and caregivers a sense of control in a world that often feels anything but. When we're open, we invite them to co-author the journey, not just to follow directions, but to influence the direction itself. Openness doesn't mean we hand over all control. It means we honor the wisdom others carry. We don't build trust with compliance. We build it with collaboration. While we may be the experts in the room on pedagogical practices, we are not the experts in the room regarding the lived experience of the humans we are teaching.

Teacher Practice Shift: From Presentation to Partnership

For too long, we've been taught that structure equals safety. That leadership means having a plan and sticking to it. Yet, students impacted by trauma aren't looking for adults with perfect plans. They're looking for adults who are willing to listen during the process. Openness lives in small, intentional shifts:

When we explain why a consequence is being assigned instead of just what it is.

When we stop mid-routine to say, "This doesn't seem to be working. How could we do this better together?"

Openness means being flexible enough to adapt, and steady enough to hold space while we do it. That's why tools like the SiNoC Interview Protocol and the Caregiver Interview Protocol are so powerful. They aren't forms to check off. They're relationship builders. They are tools designed to support trauma-responsive, relationship-centered planning and care.

Rather than relying solely on observation or adult interpretation, these protocols invite students and families to speak directly into the support process. The SiNoC interview enables students to reflect on their school experience, share what helps them feel seen and safe, and identify strengths that may otherwise go unnoticed. The caregiver protocol enables families to share important context about their child's history, needs, and what partnership means to them.

These interviews are most powerful when used before or during the creation of a connection plan, MTSS intervention, or re-entry process after a behavior event. They are not scripts, but starting points, tools for restoring dignity and voice in systems that too often silence both. A complete version of each protocol, along with sample plans and implementation guidance, can be found in the Appendix of this book. The questions we ask aren't just informational; they shift the dynamic.

"What helps you feel like you belong here?"

"What's something you're doing on purpose—even if it's small?"

"What would it take for you to feel that this team is working with you?"

They say: 'We don't just want your signature. We want your insight.' Even the closing rituals matter. When students choose a word to represent their strength, or caregivers are asked to share what they're proud of, these small moments reinforce a deeper truth: You belong in this process. Your story matters here.

A Closing Thought

Openness isn't soft. It's strategic. It's not about handing over control; it's about building enough trust to share it. It's about having the courage to pause, the humility to listen, and the wisdom to include. When students and families feel heard, they lean in. When they're invited to shape the plan, they're more likely to stay part of it. When we practice openness, we send a message that is both simple and transformative: "You don't have to earn your voice here. It's already yours."

Visit the book companion site for additional materials related to this chapter.

Book Companion Resources

- SiNoC Interview Protocols

✥ reflection ❧

Think of a student like Malik, someone whose behavior you've planned for without fully inviting their voice to be heard.

What do you think they would say if asked?

What's one classroom routine or behavior response you could revisit in partnership with students?

How might you shift your next family meeting from presentation to conversation?

When I slow down and invite a student's or caregiver's voice, I learn _____.

One place I want to practice more openness is _____.

I believe that co-creating with students and families leads to _____.

⋙ twenty-one ⋘
Intentionality

Every moment is a choice: to repeat old patterns or to practice something new.

Choosing the Next Right Thing

There's a line I find myself coming back to again and again: *"What we do, we do on purpose."* That's the heart of intentionality. It's not just about doing things right; it's about doing the right things *on purpose*, in alignment with who we say we want to be. In trauma-informed practice, this kind of intentionality is non-negotiable.

Because let's be honest: we've all had those days where survival mode takes over. We're just trying to make it through the day without a referral, a meltdown, or another policy email. That's where intentionality becomes the anchor. In trauma-informed practice, intentionality means that we don't just react; we respond. With purpose. With clarity. With alignment to our values. Every choice we make, from how we set up our classroom to how we respond to misbehavior, how we grade, and how we speak, either moves us closer to or farther from becoming a safe, healing-centered school.

The Resilience-Building Self-Assessment Tool[94] (found in Chapter 32 and on the Book Companion) reveals what that journey entails. At one end, we see schools where punitive practices are normalized, including public shaming, rigid behavioral systems, and a complete disregard for felt safety. On the other end are trauma-informed schools, where safety is not just a word on a poster but a felt experience and where relationships are the cornerstone of discipline. Where students are seen, not just managed, these shifts don't happen by accident. It requires sustained, deliberate, and intentional choices at every level.

The Challenge: Working Inside the Fence

I once heard another facilitator share an analogy of trauma-responsive intentionality. She started her explanation not in a classroom, but in a horse pen. Imagine we run a horse-breaking facility. A particularly difficult horse arrives, angry, unpredictable, "uncooperative." We build a round pen, maybe even add an electric fence, to keep everyone safe. Yet, here's the thing: those fences and boundaries don't *teach* the horse anything. They just contain it.

If all we do is restrain and correct the horse, we don't help it learn. The horse doesn't need more consequences; it needs connection. It needs calm. It needs to learn what *to* do, not just be punished for what *not* to do. The round pen becomes a space of mutual trust, where the trainer and horse build a relationship that makes learning possible. Where growth is structured but never forceful, that pen becomes a place of intentionality.[95]

Now, let's translate this analogy to education. Imagine we're not breaking horses, but helping children grow and learn in school. From preschool to high school, the goal remains the same: we aim to prepare children to succeed and thrive. Let's say a child enters preschool and immediately has difficulty adjusting, following rules, and staying out of trouble. As educators, what do we do? We might implement strategies like setting clear boundaries or administering consequences for misbehavior, but these responses alone won't ensure the child's success. They may be helpful to an extent, but they don't address the root cause of the child's struggles.

As the child progresses to elementary school, we may continue using similar methods, such as punishments, rewards, or structured routines, to support their development. However, if the behaviors persist, what do we do then? In middle school, when a child's struggles continue, we may increase the severity of consequences or try more intensive interventions. Finally, by high school, the child may be facing more serious consequences for their behavior, but are we truly helping them? Are these strategies working, or are we simply reinforcing a cycle that pushes the child further away from success?

This brings us to the core issue: punishment might work for some children, but for many, it simply doesn't. Just like a horse in a pen, children might comply temporarily, but the underlying issues remain unresolved. The "fence" we've built to keep them safe may be limiting their ability to grow, and over time, we lose a lot of children in this process. The fences we build—rules, boundaries, and consequences—aren't inherently bad, but they lack something crucial.

So, what's missing? The missing piece is the relationship. While the safety measures of the fence (rules and consequences) are necessary, they are only effective when paired with a strong foundation of trust, communication, and support. Relationships are the cornerstone of discipline. Without them, we fail to teach the child the underlying skills they need for success, like self-regulation, accountability, and emotional intelligence.

Now, imagine a school system where discipline is built around relationships first, and accountability second. The "fence" in this case would not just be a set of rules, but a supportive and nurturing environment where children are encouraged to learn from their mistakes, make amends, and grow. When children feel safe, understood, and supported, they are more likely to engage in the learning process and be held accountable in a positive way. This is where actual growth happens, both for horses and for children.

By focusing on relationships and building accountability within that framework, we create a system where children are not only punished but also taught, nurtured, and empowered to succeed. The results may be slower and more challenging to measure at first, but they will ultimately lead to stronger, more capable individuals who are equipped to navigate the world with confidence.

Rooted in Hope Focus: Intentionality

Intentionality prompts educators to pause and reflect on alignment: Are my actions aligned with my purpose? Am I responding with curiosity or control? Am I shaping this space to support regulation, connection, and growth?

To help educators assess their current situation and their desired goals, we utilize a tool called the Trauma Continuum Self-Assessment, which is available in its complete version in Part Five. This rubric outlines key domains: relationships, behavior, responsibility, regulation, academics, and felt safety, and identifies six levels of trauma alignment, from trauma-inducing to trauma-informed.[89] Our goal is not judgment. It's movement. When we choose intentionality, we commit to shifting at least one step to the right in each domain. Small, steady progress creates lasting change.

What Does Intentionality Look Like?

Intentionality is a practice. It's not just about being organized or having good plans. It's about aligning our daily actions with the kind of community we're trying to build. That means slowing down enough to ask:

Is this decision trauma-inducing or trauma-responsive?

Is this classroom setup welcoming to all students or only to those who already know how to do school?

Is my feedback building self-worth or reinforcing shame?

Am I holding this student accountable in a way that connects and teaches, or isolates and punishes?

We can't pretend our intentions alone are enough. Many systems are stuck in the middle of the trauma continuum, doing no intentional harm, but doing very little intentional healing either. Neutrality is not enough. Trauma-responsive practice requires deliberate action.

For students like Meredith, Malik, Marisol, and Isaiah, who carry the weight of trauma, dysregulation, cultural misunderstanding, or simply a different way of being, school has often felt less like a place of learning and more like a place of control. Over the years, the strategies intended to *manage* them have typically focused on containing them, making them comply, or punishing them for behaviors that were, in truth, signals of unmet needs.

Containment shows up when students are physically isolated from their peers, sent to hallways, offices, or behavior rooms under the guise of a "cool down" with no plan for reconnection. It looks like silent lunches, recess detentions, and adults who supervise instead of support. It's in the seating charts that push students to the margins and in the decisions that deny access to enriching spaces, such as art or music.

Compliance tactics, meanwhile, focus on outward obedience, employing tools such as clip charts, token economies, and reward systems that quietly reward the compliant and exclude those struggling. Scripts replace relationships.

Directives overwhelm students who are already dysregulated. We correct posture, tone, and eye contact without asking what lies beneath. Then there's punishment, including suspensions for defiance, names on the board, revoked field trips, and apologies demanded without repair. These responses send a clear message:

You are a problem to be managed.

Behind every outburst, shutdown, or refusal is a child trying to make sense of something too big for them to carry alone. When we rely on control instead of connection, we miss the invitation to understand.

By the time students reach middle or high school, they've internalized a message:

I'm too much. I'm not safe here. I'm a problem to be solved.

When we see shutdown, refusal, or pushback, it's not defiance; it's often defense. They've spent years navigating systems built to contain them, rather than connect with them.

Systems that used behavior as the benchmark of worth and compliance as the price of inclusion. If these strategies worked, this book wouldn't be necessary. The fences we build are only effective when someone is working *inside* them. Someone teaching. Co-regulating. Connecting. Intentionality asks: Are you working inside the fence, or relying on it to do your job?

Teacher Practice Shift: Being the Teacher Inside the Fence

When we talk about working inside the fence, we're not talking about adding one more thing to your already overloaded plate. We're talking about choosing a different way of being, a slower, more intentional posture of teaching that doesn't require heroics, just consistency and care. This is the work of building genuine, healthy relationships —both in school, at home, and in life.

The teacher inside the fence doesn't rely on systems of control; they cultivate conditions for growth. They aren't just enforcing boundaries from the outside; they're co-regulating, modeling, and teaching within them. They understand that discipline is not something we do to students, but something we build with them. Yes, it still comes back to the relationship. Not in a fluffy, superficial way. In a deeply practical, skill-driven way:

From the chapter on Resilience: Believe every student holds potential, even when they're struggling to access it. Don't mistake survival strategies for fixed traits.

From Origin: Approach students with curiosity, understanding that trauma, culture, neurodiversity, and adversity shape behavior. Don't jump to conclusions; ask better questions.

From Openness: Be willing to look inward. Examine your discomfort, bias, and assumptions without shame and weaponizing guilt.

From Trust: Show up consistently. Don't make promises you can't keep. Understand that trust isn't earned once; it's built daily, in micro-moments.

From Engagement: Design environments where every child, not just the regulated, compliant ones, has access to learning. Understand that connection *precedes* cognition. If a student is disengaged, don't take it personally; take it seriously.

From Neuro-Informed: Teach in ways that honor the brain. Understand that regulation isn't just emotional, it's physiological. Believe the nervous system has a language, and learn how to listen. Create calm spaces, reduce sensory overload, and recognize that shame can shut down the very parts of the brain we need for learning.

From Discernment: Don't just react to behavior— respond with discernment. Ask: *Is this decision reinforcing fear or building safety? Is this rule helping the student grow, or is it helping me feel in control?*

In these ways, you will create environments where felt safety is real, accountability is relational, and every student knows—someone is working with me, not against me. They don't show up to "fix" kids. They show up to walk with them. To teach regulation, to restore connection, to offer another chance. Again and again.

So yes, we're tired of being told to "build a relationship." However, when we strip away the noise, we find this simple truth: relationships are the vehicle for every single thing we hope to teach. If we're honest, what we're really tired of… is trying to do this work without them. This isn't just about classroom management. This is about shaping humans. If we want students like Malik, Marisol, Isaiah, and Meredith to thrive, we have to stop yelling from the outside of the fence and start stepping in with presence, purpose, and hope.

From Trauma-Inducing to Resilience-Building: The Role of Intentionality

Every classroom lives somewhere on the trauma-informed continuum. Where we fall often depends not on how much we care, but on how intentional we are. This continuum moves from trauma-inducing to resilience-building.

Trauma-inducing environments often rely on unexamined habits, such as yelling across the room, zero-tolerance policies, grading as a form of punishment, or shaming students for behaviors they haven't yet mastered. These responses feel "normal" in many schools, but they're reactive, misaligned, and often harmful.

Trauma-indifferent spaces aren't actively harmful, but they also aren't healing. Well-meaning educators may be operating on autopilot, relying on outdated systems simply because that's how it's always been done. Without reflection, nothing changes.

Trauma-aware teams begin to notice the impact of trauma, learning the language of dysregulation and resilience. This is a critical first step in many trauma-informed journeys, but awareness without action keeps us stuck. We may name what we see, then still send a student out of the room without co-regulating. Failure to move past this stage is where *intentionality* becomes the missing link.

Trauma-sensitive efforts are evident in structural changes, including the implementation of mentoring programs, revised discipline policies, and the adoption of restorative practices. However, without a shared mission, these efforts often rest on the shoulders of a few "true believers," while others continue business as usual. Burnout rises, progress stalls.

Resilience-building systems reflect committed, aligned action. Educators co-create norms with students, hold boundaries without shame, and resist "that's just how we do it" thinking. At this level, purpose and practice converge.

Resilience-building schools are grounded in collective clarity. Every adult, from paraprofessional to principal, shares a common goal: to create a safe environment, promote healing, and ensure students feel seen, supported, and valued. It's not about perfection. It's about knowing how to return, repair, and recommit when we fall short.

Across this continuum, we assess six core areas that reflect the heart of a resilience-building classroom: relationships, responsibility, regulation, behavior, academics, and felt safety. None of these exists in isolation. Each is shaped by the choices we make daily—how we speak, structure, respond, and repair.

Relationships don't happen by accident. They are built through intentional practices, including check-ins, morning meetings, advisory structures, and everyday moments that convey, *"You matter here."* In classrooms rooted in connection, every student should be able to name at least one adult they trust.

Behavior becomes a space for teaching, not shaming. When students make mistakes—and they will—we shift the script. Instead of What's wrong with you? We ask, What happened? What's needed? Relational accountability steps in where humiliation once prevailed.

Responsibility can't be demanded; it must be nurtured. It can only grow in spaces where students feel safe enough to take risks. Our message becomes: You can—and I'll help you.

Regulation always begins with us. Students cannot be expected to self-regulate in environments that are chaotic, punitive, or led by adults whose own nervous systems are constantly in a state of fight-or-flight. Resilience-building classrooms are anchored in predictability, co-regulation, and the quiet power of rhythm and repair.

Academics are not lowered. They're scaffolded. High expectations remain—but they are paired with high support. Flexibility and structure are not opposites here; they are partners. Together, they create a path to success that is accessible, equitable, and rooted in dignity.

Felt safety lives in the environment itself. Lighting, sound, seating, visuals—these are not extras. They are messages to the nervous system that say, You belong here. You are safe. You are seen.

If you'd like to see where your practice currently falls, you'll find the full Trauma-Informed Continuum Self-Assessment in Part Five. You're welcome to skip ahead now, or read on, and return to it when you're ready to reflect more deeply.

A Closing Thought

We cannot afford to leave safety, healing, or equity to chance. Intentionality is not about perfection; it's about direction—every single step matters. The trauma our students carry is not their fault, but how we respond is our responsibility. The good news? We're not alone. Change doesn't come from heroic teachers; it comes from committed ones, making one right choice after another, on purpose. Our students don't need a stronger fence. They need someone willing to meet them inside it.

Visit the book companion site for additional materials related to this chapter.

Book Companion Resources

- **Resilience-Building Self-Assessment (also found in Chapter 32)**

❧ reflection ❧

In what ways have you allowed routine or urgency to drive your teaching rather than intentionally aligning it with your values?

Which of the Trauma Continuum Self-Assessment domains do you currently find yourself operating from a trauma-indifferent or trauma-aware space?

What does "working inside the fence" look like in your classroom?

Where have you seen compliance without growth, and what might a more intentional response look like?

What support do you need to shift one column to the right?

If I want to be a teacher who works inside the fence, I need to let go of _____ and practice _____.

⋙ twenty-two ⋘
Hope

Hope is not a feeling we give students. It's a capacity we help them build.

Creating Conditions for Students to Believe in Possibility Again

We often talk about hope as if it were a personality trait. As if some people have it, some don't. In trauma-informed schools, we don't treat hope as a concept. We treat it as a practice, one that is *felt* in every intentional interaction and *grows* through connection, safety, and voice. This chapter isn't about the teacher's hope. It's about what happens when we create classrooms where students start to believe in themselves, others, and the future again.

Hope is not naïve optimism or shallow cheerfulness. It's a neurobiological and psychological process, a future-facing belief system built on the accumulation of safety, voice, and meaningful success. It's the belief that tomorrow can be different than today *and* that I have a role in making it so.

Here's the truth: many students arrive at school with their hope systems in pieces. They've experienced too much instability, too much loss, too many adults who gave up before the relationship got hard. Their nervous systems are wired for protection, not planning. Their beliefs about the future are shaped by pain, not possibility. Our job is not to force hope. Our job is to create the conditions where hope can return.

The Challenge:

In Part One, hope was introduced as an active process that builds resilience. This chapter examines the application of hope as a strategy. Let's consider Jayden and Marisol.

Jayden enters the classroom with quiet confidence. He has a stable home life, two engaged parents, and a calm presence that steadies the room. He participates, offers help, and stays grounded, but hesitates to take risks. He second-guesses himself and only raises his hand when he's sure. He's hopeful, but his perfectionism limits his agency.

Marisol, on paper, is excelling. Her work is immaculate and always tuned in early. She's responsible, helpful, and constantly checking in: "Is this okay?" "Are you mad?" At home, she breaks down. Her mother shares that she cries under the pressure—pressure no one is overtly putting on her, but that she carries anyway. Her achievement is armor. Her control is survival. She's not driven by hope, but by fear of falling apart.

Both students completed the Children's Hope Scale, which measures agency and pathways thinking.[96] Jayden scored high; he believed in his ability to reach his goals, even if he hesitated to act. Marisol scored low. She could name goals but didn't believe she could reach them. Her hope was external, not internalized.

That contrast reminds us that low hope doesn't always show up as sadness or disengagement. Sometimes it hides behind control, silence, or even perfectionism. The student who looks the most "put together" on the outside may be carrying the heaviest weight of hopelessness on the inside.

Rooted in Hope Focus: Hope

Hope is not the result of telling students "things will get better." It grows when students repeatedly experience that they can make things better, provided they have the support, autonomy, and space to grow. In the Rooted in Hope framework, hope isn't a wish; it's a way forward, built through intentional practice.

Hope takes root when students experience consistent care from adults who stay, especially when things get hard. It grows when they're invited to contribute in meaningful ways, not just comply. It deepens when students see themselves in the curriculum, in stories, in leaders, in the questions being asked. It strengthens when failure isn't final, but part of a process they're trusted to repair and recover from.

Most of all, hope flourishes when students can imagine a future self and are given real, supported steps to begin walking toward it. Hope grows from evidence, not encouragement. It lives in the space between *"I believe in you"* and *"Here's how we'll walk this together."*

Teacher Practice Shift: From Promising to Proving

Building hope doesn't require a big shift in curriculum. It requires a change in what we reflect to students about who they are becoming. We build hope when we let students re-try, repair, and rebuild without shame, when we highlight growth rather than perfection. When we catch them doing something right and say, "I saw that. That matters." When we involve them in setting goals and remind them that progress isn't linear, but they're still moving forward.

Tools like the Student in Need of Connection Interview Protocol help us recognize what students already possess: the strengths they've used to survive, the relationships they rely on, and the moments when they feel most seen. That's where hope begins, not with external validation, but with the internal realization: *Maybe I'm not stuck forever. Maybe I can do this. Maybe I'm not broken, just learning.* For Jayden, hope means nudging him gently into risk and reminding him that failure won't define him. For Marisol, hope means releasing her from the need to be perfect to feel worthy.

Hope-Building Strategies: Practical Approaches from Dr. Shane Lopez

Hope is not fluff. It's a measurable predictor of success, more closely linked to academic achievement and emotional well-being than IQ or socioeconomic status.[97] However, trauma interferes with the brain's ability to imagine the future.

Students who have been hurt in the past might stop looking ahead. Trauma-informed, restorative classrooms are fertile ground for rebuilding hope. They offer more than safety; they offer *possibility*.

In these spaces, students encounter predictable environments where the rhythms are steady and the expectations clear. They experience an authentic connection with adults who see them, not just their behavior. They're given opportunities for agency, to make choices, to lead, to shape their learning. They taste success, not because the bar is lowered, but because support is raised. Perhaps most powerfully, they witness resilience in action.

Adults who model reflection, repair, and persistence send a powerful message: *You can struggle and still move forward.* In these classrooms, hope isn't abstract. It's practiced, embodied, and real.

Dr. Lopez reminded us that hope is a teachable skill. It's not just a mindset, it's a skill set. His work provides simple yet powerful ways to help students build hope in real time. These aren't nice extras. In trauma-impacted classrooms, they're foundational.[98] Let's take a look at how these strategies show up in our everyday practice:

Imagining Hope: Helping Students See It

Many students, especially those with trauma histories, have learned to stop imagining the future because the past has taught them it's not safe to look forward. Imagining hope is the practice of inviting students to picture a future self or moment worth moving toward. Try asking:

"What's something you're looking forward to, even a little?"
"If things went well for you this week, what would that look like?"
"Who's the person you most want to become?"

These aren't career questions. They're regulatory questions. They help widen the window of tolerance and re-engage the prefrontal cortex. Even if the answer is small, "Friday," "basketball practice," "getting to recess without getting in trouble" — it's a beginning.

Next-ing: Focusing on Just the Next Step

Students stuck in hopelessness don't need a five-year plan. They need a next step they can take today. Next-ing is the art of zooming in on what's possible right now, not to oversimplify the big picture, but to *make it feel manageable.*[99] Try saying:

"What's the very next thing we can do?"
"Let's just get through the first five minutes, then we'll check in."
"Don't worry about the whole assignment, let's start with one sentence."

Hope grows when students feel like movement is possible, even if it's slow and gradual.

Futurecasting: Naming What Could Be

Futurecasting means helping students connect today's effort with tomorrow's possibilities. It builds the skill of linking cause and effect, not in a punitive, "choices have consequences" way, but in a way that restores agency and optimism.[100] You might say:

"When you keep showing up like this, you're building a skill that's going to serve you long after this class."

"I know today felt hard, but imagine how it will feel when you finish this."

"You didn't give up. That's going to change what happens next."

Futurecasting gives students narrative momentum. It helps them see themselves as characters in a story that's still unfolding.

Using Hope Maps: Naming the Now and Charting the Way Forward

When students feel stuck, they often struggle to see how to move from their current reality to a better future. Hope Maps, developed as part of hope theory research, offer students a visual and straightforward way to identify their current position, their desired destination, and the obstacles that stand in their way.[101]

A Hope Map is a simple yet powerful tool that helps students transition from mere survival to envisioning a brighter future. It invites them to pause and reflect on their current state, their Present State, and to name a meaningful goal or outcome they want to achieve, their Future State. From there, they begin to identify Pathways, the small steps, strategies, or supports that could guide them forward. Just as importantly, they are encouraged to name the Obstacle*s* they might face along the way, and to consider how they might respond with resilience rather than retreat. In trauma-informed spaces, we don't just ask students to hope; we show them how to build it, step by intentional step.

Students can draw their Hope Map or talk it through with a trusted adult. The process isn't about fixing everything; it's about making the journey visible. When students see that there *is* a path forward, even if it is a winding one, their sense of agency begins to grow. Try saying:

"Let's name where you're at and where you want to go."

"What's one possible step in between?"

"What might get in the way, and what could help if that happens?"

Hope Maps shift students from being overwhelmed by the distance to being empowered by the direction. Even naming the obstacles helps students feel less powerless, because now, they aren't facing them alone.

Borrowing Hope: Lending Your Belief

Sometimes students can't access hope on their own. Their nervous systems are too overwhelmed. Their stories are too heavy. That's when they need to borrow ours. We lend hope when we say:

"You're not the first person I've seen go through this, and I believe in you."

"I've seen you get through hard things before. I know you can do this, too."

"I'll hold onto the hope until you can pick it back up."

This isn't offering false reassurance, but presence and persistence. In trauma-informed classrooms, hope isn't something we talk students into. It's something we walk them toward.

Hope and the Brain

When hope is alive in a school, you can hear it in the voices of students. They may not use the word *"hope"* directly, but their words carry it. A student who says, *"I feel like I matter here,"* is expressing more than simple belonging—they're signaling that their identity is seen, valued, and affirmed. Another who shares, *"There's someone I can talk to,"* is describing a felt sense of safety and connection, a trust that they are not alone when life feels heavy.

Hope also appears in how students perceive mistakes. When a child can say, *"If I mess up, it's not the end,"* they are learning that failure is not final, but rather a part of growth. That's resilience in action. And when a student notices, *"I'm actually good at something,"* they are discovering purpose, confidence, and the belief that their contributions matter. Even a simple statement like, *"This year feels different,"* reveals that something has shifted—the culture, the relationships, the systems.

These are not empty platitudes or wishful thinking. They are evidence. They tell us that hope is taking root not only because of the words teachers speak, but because of the deeper, structural changes happening in the classroom and the school as a whole. Schedules are designed with student well-being in mind. Discipline policies emphasize restoration over punishment. Adults are intentional about building trust, listening deeply, and modeling regulation. The environment itself communicates, *"You belong here. You are capable. You have a future."* When students talk this way, it means hope is no longer abstract—it's a lived reality.

A Closing Thought

Hope doesn't arrive with a speech. It comes with a second chance. The rewritten plan. The moment a student is trusted with something that matters. Hope sounds like:

"You can try again."
"I still see you."
"You're not your last mistake."

In trauma-informed, neuro-aligned classrooms, hope is not a feeling we deliver. It's a system we build. One that tells students, day after day: You are not too far gone. You are not stuck. You are not alone.

Visit the book companion site for additional materials related to this chapter.

Book Companion Resources

- Hope Maps
- Guided Imagery Exercise
- Children's Hope Scale

◈ reflection ◈

What are you doing that helps students see new possibilities for themselves?

Are your consequences helping students grow, or reinforcing a sense of defeat?

What opportunities have you created recently for students to succeed in ways that matter to them?

When students leave your classroom, do they feel more hopeful or more exhausted?

When I think of a student who's quietly losing hope, I want to offer _____.

One way I can reflect growth instead of perfection is _____.

Hope, for me, looks like _____.

✦ twenty-three ✦
Ownership

Our job isn't to hold students accountable.
It's to help them become accountable, because they believe it matters.

Growing Internal Accountability, Not Enforcing Control

In many schools, the word 'accountability' is tossed around as a solution. "We have to hold them accountable" becomes shorthand for punishment, detention, suspension, loss of privilege, and exclusion. A question to ask is, *"Are we asking for compliance when we really want commitment to the community?"* Compliance may quiet a behavior, but it rarely transforms it. Obedience may earn a gold star, but it doesn't always grow integrity. Accountability isn't about enforcing control. It's about cultivating ownership, from the inside out.

In a resilience-building classroom, we shift from focusing on behavior management to emphasizing meaning-making. We help students connect their actions to their values, to the impact on others, and to the kind of person they want to become. Not because we force them, but because we believe they're capable of growth. Ownership doesn't emerge from shame. It grows in the presence of safety, relationship, and reflection.

The Challenge: Why Traditional Accountability Works for Some Students, and Not for Others

Let's talk about Jayden and Isaiah.

Jayden is the kind of student most teachers wish for. He's kind, consistent, and eager to please. If he forgets a homework assignment or gets a little off-task, a gentle reminder is enough to reset him. He might blush, apologize, and even over-correct. A missed assignment turns into a fulfilled promise of doing better next time. He owns his mistakes quickly, not because he's afraid, but because he believes his choices matter and trusts the adults guiding him. That's what secure attachment does. It lays a foundation where correction feels safe, and repair feels possible. When Jayden is held accountable, he hears, "You're better than this. I know you can do better," and he believes it.

Then there's Isaiah. When Isaiah is corrected, he explodes. A calm redirection turns into a power struggle. He walks out. He yells. He refuses to apologize. You might think he doesn't care—but that's not it. Isaiah cares deeply, so deeply that shame sends him into a state of survival mode. He's been through the system, removed from his home, bounced between placements, and told, both in words and actions, that he's the problem. Correction doesn't feel like care to him. It feels like betrayal. Like rejection. Like every other adult who gave up. So when you say, "We're going to hold you accountable," Isaiah doesn't hear a chance to grow.

He hears, "You're too much again."
He hears, "Here we go again."
He hears, "You're on your own."

Jayden can receive accountability. Isaiah has to be taught ownership. That's the difference.

Rooted in Hope Focus: Ownership

Ownership isn't about getting it right the first time. It's about giving students the tools, space, and relationships to get it right the next time. In trauma-informed classrooms, ownership isn't demanded; it's cultivated. It grows when students are invited to reflect before they're corrected, supported in making things right without being shamed, and given real opportunities to lead, contribute, and practice responsibility.

Ownership deepens when we remind students of their strengths, even in moments of struggle. At its core, ownership communicates this truth: *You are not defined by what you did. You are responsible for the choices you make next.* That kind of responsibility can't be lectured into a student. It has to be modeled, nurtured, and walked out together. We don't build ownership by talking *at* students. We build it by walking with them.

Accountability vs. Ownership

Holding a student accountable is often confused with control. It might look like issuing a consequence, insisting on compliance, or monitoring behavior to ensure obedience. However, true accountability—resilience-building accountability—goes deeper.

Helping a student become accountable means teaching the why behind the expectation, not just enforcing the rule. It means involving them in the repair process when harm occurs, not just assigning a punishment. It means giving them space to reflect, restore, and reset.

Above all, it means believing, sometimes before they believe it themselves, that they are capable of making different choices. Ownership is rooted in dignity. It says to the student: *You are not defined by what you did. You're responsible for what you choose next.*

Teacher Practice Shift: From Correction to Co-Responsibility

Ownership doesn't mean there are no consequences. It implies the consequence is connected to something more than control. Let's walk through some shifts that build internal accountability in students—especially those like Isaiah, who need something more than a color chart and a reminder.

Restore Before You Consequence

In traditional models, we correct first and connect later, if at all. In trauma-informed classrooms, we flip the order. Instead of:
"You broke the rule, so here's the punishment."
Try:
"Something didn't go right. Let's talk about it first."

Give the student a chance to share their story, regulate their body, and join in deciding what happens next. This doesn't excuse behavior—it humanizes the process.

Use Reflective Questions That Build Internal Scripts

Over time, the way we talk to students becomes the way they talk to themselves. Equip them with the right questions:

"What happened from your perspective?"

"Who was impacted?"

"What can you do to make this right?"

"What support do you need to follow through?"

These questions create a pause between mistake and response—an internal pause students can carry with them long after they leave our rooms.

Spotlight Strength-Based Ownership

When students name their strengths, their capacity to take responsibility expands. From the SiNoC Interview:

"What's something you're proud of—even if nobody sees it?"

"What's something you want to take more responsibility for?"

We don't just ask these questions once; we revisit them. We reflect them. We celebrate not just when students behave, but when they restore, regulate, and try again.

Scaffold Without Shame

Isaiah doesn't need a lighter consequence. He needs a plan that matches his nervous system's capacity. That might mean breaking the repair process into steps, practicing self-advocacy scripts ahead of time, co-creating behavior plans with family input, and allowing for emotional recovery before engaging in logical discussion. We can't shame students into growth. However, we can support them in taking on self-responsibility.

A Word About Consequences

As we discussed in the chapter on Discernment, consequences still matter—but only when they serve as a teaching tool. A trauma-informed consequence isn't about proving authority; it's about guiding growth. It's logical because it connects directly to the harm. It's restorative, because it invites repair. It's delivered relationally, protecting dignity in the process. And it's always regulation-checked, never handed down in the heat of the moment.

Think back to the Social Discipline Window and ask yourself: *Is this consequence about teaching, or about proving I'm in control? Am I leaning toward permissive, neglectful, punitive, or restorative practices?*

When the balance is right, students don't just comply—they begin to take ownership of their behavior. You'll hear it in their words:

That wasn't okay, and I want to make it right.
Can I try again?
I messed up, but I don't want to stay stuck.
I want to do better, and I know how.

That's not compliance. That's becoming.

A Closing Thought

You don't build ownership by holding students tighter. You build it by inviting them into a process that says, 'You can grow here.' By modeling reflection. By offering restoration. By trusting that even the students who resist the hardest are the ones who need that trust the most. Every time we give a student the chance to make things right, not to earn our approval, but to rediscover their integrity, we walk them a little closer to becoming the kind of person they already want to be.

❧ reflection ❧

Where in your current discipline system do you rely more on control than on co-regulation?

When students make mistakes, do you offer a path to repair—or just a consequence?

How are you helping students develop a sense of identity as individuals who can take responsibility for their actions?

One moment this week when I helped a student build ownership was _____.

 A consequence I've used in the past that may have communicated control more than teaching is

_____.

To help my most disconnected student grow internal accountability, I can _____.

❧ twenty-four ❧

Purpose

Purpose isn't what students achieve. It's what they believe they were made for.

Helping Students Remember They Matter

In Rooted in Hope classrooms, purpose is not a standalone goal; it's an outcome. When we create resilience-building, neuro-informed spaces where students experience safety, voice, and connection, something transformational begins to emerge: they remember who they are and start imagining who they could become.

Purpose is intertwined with engagement. It is both a driver of motivation and a sign that students feel seen, safe, and significant. It grows alongside other key outcomes of resilience-building practice, hope, ownership, and empowerment. When students reconnect to a sense of purpose, they don't just participate; they invest.

Purpose isn't something we hand students. It's something we cultivate through presence, possibility, and practices that say, "You matter here."

The Challenge: When Purpose Is Missing

Jayden and Malik aren't in the same class, but they remind us that every student carries a story, and those stories shape how purpose is built, lost, or recovered. Jayden comes from a stable home and shows up with a ready-to-learn attitude. He's kind, consistent, and often the first to lend a hand. However, he is also hesitant to take academic risks. His teacher sees the potential in him, not just for success, but for leadership. Jayden doesn't need rescuing. He needs to be stretched with purpose, something that invites him to invest, not just perform.

Malik, on the other hand, carries a much heavier load. He's creative, quick, and full of potential, but avoidantly attached and distrustful of adults. He disengages easily. Compliance-based systems don't work for him. What he needs isn't tighter control, it's a deeper reason to try. Purpose isn't just a motivator for Malik; it's a lifeline. It's the thread that could pull him back into belonging.

When students like Malik are given the chance to lead, contribute, and be seen for their strengths, purpose starts to take root. When students like Jayden are trusted with more than compliance, they begin to stretch toward who they're becoming.

Rooted in Hope Focus: Purpose

Purpose is more than a future goal—it's a present identity. It tells students, *You're not just here to behave or perform. You're here because you bring something no one else does.* In Rooted in Hope classrooms, purpose isn't a distant aspiration; it's something we cultivate daily. We grow purpose by reflecting on students' strengths before correcting their behavior. We offer meaningful roles that communicate trust, not just busywork to keep them occupied. We connect content to culture, creativity, and community, making learning feel alive and relevant. When we help students name what they care about—and why it matters— they begin to see school not just as a place to earn points, but as a space to live out their values.

Purpose is also protective. It regulates behavior, builds resilience, and increases motivation—not through pressure, but through a sense of belonging. Students who believe they have something to offer are more likely to stay when things get hard. For students like Malik, purpose may be the difference between checking out and buying in.

Teacher Practice Shift: From Managing to Meaning

We don't grow purpose through compliance charts. We grow it through connection and contribution. Let's look at how purpose can be embedded into everyday practice:

Replace Tasks with Roles That Matter

Building on our discussion in the chapter on Engagement, instead of using classroom jobs to manage behavior, utilize them to foster identity.

> *The line leader becomes the Community Coordinator.*
> *The student who paces becomes the Movement Manager.*
> *The class clown becomes the Morning Meeting Host.*
> *The withdrawn student becomes the Reflection Partner.*

Every role becomes an opportunity for students to see themselves as capable and valued.

Use Strengths-Based Reflection to Reclaim Identity

Ask students what they're proud of, even if no one else notices. Ask what they want to be remembered for. Ask caregivers what dreams they still hold for their child. These questions help students rewrite their internal stories, not to erase what's been hard, but to see what else is true. It shifts the narrative from "I'm the one who gets in trouble" to "I'm someone becoming."

Make Learning Matter Beyond the Classroom

One of the most powerful ways to build purpose is to anchor learning in the real world. When I taught science in an inner-city school, I began using current events to ground every lesson. This wasn't about relevance alone; it was about connection and contribution.

When I taught fourth grade, we studied water conservation. My students read articles about the global water crisis, especially the lack of clean water in developing countries. A group of students became so passionate that they designed a water filtration system out of recycled materials. After realizing it mirrored an actual model that could be purchased affordably, they started selling water at lunch to raise money. They raised enough to buy and ship multiple filters overseas.

Another year, while reading a novel that touched on grief, several students opened up about recent losses in their families. They decided to raise money for our local Cancer Council, which had supported their loved ones. Two local businesses matched their efforts. It was healing. It was powerful. And it was purposeful. That's what happens when content connects to character and community. School stops being something students endure and starts becoming something they own.

Help Students Name What They Stand For

Purpose isn't just what you do. It's what you stand for. Try this exercise, inspired by the Ikigai model:[102]

What do you love?

What are you good at?

What does the world need?

What can you be paid or recognized for?

The overlap? That's the beginning of purpose. Now simplify it: Invite students to choose a core value word, such as kindness, creativity, justice, or strength, and ask:

"What's one way you can live into value this week?"

"What would it look like if this classroom protected that value?"

It's not about having all the answers. It's about inviting students to see themselves as people who matter.

Trauma and the Loss of Purpose

Trauma has a way of collapsing time. It pulls students into survival mode, disconnecting them from future thinking and distorting their sense of identity. When students stop imagining what *could be*, they start bracing for what might go wrong. That's where purpose comes in. Purpose interrupts the cycle. It offers a reason to stay when learning becomes challenging, a framework for understanding, and a steady reminder: *You are not defined by what has happened to you.* In classrooms rooted in hope, purpose is not just a concept; it's a compass.

For Malik, purpose is the bridge between his protective detachment and the possibility of contribution. For Jayden, purpose is the next step toward self-led engagement and courageous growth.

For both, purpose is the thread that ties belonging to becoming.

Present Purpose

When students discover a sense of purpose, it doesn't just shape who they want to become someday—it steadies them in the moment. Purpose is a critical weight on the Regulation Fulcrum, tipping students back toward safety and engagement when stress threatens to pull them off balance. A student who knows *why* they matter and *what* they bring begins to regulate more effectively, because the pull of meaning is stronger than the push of fear.

This is why purpose is not only about the future but also about the present. It reframes difficulty as part of growth rather than proof of failure: a challenging assignment becomes a practice in persistence, conflict becomes an opportunity to repair, and even failure becomes a doorway to resilience. In this way, purpose shifts focus from survival to contribution, from "just get through the day" to "this is who I am becoming." It grounds students in strength today while opening doors to possibilities tomorrow.

A Closing Thought

Purpose doesn't emerge because we say the right words. It emerges when students feel seen. It grows in relationships that protect their identity, and in classrooms that invite contribution before compliance. In Rooted in Hope classrooms, students begin to believe:

"I am more than what happened to me."

"I belong here."

"I have something the world needs."

When that belief takes root, students don't just survive school; they thrive. They transform through it.

❧ reflection ❧

What opportunities do students have to lead, shape, or contribute in your classroom?

Are you reinforcing the idea that they are someone, or that they must earn value through behavior?

What future vision of themselves are your students rehearsing each day here?

Who is helping your most discouraged student believe they have a reason to try again?

One student who seems disconnected from purpose is _____.

I could begin to rebuild that by _____.

If I asked students what they want to be remembered for, I hope they'd say _____.

❧ twenty-five ❧
Empowerment

Empowerment isn't something we give students.
It's what they remember they already have.

Reclaiming the Power Within

Every student walks into school with intrinsic power, the power to feel, to choose, to connect, to heal, and to grow. It is not distributed by ability, behavior, background, or compliance. It's inherent, because they are human. Yet, too often, the systems around them are built on power-over models.

Rules without voice. Consequences without context. Instruction without relevance. Compliance mistaken for character. In these systems, students may learn to behave, but not to believe in their capacity. They may learn to obey, but not to own. The work of resilience-building education is to shift from managing students to equipping them, to move from controlling behavior to cultivating belief.

The Challenge: When Empowerment Feels Out of Reach

Jayden rarely needed reminders. He showed up, did the work, and followed the rules. Adults praised him for his consistency and self-control. Yet, when given the chance to lead or try something new, he hesitated. "What if I mess it up?" he'd whisper. His teachers noticed he preferred following instructions over making decisions. He was capable, but he didn't always trust himself. Jayden was empowered in structure, but not in voice.

Meredith, on the other hand, had no trouble using her voice at home. At school, it was a different story. After experiencing dismissal, judgment, and even public discipline for expressing discomfort or asking questions, she learned to stay quiet. She learned that pushing back, even respectfully, meant being labeled disrespectful. Her confidence withered. Not because she lacked ability, but because she'd learned that her voice wasn't safe here.

These two students seem like opposites, but they both highlight the same truth: empowerment doesn't grow in silence or obedience. It grows in practice, in spaces where voice, choice, and trust are authentic.

Rooted in Hope Focus: Empowerment

In the *Rooted in Hope* framework, empowerment signifies the transition from mere survival to self-determination and autonomy. It's not about giving students power; they already have it. It's about helping them access, trust, and direct that power with purpose. This facet calls educators to reflect deeply:

Where might I be holding power in ways that silence voice, limit autonomy, or constrain growth?

True empowerment means moving beyond behavioral control and toward co-creating spaces where students build capacity, both academically and emotionally, and relationally. It asks us to examine our beliefs and systems, making intentional shifts that invite agency rather than compliance. Empowerment flourishes when students are not just seen as participants, but as partners in their learning and healing.

A Note on Control

Many students arrive at school each day with very few real choices. From what they wear (due to uniforms or dress codes), to when they can sharpen a pencil, to how and when they use the restroom or get a drink, their autonomy is stripped away in hundreds of small ways. We control their bodies, their movements, their time, and even their tone of voice. Then we act surprised when they don't know how to make decisions or advocate for themselves. It's not that they lack the capacity for decision-making; it's that they haven't been trusted to practice it.

Teacher Practice Shifts That Empower Students

Create Choice-Driven Structures

Trauma often strips students of the ability to choose. Rebuilding autonomy doesn't mean chaos; it means creating systems where choice is expected, not exceptional.

> *Examples:*
> *Offer multiple ways to complete a task*
> *Let students help co-design classroom norms*
> *In behavioral plans, allow them to choose which regulation tool or adult support they want to access*

From the Student in Need of Connection Interview:

> *"What would help you feel more in control or heard here?"*

Engage in Shared Power with Families

From the Parent/Caregiver Interview Protocol:

> *"Are there ways you'd like to be involved in supporting your child at school?"*
> *"What would it take for you to feel this team is working with you?"*

When families are seen as collaborators, not compliance targets, students feel their identity and experience affirmed, not erased. That's empowerment through belonging.

Teach the Language of Regulation and Choice

When students can name what they feel, identify what they need, and choose a tool or strategy, they reclaim internal power—power that has been hijacked by stress, shame, or disconnection.

Start small:

"Do you want to talk about it or take a quiet space?"

"Would a walk, music, or water help your body feel better?"

Letting students choose how to regulate doesn't just calm behavior. It reinforces agency over reaction.

Recognize and Reflect Student Strength

From the interview protocol:

"What are you proud of, even if others don't see it?"

Empowerment grows when students feel seen not just for their effort, but for their essence.

Try:

"I noticed how you supported your classmate when they were upset. That's leadership."

"It took courage to start over. That matters more than perfection."

Empowerment is not praise for compliance. It's recognition of intrinsic capacity.

Disempowerment vs. Empowerment

Disempowerment is rooted in control, compliance, and fear—"Do what I say or else." It relies on punishment, one-size-fits-all plans, and routines that silence student voice. Empowerment, on the other hand, is about partnership. It says, "Let's figure this out together." It embraces learning from mistakes through rupture and repair, creates personalized interventions, and builds structures that actively invite student voice and feedback.

Empowerment doesn't mean lowering expectations or giving up authority. It means using authority relationally, guiding students to build agency, accountability, and ownership. When we move from disempowerment to empowerment, students aren't just compliant for the moment; they're equipped with the skills, confidence, and resilience to thrive long after they leave our classrooms.

Disempowerment	Empowerment
Control over students	Partnership with students
"Do what I say or else."	"Let's figure this out together."
Punishment for mistakes	Learning from rupture and repair
One-size-fits-all learning or behavior plans	Personalized, choice-based interventions
Voice-less routines	Structures that invite voice and feedback

Empowerment in Action

When Jayden was asked to lead a classroom discussion, he initially declined. However, with encouragement and scaffolding, he agreed to co-lead with a peer. The following week, he asked to lead alone. He shared insights, invited others to contribute, and ended by saying, "That felt good."

During the school shutdown due to COVID-19, Meredith was given the opportunity to design a passion project, and she lit up. Her proposal? A student podcast on mental health, featuring interviews, original music, and coping tips. She wasn't just doing an assignment. She was reclaiming her voice and her power.

When students are empowered, something shifts. They begin to advocate for themselves with both respect and clarity, recognizing that their voice has weight. Challenges no longer feel like threats; they become opportunities to grow, reflect, and try again. Most importantly, empowered students start to imagine futures where they are not passive observers, but the main characters, shaping their story, not just surviving it. Empowerment isn't just a skill; it's a way of being in the world. When we nurture it, we don't just change outcomes, we change identities.

A Closing Thought

Empowerment is not soft. It's sacred. It's the quiet strength of a student who says, "I know what I need." "I'm proud of how I handled that." "I'm choosing differently today." In Rooted in Hope classrooms, we don't give students power; they already have it. Our role is not to grant it, but to create conditions where they can trust and be trusted. Many of us were never taught how to share power without losing authority, or how to support agency without losing control. The shift is working to build the kind of relationships, systems, and expectations that help them rise into their power—not taking it away, not holding it over them, instead walking alongside them as they learn to carry it well.

Visit the book companion site for additional materials related to this chapter.

Book Companion Resources

- SiNoC Interview Protocols

⋅s reflection ɣ⋅

What assumptions do you hold about how much power students "should" have?

Where in your day do you unintentionally prioritize control over connection?

How do you respond when a student exercises agency? Do you feel threatened or inspired?

What's one system you could redesign to include more student choice or voice?

One way I reinforced student agency this week was...

A moment I saw a student act from a place of inner power was...

If empowerment is remembering you have a say in your own story, then my classroom must...

✺ part three reflection ❧
The Rooted In Hope Framework

Take a moment to breathe.

You've just walked through twelve chapters that asked you not just to learn, but to feel, to reflect, and to reconsider what it means to be an educator in the lives of students navigating pain, brilliance, trauma, humor, creativity, loss, and potential. This is more than professional development, it's personal formation.

You've met students like Jayden, Malik, Marisol, Isaiah, and Meredith. Their stories weren't included as examples. They were invitations. Invitations to reimagine your role, not as an enforcer or fixer, but as a steady, curious, compassionate presence who helps students return to safety and grow into their strength. As you move through this reflection, don't rush. Let it be a mirror.

Use the Part Three ROOTED IN HOPE Reflection found in Part Five on page 277 or by scanning the QR code below to organize your thinking to organize your thinking and start planting seeds of change in your practice.

Visit the book companion site for additional materials related to this chapter.

Book Companion Resources

- Part Three Reflection

✍ part four ✒
From Insight to Implementation

Part Four marks a turning point in this journey. Where earlier sections explored the *why*, the science, stories, and self-awareness that shape resilience-building practice, this section shifts into the *how*. It's where insight becomes implementation. Where reflection becomes design. Where we stop asking what's wrong with students and start building the environments, systems, and supports they need to thrive. This is where we implement resilience-building practices through four core practices.

Attend to the Physical Environment

We begin with Creating Spaces That Heal, an in-depth exploration of how physical and relational environments influence students' nervous systems. Classrooms, calm rooms, hallways, bathrooms, and in-school suspension rooms are reimagined not just as functional spaces, but as interventions, each one holding the power to reinforce dysregulation or to invite safety, dignity, and connection.

Teach Emotional Awareness

Next, we explore Building Emotional Regulation. Through core emotional language, daily check-ins, grounding strategies, breathwork, and reflection, we explore what it means to equip students with the tools they need to navigate stress, rather than just avoid it. These are not soft skills; they are survival skills.

Develop Competence in Co-Regulation

To intervene effectively, we need to view the Co-Regulation Process as a stage-based roadmap for supporting students through dysregulation with empathy, clarity, and relational presence. This is where theory meets the moment, in the hallway, in the heat of a crisis, in the quiet after a rupture. We walk through what to notice, what to say, how to respond, and how to recover, together.

Identify and Respond to Students in Need of Connection

Finally, we bring it all together with the Student in Need of Connection (SiNoC) Process, a comprehensive framework for responding to students who are showing signs of disconnection, distress, or unmet needs. Grounded in story, not just data, the SiNoC process helps educators build student-centered profiles, map patterns of resilience and risk, and design interventions that are relational, strategic, and equity-driven. It integrates everything we've learned, neurobiology, attachment, motivation, behavior, and identity, into one cohesive support tool.

✒ twenty-six ☙
Creating Spaces and Places that Heal

Every Space Teaches

Classrooms. Calm Rooms. Hallways. Bathrooms. Libraries. ISS rooms. Each one communicates expectations and values. Each one is either a tool for regulation or a barrier to it.

We walk through these spaces every day. But do we *see* them?

Do students feel emotionally safe in our hallways?

Are bathrooms monitored with dignity, not suspicion?

Do our routines allow for pause, or only pace?

Are the adults steady and supported, or stretched thin and reactive?

These questions are not aesthetic. They are equity. Because students who are dysregulated don't need more rules, they need more alignment between the environment and the nervous system.

That begins with how we design, not just the layout, but the *experience* of being in school.

Designing Environments for Connection, Safety, and Regulation

A resilience-building school isn't built solely through training, policies, or mission statements. It's built through space, real, physical space. Classrooms, hallways, bathrooms, common areas, even the front office. Each one speaks. Each one teaches. Each one holds the power to either reinforce dysregulation or help students come home to themselves.

For students impacted by toxic stress or trauma, the environment is never neutral. Sensory overload, unpredictable transitions, harsh lighting, or a lack of privacy can activate the nervous system before a single adult has said a word.

However, the opposite is also true: thoughtful spaces convey a sense of safety, care, and belonging. They soften the stress of the day. They become stabilizing forces for students whose internal worlds may feel unpredictable and chaotic.

Healing-centered spaces aren't about trendy aesthetics or Pinterest-worthy bulletin boards. They are about intentionality, the small, consistent choices we make to ensure that our environments regulate, restore, and reconnect.

There are three essential components to consider when creating learning spaces and places that heal: relationships, safety, and regulation. These aren't one-time interventions. They're long-term commitments to how we structure our spaces, design our routines, and show up for our students day after day.

You are not expected to implement everything at once. That would be counterproductive. Instead, consider what you're already doing well, what resonates with you, and what your students might need most right now. Start there. These strategies are not about doing more; they're about doing what matters with greater intention.

Relationships: The Foundation of All Healing

As we've explored throughout this book, relationships are the heartbeat of a resilience-building learning environment. Without a strong relational connection, no amount of strategy will stick. The good news? Relationship-building is something most educators already do naturally. The goal now is to become even more intentional and strategic in cultivating connections with every student, every day.

Building these relationships starts with creating a classroom culture that feels like a family, one where students know they belong, are known by name, and are greeted with warmth. Using consistent routines, such as daily greetings and end-of-day check-ins, can provide these touchpoints.

Intentionally teaching social skills, rather than simply correcting behavior after the fact, helps students understand how to navigate relationships in ways that feel safe and productive.

When we share good news with our families, celebrate student effort, and use literature to foster empathy, we reinforce that our students are more than just their grades or behavior; they are whole individuals, worthy of connection. That connection extends beyond the classroom walls when we attend events outside of school, welcome families into the building, and create spaces where students can build peer connections through play, conversation, and shared traditions. In all of this, we are telling students: *"You matter. You belong. I'm glad you're here."*

Safety: More than Emergency Plans

When we hear "school safety," we often think of lockdown drills or emergency protocols. Yet, for trauma-impacted students, safety must go deeper. It must be felt. Emotional and psychological safety come from predictability, consistency, and an environment that reduces sensory overwhelm rather than amplifies it. The space around a student can either escalate their nervous system or help it settle.

Designing calm, organized classrooms with soft lighting, minimal visual clutter, and intentional sound can significantly impact how students perceive the space. Maintaining clear routines and practicing procedures daily helps students predict what's coming next and feel more in control. When expectations are taught explicitly and revisited regularly, they feel like scaffolding, not traps. Mantras, affirmations, and familiar phrases can serve as anchors, helping students center themselves and remember who they are, even in moments of stress.

Regulation: Teaching and Supporting Nervous System Balance

Regulation is a developmental process that is both biological and learned. We're born with nervous systems designed to up- and down-shift arousal, but those systems are immature early on. Through co-regulation—being soothed, guided, and given predictable rhythms—children gradually internalize strategies and neural pathways for self-regulation.

In other words, capacity begins in the body, grows through relationships, and becomes a skill through practice.

That's why we cannot expect students to self-regulate when they've never been taught or rarely seen it modeled. Regulation is not something students just "know" how to do. It must be taught, modeled, and supported—especially in environments where students are asked to focus, persist, and collaborate. When we understand how the brain responds to stress, we shift our goal from managing behavior to supporting regulation before, during, and after dysregulation occurs.

When students are in a regulated state, that's the ideal time to teach skills such as emotional expression, stress awareness, and basic brain science. It's when their prefrontal cortex is most accessible, and they can absorb strategies such as breathing techniques, mindfulness, and communication tools. These lessons, taught in calm moments, lay the foundation for what students will need when their nervous system is overwhelmed.

When stress begins to rise, intervention needs to happen early and gently. Offering breaks, access to water or snacks, movement opportunities, and quiet spaces allows students to reset, build capacity for stress, and prevent dysregulation. Transitions, both big and small, should be supported with clarity, consistency, and reassurance. When a student's stress response activates, co-regulation becomes our greatest tool. It's not about fixing or forcing. It's about offering our calm so they can begin to find theirs. This might look like a quiet check-in, a walk-and-talk, or simply staying nearby with a steady presence. Regulation isn't about eliminating stress; it's about helping students learn how to navigate it with support and skill.

Healing-centered environments aren't built in one training or with one initiative. They are built in moments: a steady tone, a soft light, a teacher who keeps showing up. As you reflect on these components — relationships, safety, and regulation — choose one small thing to try or revisit. You are already building spaces that heal. Let this guide you further, not into doing more, but into doing what matters with even more clarity, compassion, and purpose.

Respect Agreements

In a resilience-building classroom, safety and belonging aren't assumed; they're built together. One of the most powerful ways to begin that process is by co-creating a Respect Agreement, a living document shaped by student voice and grounded in mutual care.

As described by Joe Brummer, a Respect Agreement is not a list of rules imposed by the teacher, but a shared commitment between students and adults about how they will treat one another.[103] It is created with students, revisited often, and used as a touchstone during moments of regulation, conflict, and reflection.

One activity that helps lay the foundation for this agreement invites students to identify what they need from themselves, their peers, their teacher, and their environment to feel safe and ready to learn. While in the classroom, I had students record their answers to the following questions on sticky notes and place them on four separate charts. A full description of this activity can be found on the Book Companion site.

"To be at my best, what I need from myself is…"

"To be at my best, what I need from my peers is…"

"To be at my best, what I need from my teacher is…"

"To be at my best, what I need from the environment is…"

Regulation Rooms: Creating Space to Regulate and Return

Despite our best efforts, some students will become overwhelmed. Their stress will spill over. When it does, they need more than a hallway walk or a punitive referral. They need a structured space to regulate, reflect, and return. This is the role of the Regulation Room.

A Regulation Room is not a time-out space or a place to "sit and think" in isolation. It is a regulated, supportive space where students are welcomed, not sent. The goal is not removal. The goal is reintegration.

One thing I caution people to consider is the use of the word "calm" as part of the name. The word "calm" is perfectly acceptable and widely used, but I am not sure that it always accurately reflects the specific goals of the room. What we more accurately mean by 'calm' is 'regulated. ' Regulated is the baseline, and it isn't the same as calm or quiet. Regulation means the student's internal state matches the demands of the moment. Some other choices for the name could include:

Reset Room	Brain Break Room	The Den
Reset and Return	Holding Space	Balance Room
Regulation Station	Bridge Room	The Nest

Regulation rooms need to be staffed by a trained adult, not just someone monitoring behavior, but someone who co-regulates. This person holds space without judgment. They understand that a child's distress is not a sign of disrespect. They notice patterns. They stay calm. They guide.

The room itself is intentionally designed. The lighting is soft. Seating options are flexible, including beanbags, wobble stools, and yoga mats. Sensory tools are available, including fidgets, putty, headphones, and breathing visuals. A timer and check-in/check-out sheets provide structure. Students are guided to identify what they're feeling and what they need. They are not rushed. They are not lectured.

Time in the Regulation Room is purposeful and time-limited. Students know the expectations. Staff track entries and exits, not as a discipline record, but as data to help us understand:

When is this student most vulnerable?

What helps them recover?

How can we prevent future escalations?

Importantly, Regulation Room data is disaggregated by race, disability, gender, and grade level. This helps us identify any patterns of disproportionate use. Suppose we notice that certain groups of students, such as Black students, students with disabilities, or boys, are being sent to the room more often than others. In that case, it's a signal to pause and ask deeper questions: *Are our systems truly equitable? Are we unintentionally relying on this support more for some students than others?* When we observe patterns like this, it's not just about individual behavior; it's about how our systems are functioning and whether they need to be adjusted to serve all students better.

Call-Out Systems: When the Adult Needs Support

A well-established call-out procedure provides a safety net for teachers, enabling them to self-regulate when necessary and ensuring that educators and students are cared for in moments of heightened emotion. These systems are designed to help teachers quickly and effectively request assistance in managing students' emotional or behavioral needs. A call-out system allows teachers to signal that they need help. This might be a text message, an app-based system like GroupMe, or a walkie-talkie. Another adult, such as a counselor, coach, or administrator, arrives and temporarily takes over the role. The goal is not to "rescue" the teacher, but to prevent rupture. To say: *You are not alone in this.*

When designing a call-out system, it's essential to consider the types of situations typically encountered by teachers and create your codes based on that data. A sample system developed by Jessica Harris at Mayflower Mill Elementary in Tippecanoe, IN, can be found on the Book Companion site.[104] Typical codes include 'walk and talk,' 'hangouts,' 'flip-flop,' 'clearing a room,' 'escorting a student to another location,' and 'tap-out.'

The tap-out code can be a game-changer for teachers. Let's face it, sometimes it's not the student who needs a break, it's the adult. Every educator has a limit, and reaching that limit doesn't make us ineffective; it makes us human. In a resilience-building culture, we normalize this. We expect it, and we create systems to support it.

During the tap-out, the teacher regroups, emotionally, physically, or mentally, and returns when they are regulated. This keeps classrooms safe. It models co-regulation in action. It also protects everyone's dignity, including that of the teacher. We don't wait for burnout to offer this. We build it into the culture because adult regulation is about student safety.

Many schools are also setting up adult regulation rooms, spaces where a quick break can be taken. Often, these rooms are furnished with soft lighting, white noise machines, essential oils, snacks, and water/tea/coffee. Some even have massage chairs! This space allows teachers to care for themselves for a few moments and acknowledges that it's okay to need a moment to regulate.

In-School Suspension: Reframing Accountability

In many schools, In-School Suspension (ISS) is where students are sent when they cross a line. In trauma-responsive schools, the ISS is transformed from a holding room into a healing space, which some refer to as The Reconnection Room or The Reset Room. This room is not punitive. It is structured. Students are greeted by a trained adult who knows how to hold boundaries and extend care. Expectations are clear. There are workstations, calming materials, and a plan for how students will reflect, repair, and re-enter.

Restorative conversations are part of the process. Students aren't just "sitting it out." They're being guided through co-regulation, reflection, and reconnection. They may complete a plan, repair a relationship, or practice a skill they lacked in the moment.

Staff track entries to ISS carefully, again, not to punish, but to understand patterns and inform support. How did the student end up here? What upstream interventions were attempted? What helped them get ready to return?

When done well, the ISS room becomes not a dead end, but a detour toward a sense of belonging. A place where the message is clear: *You are still part of this community. Let's figure out how to return together.*

Visit the book companion site for additional materials related to this chapter.

Book Companion Resources

- Building Respect Agreements
- Regulation Room Considerations
- Sample Call-Out System

✤ reflection ✤

Walk through your building with your nervous system wide open.

Where do you feel tension rise?

Where do you feel calm?

Where might a student who is often in survival mode find refuge—or reinforcement of their shame?

Choose one space—your classroom, a hallway, or a common area—and identify three simple changes you could make to support regulation, trust, and connection. Not perfection. Just presence.

✎ twenty-seven ✐
Building Self-Awareness

One of the most effective ways to support regulation is to teach emotional awareness through the lens of core emotions. Teaching students (and ourselves) to acknowledge and honor emotion without judgment is one of the most powerful regulatory tools we have. We don't need to fix feelings. We just need to notice them, name them, and give them space to pass.

Emotions aren't good or bad. They're messengers. Signals. They help us identify what matters and what needs attention. When we normalize emotions, when we stop labeling them as problems to solve, we open the door to regulation. While there are dozens of nuanced feelings, most intense emotional experiences can be traced back to four foundational states: mad, sad, glad, and afraid.

Four Core Emotions

Emotional regulation doesn't begin with deep breathing or behavior charts. It starts with language that is shared, simple, and accessible, even in moments of dysregulation. When students can identify their emotions, they're better equipped to understand what they need. When adults can respond with clarity and calm, we become co-regulators, not controllers.

Emotions are like primary colors. Just as red, blue, and yellow combine to create every color on the spectrum, our emotional experiences are built from a few foundational feelings that blend and shift depending on what's happening inside and around us.

In my work, I focus on four core emotions: sad, afraid, glad, and mad. Each one has its own "color," not just for simplicity, but because colors make abstract concepts more concrete, especially for kids (and let's be honest, adults too).

All emotions are acceptable. All behavior is not. That distinction matters. Anger, sadness, fear, and joy are everyday human experiences. They belong in our classrooms. However, hurting others, destroying property, or lashing out in unsafe ways are behaviors that require guidance, structure, and support. When we validate emotion and hold compassionate limits around behavior, we create a space where students can feel deeply without fear, and still be held accountable with care.

- **Glad is yellow.** It represents a sense of balance, safety, and contentment. It's not just about joy or excitement; it's about a nervous system that feels calm and steady because its needs are met.
- **Sad is blue.** It reflects experiences of loss, disappointment, or hurt. It can also include feelings of shame when we believe we have let someone down or don't measure up.

- **Afraid is red.** It includes worry, anxiety, and fear of harm, whether physical, emotional, or relational. It often shows up in students as avoidance, control-seeking, or sudden withdrawal.
- **Mad is purple.** It covers a range from mild irritation to full-blown rage. It's often triggered by a sense of unfairness or perceived injustice, but underneath, it may hold layers of sadness or fear.

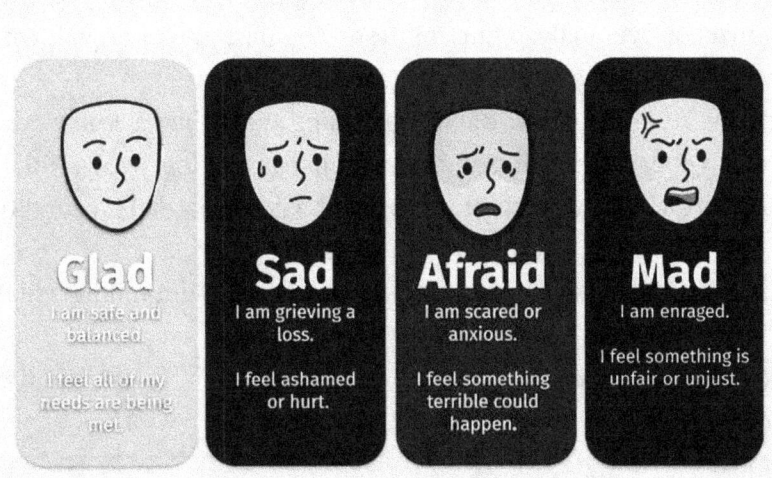

You may notice that in this model, the colors don't follow the typical "red equals mad" rule you see on posters or emoji charts. There's a reason for that. I've aligned the primary emotions with the primary colors:

Glad → Yellow

Sad → Blue

Afraid → Red

Anger, on the other hand, is not a primary emotion. It's a secondary emotion, often covering sadness or fear. Because of that, anger is represented by purple—a secondary color created by mixing the primaries of red and blue. This shift in color coding helps us see anger for what it really is—not the starting point, but the signal to look deeper.

This language provides a way to shift from reacting to behavior to understanding it. Through words to name core emotions, we can begin to decode the meaning behind behavior rather than taking it personally. When a student storms out, argues, or withdraws, we can pause and ask ourselves:

What's really happening under the mad?

What sadness or fear might be driving this response?

Naming emotions creates a bridge, giving us insight into what a student may not yet have the words to express. It doesn't excuse the behavior, but it helps us respond to the root, not just the symptom.[105]

It's also helpful to remember that emotion is energy—*e-motion*—energy in motion. Neuroscience tells us that when we allow ourselves to fully feel and name an emotion, it typically passes through the body in about 90 seconds. Dr. Jill Bolte Taylor explains,

"When a person reacts to something in their environment, there's a 90-second chemical process that happens in the body. After that, any remaining emotional response is just the person choosing to stay in that emotional loop."[106]

Most of us were never taught to get out of the loop. We were taught to suppress, distract, minimize, or overanalyze our emotions. We push the energy down instead of letting it move through, and what doesn't move often gets stuck.

Most of us are more comfortable expressing anger than acknowledging sadness or fear. Anger often appears first, loud and intense, because it feels powerful. However, underneath it, there's usually something more vulnerable. Sadness. Fear. Shame. Disappointment.

Try this: Think back to the last time you were mad, not mildly irritated, but truly frustrated, snappy, on edge. Now ask yourself:

What was I really feeling underneath that anger?

What was I sad about?

What was I afraid of?

I'll go first.

Remember the story of when I took my daughter to the dentist? As she refused to open her mouth, anger rose quickly within me. I was mad that she wouldn't cooperate. Mad that she wasn't listening. Mad that this was supposed to be a quick appointment, and now it was a scene.

However, beneath that madness, I was sad. Sad that she was afraid, and I hadn't seen it coming. I was sad that what should have been routine felt terrifying to her. And I was afraid. Afraid that the dentist and staff were judging me. I was afraid I looked like a bad mom who couldn't get her kid under control. Afraid that if she didn't get this cavity filled, her teeth would rot out of her head, and it would somehow all be my fault.

Mad was the surface emotion. It was loud, but it wasn't the whole truth. In that moment, the anger gave me emotional permission to pass the feeling on to her. Misery loves company, and when we don't process the emotion, we tend to either try to toss it to others or stuff it down deep inside. If I had only responded from that anger, I would have missed the opportunity to meet her where she was: in fear, in overwhelm, in need of comfort, not correction.

Identifying Emotions

Anger rarely stands alone. Often, it covers more vulnerable feelings, such as sadness or fear. This exercise helps you notice what's beneath anger and how your body shifts when you connect with core emotions.

Recall the moment.
Think of a specific situation that made you feel mad. Hold that memory lightly—just enough to remember, not to relive it.

Describe "mad" in your body.
Notice where anger lives inside you. Use your imagination to give it form:

- Where do you feel it?

- If it had a shape, what would it look like?

- What material is it made of?

- What temperature does it carry?

- If it had a smell or texture, what would it be?

Go underneath.
Anger is often a secondary emotion. Ask yourself: Underneath the anger, do I feel more sad or more afraid?

Explore that primary emotion. Choose the one that comes up more strongly—sadness or fear. Describe it in your body the same way you did for anger. What changed?

- Where do you feel it?

- If it had a shape, what would it look like?

- What material is it made of?

- What temperature does it carry?

- If it had a smell or texture, what would it be?

Explore the other one.

- Where do you feel it?

- If it had a shape, what would it look like?

- What material is it made of?

- What temperature does it carry?

- If it had a smell or texture, what would it be?

Reflect.
As you moved through these layers:

- What did you notice in your body?

- If you had been able to act from sadness or fear instead of anger, what might you have done differently in that moment?

- How does connecting with primary emotions change the way you understand yourself?

This is why shared emotional language matters. It's not just about giving students vocabulary—it's about helping *us*, the adults, stay grounded and honest, too. When we can name what we feel and trace it back to its roots, we stop reacting and start responding. We lead with compassion instead of control. Through this example, we show our students that emotions are not problems to fix. They are signals to follow.

Daily Check-Ins

One way to model and practice emotional awareness is through a daily check-in with students. Daily emotional check-ins are such a powerful tool in the resilience-building classroom. They don't need to be complex or time-consuming. A consistent and straightforward invitation to name and explore feelings can foster emotional literacy and connection over time. You might ask students individually, in small groups, or as a whole class: *"Which of the core four are you feeling right now, mad, sad, glad, or afraid? What is that most about?"* You might use visuals, colors, or gestures to support the check-in. You may need to adjust based on age or environment. The format doesn't matter as much as the intention: to help students feel seen, known, and supported.

Emotional check-ins aren't just for calm moments. In times of dysregulation, returning to this shared language can offer clarity and grounding. A quiet, curious question like, *"Are you feeling more mad, sad, or afraid right now?"* can shift the moment from chaos to curiosity. It helps both the adult and students identify their feelings and understand what is happening within their nervous system to determine the type of support needed.

When we use a shared emotional language across the classroom or school, we make emotions less mysterious and more manageable. We reduce shame, increase connection, and provide students with one of the most essential tools for resilience: the ability to understand themselves. We are sending the message: *You're more than your behavior. You're a human being with feelings that matter—and I'm here to help you understand them, not silence them.*

Supporting Regulation Through Grounding, Breath, and Reflection

When students are dysregulated, they are not ready to reason, reflect, or take responsibility. They are simply trying to survive the moment. In these instances, what's needed first is not logic, but regulation. Our role is to help them transition from bottom-up brain states (driven by instinct and emotion) to relational and, ultimately, thinking brain states, where accountability becomes possible.

To support that shift, we begin not with correction, but with connection. Grounding, breathwork, and gentle reflection help bring the nervous system back to balance, allowing students to re-enter the classroom, reconnect with their relationships, and reconnect with themselves.

Grounding: Reorienting to Safety and the Present Moment

When a student is overwhelmed, grounding can help them reconnect to their body and the present moment. These techniques aren't about fixing emotions but about creating just enough internal space for the brain and body to reset. Students who are dysregulated may exhibit signs such as a heightened startle reflex, rapid speech, delayed responses, tremors, or hypersensitivity to sound. These are clues that their nervous system is activated and in need of support.

Grounding doesn't need to be complicated. It can be as simple as a 5-4-3-2-1 senses check: *five things you can see, four you can hear, three you can touch, two you can smell, one you can taste.* This short exercise helps students reorient to their environment using their senses.

Tactile objects, items with texture, weight, or temperature differences, can also offer comfort. A small basket containing fabric swatches, foam blocks, rubber bands, or textured stones provides students with an object to hold onto when emotions feel overwhelming.

Some students benefit from physical tension release techniques, such as progressive muscle relaxation, where they slowly tense and release various parts of the body to help discharge stored stress. Others may benefit from water or strong tastes; peppermints, sour candy, applesauce, or a drink of cold water can help re-engage the body's regulation systems.

Still others may need guided meditation or visualizations. Tools like the Calm app (free for teachers) offer short, student-friendly practices that can support classroom regulation without requiring the adult to lead the experience directly.

Grounding doesn't "fix" the emotion. It provides a pause, a regulated breath in the storm, allowing students to regain their composure.

Breath: Resetting the Nervous System

Breath is the body's built-in regulation system, and it's one we can access anytime, anywhere. When students breathe with intention, they reduce cortisol, restore oxygen flow, and send messages of safety back to the brain. Shallow, rapid breathing; chest rising instead of ribcage expansion; mouth breathing; or frequent yawning are all signs of nervous system activation. Many students don't yet know how to take deep, restorative breaths. In moments of stress, even those who do may forget how.

Invite students to sit up straight and focus their attention on their breath. Nasal breathing is ideal; it engages the parasympathetic nervous system and helps maintain internal balance. From there, introduce a rhythm.

Box breathing is simple: inhale for four counts, hold for four, exhale for four counts, and hold for four. Then repeat.

4-7-8 breathing builds deeper regulation: inhale through the nose for four counts, hold for seven, and exhale slowly through the mouth for eight.

Belly breathing teaches students to engage their diaphragm. Encourage them to place a hand on their belly and feel it rise and fall as they breathe, helping the breath drop lower into the body.

Some students respond to visual breathing exercises, such as tracing an infinity sign (∞) with their finger while breathing in and out at each loop. Others may benefit from breath walking, which pairs gentle movement with intentional breathing to re-anchor the body.

These tools are especially powerful because they are teachable, portable, and remain available long after the crisis moment has ended.

Reflection: Reconnection Without Correction

Once a student begins to return to baseline, when their eyes refocus, their speech slows, and their breathing becomes more even, we can invite gentle reflection. This is not the time to assign consequences or dissect what went wrong. It is the time to say, "I'm still here. You matter more than the mistake."

Reflection strategies help rebuild self-awareness and dignity after dysregulation. They offer students the opportunity to come back into relationship, not by being forced to explain or apologize too soon, but by being reminded of their worth and their voice.

Affirmations like *"I am loved," "I am safe,"* or *"I am good"* can rewire inner narratives that have been shaped by shame. These mantras work best when developed with students ahead of time and then used when needed, much like breathing techniques.

A mini-timeline, naming five things that went well today, shifts focus toward agency and competence. It helps students remember: *"I've already done hard things today. This moment doesn't define me."*

Nexting fosters hope. Asking, *"What's one thing you're looking forward to next?"* brings the brain out of fear and into future-thinking.

Journaling or creative expression can also offer a safe way to explore emotion. Prompts like *"If this feeling were a color..."* or *"If this feeling were music..."* allow students to give language to what they may not yet be ready to say directly.

Reflection is not about evaluation. It's about re-grounding identity. You're not just a student who had a hard moment. You are someone still becoming, still loved, and still worthy of support.

Self-Assessment: Safety, Connection, and Regulation

To help students recognize their state of regulation, we can teach them to check in with themselves using simple 1–10 scales:

> *"On a scale of 1–10, how stressed are you right now?"*
>
> *"On a scale of 1–10, how much do you feel like you belong here at school?"*
>
> *"On a scale of 1–10, how physically safe do you feel in this space?"*

These numbers aren't about grading emotions. They're about building internal awareness. They offer the adult insight, too: if a student's stress is above a 4, our job is to slow down—not speed up. When we push too soon for reflection or accountability, we risk reinforcing shame and re-triggering the stress response. Instead, we create healing by meeting students where they are, then walking with them, step by step, back to safety.

In a resilience-building culture, we don't ask students to rejoin us in thinking mode until we've walked with them through feeling mode. That process might take anywhere from ten minutes to twenty-four hours. Every nervous system is different. What matters is that we wait long enough for the student's thinking brain to come back online, and we stay long enough to remind them they're not alone.

Visit the book companion site for additional materials related to this chapter.

Book Companion Resources

- Daily Check-in Resources
- Grounding Strategies
- Breathing Strategies
- Reflection Strategies

☙ reflection ❧

When was the last time you reacted from anger, only to realize later that sadness or fear was underneath?

Which of the four core emotions—mad, sad, glad, afraid—feels easiest for you to notice in yourself? Which is hardest?

How does your body typically signal that your nervous system is dysregulated?

What strategies help you pause long enough to notice and name your emotions before reacting?

How might modeling honest emotional awareness with students change the climate of your classroom?

When I notice myself getting angry, it often means I am really feeling _____.

If I can pause and name that truth, I am more likely to _____ instead of reacting in ways I regret.

❧ twenty-eight ❧
Develop Competency in Co-Regulation

We've already learned that regulation isn't always a quick process. It requires transitioning from the survival brain (brainstem) to the relationship brain (limbic system) and then to the thriving brain (prefrontal cortex). However, the path to regulation doesn't start with logic; it starts with connection. The bridge between dysregulation and choice is *relational.* That's why co-regulation is not just helpful; it's essential.

Co-regulation is the process by which caring adults help children manage emotional arousal, reduce stress, and return to a state of safety. It's a moment-by-moment interaction that builds the scaffolding for long-term self-regulation. While it may appear differently at various stages of development, co-regulation remains a critical resource throughout development. Researchers Rosanbalm and Murray stated,

> "The capacity for self-regulation develops over time, from infancy through young adulthood (and beyond). Consequently, the amount of co-regulation a child, youth, or young adult needs will vary as they grow."[107]

The Role of Environment and Experience

Not all students need the same level of co-regulation. Differences in biology, temperament, and early experience create vastly different starting points. Trauma and chronic stress sensitize the brain, heightening emotional reactivity and reducing access to the thinking brain.

This means some students need more co-regulation, not because they're defiant or manipulative, but because their systems have been shaped by instability. In these cases, predictable, responsive, and supportive environments are the intervention. They are the strategy. They become the relational reset button through which students begin to access and build self-regulation capacity.

Timing Matters: Developmental Windows of Opportunity

Children's brains develop from the bottom up, from survival to reasoning. While the brain is continually growing, there are two key developmental windows during which the brain becomes especially ready to learn and integrate new self-regulation skills: early childhood (ages 3–5) and early adolescence (ages 12–18). In early childhood, the brain creates a surplus of synaptic connections.[107]

What gets used, stays. What doesn't fade. Social interactions during this time sculpt the brain's architecture, reinforcing or weakening the circuits responsible for communication, empathy, and self-control. In adolescence, the prefrontal cortex, the part of the brain responsible for reasoning, reflection, and decision-making, begins its final, and most dramatic, stage of development. This makes middle and high school a critical period for coaching, not punishing regulatory skills. That's why your presence matters so much.

Even when students appear old enough to "know better," they may still *need* co-regulation —your calm, your clarity, your coaching —as they navigate increasing demands, shifting identities, and a rapidly changing brain. Effective co-regulation doesn't just manage behavior in the moment. It builds the long-term capacity for students to regulate themselves.

Key Elements of Co-Regulation:

Empathy: Recognize that the child's behavior reflects their internal state, not their intent to challenge authority.

Connection: Build trust by being present, patient, and responsive to their needs.

Support: Modify the environment or provide accommodations that help the child feel safe and capable.

Revisiting the Co-Regulation Process

We often talk about regulation as something internal, something a student either has or doesn't. However, for children, especially those impacted by trauma, regulation is a relational process. It's not something we *do to* students; it's something we *do with* them. It's shaped by our presence, our tone, our attunement. It starts before the outburst and continues long after the room quiets down.

Understanding the landscape of escalation helps us know when and how to intervene. When we can recognize the early cues, restlessness, irritability, and withdrawal, we're more likely to respond in ways that prevent a full escalation. When we understand what's happening neurologically during the peak of a meltdown, we shift from trying to reason with logic to offering co-regulation through calm, consistent support. When the storm passes, we know that recovery is not the end—it's the beginning of repair, reflection, and skill-building.

Let's revisit the stages of the Escalation Cycle, this time viewing it through the lens of neuro-informed co-regulation.[109]

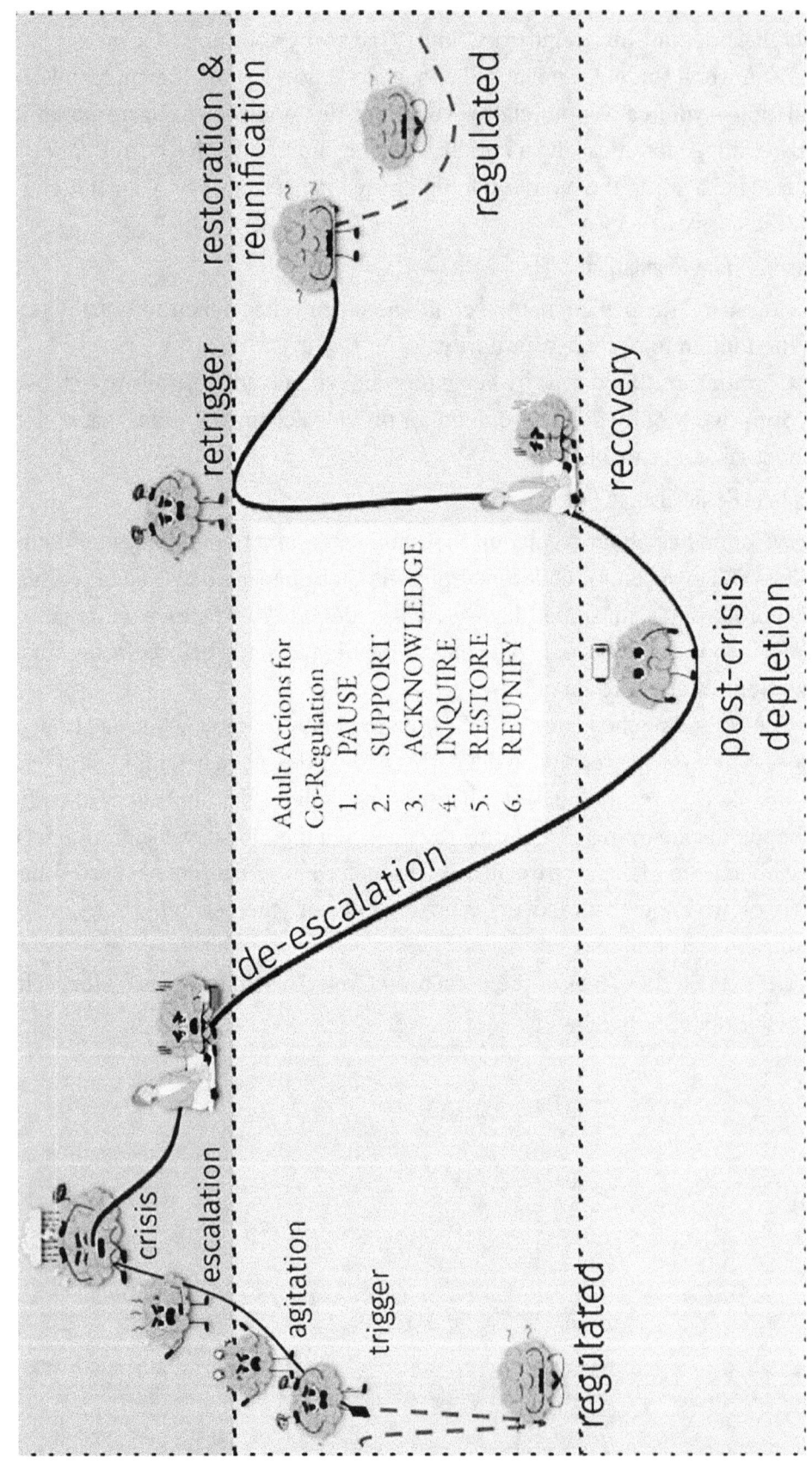

Regulated

Regulated is the baseline state where stress levels are low or tolerable, and the individual feels safe, supported, and regulated. Needs are met, and the brain operates in its optimal, thriving mode. This state does not just mean calm or compliant. It is more accurately described as being in a state where a person's energy matches the task. For example, a child laughing loudly and doing cartwheels in class is not regulated to participate in math class, but the same behavior is appropriately regulated for recess.

Stage	Notice	Adult Response

Brain State: Survival Brain
 	
 Escalation Cycle:

 Trigger

 Agitation

 Escalation

 Crisis
	Student's Regulation
	 • Breath Rate
	 • Tension in the body
	 • Speech patterns
	 Use an oximeter or a similar device to check the heart rate of students and adults.
	
	 Your regulation:
	 • Be mindful of your power and position
	 Adjust body language, voice tone, and volume to co-regulate and communicate warm regard
	
	 Assess your capacity to respond.
	 • Are you too dysregulated to be of benefit?
	   ○ No? Ground yourself
	   ○ Yes? Find another adult to support the student, and then ground yourself.
		Non-verbal
		 • Sit/Stand at the same level as the student, side by side
		 • Don't demand eye contact
		 • Listen to connect
		 • Use grounding strategies
		
		 Verbal
		 • Use few words and simple language
		   ○ Use phrases like "I'm here to help."
		 • Clarify and affirm emotions
		   ○ "You're upset. That makes sense."
		 • Love unconditionally.

Trigger

A trigger disrupts the child's regulated state, putting them at risk of dysregulation. Triggers can include repeated frustrations, a lack of positive reinforcement, sensory overload (e.g., noise or bright lights), or internal issues such as hunger or fatigue.

The best time to provide an intervention at the Trigger Stage

Identify the Trigger: Notice cues and determine what caused the disruption.

Modify or Remove the Trigger: Adjust the environment (e.g., reduce noise or offer a break).

Provide Opportunities for Success: Encourage the child with tasks they can accomplish easily to build confidence and reduce frustration.

Address Internal Needs: Offer snacks, hydration, or time to rest, and check if the child is experiencing physical discomfort.

Agitation

If the trigger is not addressed, the child becomes agitated, and signs of dysregulation become apparent. Behaviors include whining, complaining, resisting transitions, or withdrawing from activities.

The second-best place to provide an intervention is in the agitation stage.

Understand the Behavior's Purpose: Identify what the child is trying to communicate through their actions.

Make Environmental Modifications: Change the setting or offer a calming activity.

Offer Choices: Giving the child options restores a sense of control.

Match Communication: Speak in simple, short phrases and allow extra time for the child to process.

Reinforce Positivity: Look for opportunities to acknowledge positive behaviors or efforts.

Escalation

At this point, the child is entirely outside their Window of Tolerance, and the situation may escalate to severe behaviors such as hitting, screaming, or aggression.

If the cycle reaches the escalation stage, it is most likely to progress to a crisis.
> **Ensure Safety**: Remove dangerous objects and give the child space.

> **Use Non-Violent Crisis Intervention**: Avoid physical contact unless the child is in immediate danger.

> **Disengage Verbally**: Minimize talking, as the child cannot process language effectively during this stage.

> **De-Escalation Techniques**: While prevention is preferable, employ techniques like deep breathing or calming body language to signal safety.

Crisis

Crisis is the peak of escalation, where behaviors are most intense and dysregulation is at its highest. The child operates entirely from their survival brain.

Once the crisis stage has been reached, co-regulation is essential.
> **Focus on Safety**: Continue to prioritize the safety of everyone involved.

> **Minimal Communication**: Use body language and proximity rather than words to convey a sense of safety.

> **Stay Calm**: Your demeanor can influence the environment and promote eventual de-escalation.

Stage	Notice	Adult Response
Brain State: Relationship Brain **Escalation Cycle:**  De-escalation 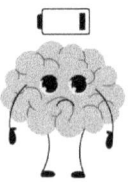 Post-Crisis Depletion  Recovery  Retrigger	**Student's Regulation** You will continue to see signs of dysregulation. Students will likely use a variety of coping strategies to calm and self-soothe. The fight, flight, or freeze response is still easily triggered in this stage. Pay attention to the students and your: • Breath rate • Tension in the body • Speech patterns. It is normal for this part of the conversation to send a student back into a dysregulated state. Check in on the nervous system and use grounding and breathing strategies to promote regulation.	**Assess emotional state and perception:** Ask: Are you mad, sad, glad, or afraid? What is that mostly about? **The key is listening -** remember that perception is reality. **Focus on:** • Connection before correction • Empathy **What happened?** Establish a shared narrative, but don't get stuck here. **How did we get here?** Uncover the needs the student was trying to meet through the observed behavior? **Who/What has been impacted?** If the student gets defensive, remind them of their worth. Remind them they are safe. Remind them that you are here to help.

Deceleration

After the crisis, the child's behavior begins to subside. They may appear confused, withdrawn, or emotionally overwhelmed.

Maintain Safety: Continue creating a calm and safe environment.

Avoid Blame: Refrain from reprimanding or forcing apologies.

Post-Crisis Depletion

At this stage, the child is emotionally and physically drained. They need time to recover and re-establish a routine.

Reassure and Reset: Help the child regain a sense of normalcy.

Reintroduce Routine: Gradually guide the child back to their schedule.

Recovery

Once the child has returned to a regulated state, it's time to reflect, teach, and prepare for future challenges.

Reflect Together: Discuss what happened, identify the triggers, and plan for more effective responses in the future.

Teach Replacement Behaviors: Demonstrate calming strategies and alternative ways for the child to express frustration.

Provide Consequences: Use this time to deliver consequences if needed, ensuring they are logical and restorative rather than punitive.

Retrigger

There is a possibility of slipping back into hyperarousal as the child prepares to return to the learning environment. This is often due to feelings of guilt, shame, and fear of how the restoration and reunification process will unfold.

Acknowledge this as a normal reaction.

Regulate: Take a moment to do a breathing or grounding exercise.

Revisit the plan for restoration and reunification.

Stage	Notice	Adult Response
Brain State: Learning Brain **Escalation Cycle:** Restoration and Reunification Regulated	**Student's Regulation:** Breath is controlled Eyes are focused Normal speech patterns Body movements are calm Thoughts are focused Be sure that the student is regulated before returning to class. Consider doing a grounding/breathing or mantra exercise before heading back to class. Support the student's needs in their return to the learning space to ensure that they are welcomed back and transition does not cause dysregulation.	**Revisit the emotions:** Acknowledge and validate that the emotions are welcome, but not all behaviors are acceptable. **Problem solve:** Ask: If you truly knew that you were safe, loved, and trusted, and that your needs would be met, how would you have shown up to this situation? What might you do next time if you knew those things were true? **Discipline:** Explain: My number one priority is to ensure everyone's safety, and we are all accountable for that, so there are consequences for our behavior. **Discuss Consequences:** Ensure that the student understands the consequences and recognizes that they are still valued and safe. **Determine Plan:** Ask: What do you think needs to be done to repair the harm? Work together to create a plan for reunification, repair, and restoration.

Restoration and Reunification

Finally, focus on reintegrating the child into the learning environment and fostering a sense of belonging.

> **Collaborate**: Work with the child to determine how they can repair relationships and restore trust.

> **Check-In**: Offer ongoing support and ensure they feel understood.

> **Welcome Back**: Use a kind tone and give clear, simple directions to help the child reintegrate smoothly.

By understanding and navigating the Escalation Cycle, we can better support children during dysregulation, ensure their safety, foster emotional resilience, and ultimately help them thrive.

Teaching Regulation at Tier 1

When regulation is understood and practiced at the Tier 1 level, it becomes an integral part of the school's emotional ecosystem. We teach students to name their internal state before it becomes explosive. We practice the Core Four—mad, sad, glad, afraid—as a way to simplify complex emotions. We build check-ins into our routines. We normalize the ups and downs of being human.

These aren't soft practices. They are *skill-building systems*. They equip students with the language, tools, and trust to stay in their Window of Tolerance longer and return to it more quickly when they fall out of it. When students see that they are not punished for dysregulation, but supported through it, they begin to trust not just us, but themselves. They begin to believe:

Maybe I'm not broken.
Maybe I'm just learning.

Supporting a Colleague After Co-Regulation

Co-regulation is a relational, exhausting, and deeply human process. While much focus is placed on the student's experience, we must also tend to the adult who offered their nervous system in service of regulation.

After a dysregulated moment, teachers often feel emotionally flooded, uncertain about what happened, or unsure how to move forward. That's where colleague support matters most. As leaders, coaches, or fellow educators, our role is not to critique, but to hold space, offer clarity, and foster reflection without shame. These moments can either reinforce burnout or strengthen resilience, depending on how we process them together.

A Four-Step Framework for Post-Co-Regulation Support
Acknowledge Emotions and Thoughts

Start by offering space for your colleague to name what's real in the moment. Dysregulation affects everyone involved, and holding that weight alone can lead to emotional shutdown or internalized blame. Ask simple, grounding questions like:

> *"What are you thinking about right now?"*
>
> *"How are you feeling after that interaction?"*

These questions are not about fixing, they're about naming. Naming allows separation between the educator's emotional response and the student's needs. It brings perspective back online.

Clarify What Was Needed—For the Student and the Adult

Shift the focus toward understanding the situation, not in hindsight, but in terms of the needs it presents. Consider:

> *"What do you think the student needed most in that moment?"*
>
> *"What might you have needed to feel more supported?"*

This reflection helps identify patterns and gaps. Maybe the room was overstimulating. Maybe a tap-out system wasn't available. Perhaps the adult needed a walk before re-entry. Asking these questions supports both empathy and system improvement.

Invite Self-Awareness Without Shame

This is where professional growth lives—not in guilt, but in discernment. Help the educator reflect gently on their role in the interaction, not as a measure of failure, but as a mirror for growth:

> *"How do you think your response impacted the student?"*
>
> *"Is there anything you might reinforce or adjust if this happened again?"*

This step isn't about what went wrong. It's about what was learned—and how that learning becomes practice.

Anchor Forward in Strength

End with affirmation. Embed hope. Co-regulation is hard, and every time we engage in it, we get better. Try:

> *"What's one key learning you're taking away from this?"*
>
> *"How can you use this experience to inform future moments?"*

Then say it plainly:

> *"You stayed. You regulated. That mattered more than perfection."*

Leadership Communication After Co-Regulation

One of the most common frustrations teachers express is this:

"I called for help. Admin came, took the student out for two minutes, and then brought them back with a lollipop. There's no accountability anymore."

When communication breaks down between support staff and classroom teachers, it creates confusion, distrust, and missed opportunities for consistency and alignment. That's why post-regulation communication isn't optional; it's an essential step in trauma-responsive culture. This doesn't require a formal meeting every time. A five-minute check-in can go a long way toward transparency, collaboration, and shared support.

A Process for Post-Regulation Communication

Make Space for Timely Conversation

Aim to debrief while the incident is still fresh. A hallway check-in, an email summary, or a quick chat after dismissal can all serve the purpose.

Provide an Overview of the Co-Regulation Process

The adult who supported the student should share:

> What triggered the dysregulation
>
> What co-regulation strategies were used
>
> How the student responded
>
> Any key emotional insights or shifts

This helps the classroom teacher reframe what happened and know how to support the next steps.

Clarify Any Consequences or Follow-Up

If discipline was involved, clearly communicate it. Did the student lose privileges? Were restorative steps discussed? This ensures alignment and avoids confusion.

Collaboratively Plan for Re-entry

Together, decide:

> What the student needs to re-enter safely
>
> How the teacher might adjust tasks, expectations, or peer dynamics
>
> How connection will be re-established—without shame

This is where we shift from punishment to repair.

Reflect on the Experience Together

Give the support staff space to name what went well and what felt hard. Invite the teacher to do the same. These shared moments of reflection build trust and professional wisdom.

Recommit to Ongoing Communication

Agree on how you'll stay connected regarding the student's progress, including quick updates, check-in slips, and brief notes. Small gestures go a long way in making teachers feel supported, not sidelined.

Document Key Agreements (If Needed)

Sometimes it's helpful to jot down shared next steps, especially for students with ongoing support needs. This isn't about compliance documentation, it's about clarity.

Addressing the "Lollipop Problem": Regulation and Accountability Must Coexist

Let's go back to that quote about lollipops... this isn't just a gripe; it's a reflection of something deeper — a perceived disconnect between support and structure, between trauma-informed care and meaningful accountability. Unless we address it directly, it risks undermining trust between staff and leadership.

Here's the truth: in resilience-building schools, regulation is the first step, not the only step. Sometimes, when a student is highly dysregulated, food or sensory tools are used to support their nervous system. A peppermint can help bring awareness back to the present moment and cool the body. Drinking a bottle of water helps to flush cortisol, the stress hormone, from the body. Chewing on taffy or jerky can physiologically shift a child out of fight, flight, or freeze mode by activating the vagus nerve. These are tools, not treats, but unless they're framed that way, they can appear to others, especially teachers who have just experienced the brunt of a student's dysregulation, as rewards for misbehavior. That's where things break down.

Leaders, here's what matters most:

Explain the tool. Tell the student: *"I'm giving you this peppermint to help your body feel more regulated. This isn't a treat; it's to help you come back into your thinking brain."*

Use it intentionally. Don't send students back into the classroom while they're still holding the tool. Not because the tool is inherently harmful, but because optics and relational trust are essential considerations. It helps the teacher hold boundaries without resentment.

Follow with accountability. Regulation opens the door for reflection, repair, and re-entry. It is not a substitute for those things. Once the student is regulated, they should reflect on the impact of their actions, take ownership in developmentally appropriate ways, and re-engage in the classroom community with support and clarity.

Communicate with the teacher. Let them know what happened, the regulatory strategies employed, and the follow-up steps in place. This step is crucial for maintaining a cohesive and trusting staff culture.

Finally, remember this: a trauma-informed approach without accountability becomes enabling. Accountability without regulation becomes punitive. We need both. The lollipop might be part of the solution, but only if it's part of a bigger system of co-regulation, communication, and compassionate structure. When done right, it isn't a bribe. It's a peace offering. A doorway back into trust. A sign that we care enough to calm first, and correct with connection.

Visit the book companion site for additional materials related to this chapter.

Book Companion Resources

- **Printable co-regulation resources**

❧ reflection ❧

Which environmental triggers in your room (noise, transitions, peer proximity, tasks) most often precede dysregulation—and what's one change you can make tomorrow?

How do you differentiate responses for trigger vs. agitation vs. escalation vs. crisis vs. recovery?

When safety is secured, how do you signal "connection before correction" without losing boundaries?

What's your agreed re-entry routine (welcome, task scaffold, relationship repair), and how consistently do you use it?

After a challenging incident, how do you debrief with a colleague so the load is shared, rather than stored?

When I notice early signs of dysregulation (mine/the student's) such as _____,

I will first do _____ to co-regulate, then communicate _____, and

after recovery I will follow through with _____ to ensure accountability and repair.

◄ twenty-nine ►
The SiNoC Process

The Student in Need of Connection (SiNoC) process doesn't begin with a form or a meeting. It starts with a teacher's intuition, an uneasiness, a pattern, a child slipping further and further from connection.[110] Maybe the student is shutting down, acting out, disengaging from learning, or becoming increasingly reactive. Whatever the behavior, something in the teacher's nervous system says, "*This student needs me to pay closer attention.*"

So the teacher leans in. They take small but meaningful steps, checking in more often, offering co-regulation, trying the 2x10 strategy, and using strength-based engagement. Sometimes, that's enough. The student starts to soften. They begin to trust, to engage. In those moments, no formal intervention is needed. The teacher simply keeps showing up, keeps staying close, and continues to support the student with consistency and care.

However, sometimes the concern grows. Despite best efforts, the student continues to struggle, emotionally, behaviorally, or academically. When that happens, the teacher initiates the SiNoC process by requesting and completing the SiNoC Profile. This profile is more than a referral form; it's a window into the student's story. It includes data, observations, prior interventions, and a reflection on what has been tried and what remains unknown.

Before the team gathers, the facilitator (often a counselor, social worker, or MTSS lead) prepares by gathering relevant information such as behavior logs, academic data, work samples, and, if possible, input from the student's caregiver. It's also important to identify and invite at least one adult in the building who has a strong relationship with the student. Sometimes that's the classroom teacher. Other times, it's someone less obvious, like a para, coach, lunchroom supervisor, or art teacher. Whoever it is, that voice matters. We want the whole picture, not just where the student struggles, but where they shine.

At the next scheduled meeting, the SiNoC Team Lead adds the student to the agenda and opens the conversation. The referring teacher is present and shares context and concern. Other teachers and staff who know the student contribute their experiences. We begin with strengths, not as a formality, but as a necessity. We ask:

When have we seen this student at their best?
What are they good at? Who do they connect with?
Where do they feel most like themselves?

These answers often hold the key to re-engagement.

Then we clearly and honestly name the concern. We use the SiNoC profile to identify patterns. Are academic struggles linked with behavioral outbursts? Does the student shut down during transitions? Are they avoidant, anxious, explosive, or withdrawn? The team is encouraged to stay grounded in observations rather than assumptions. This is a time for clarity, not labels.

At this point, the team determines the next course of action. If the core issue appears to be rooted in a relational or environmental mismatch, the team may offer support directly to the teacher, including coaching, modeling, or adjusting classroom practices, without proceeding with a formal plan. However, if the concern reflects unmet needs that require broader or deeper intervention, we move forward with developing an action plan.

That plan isn't a laundry list. It's two or three clear, actionable, relationship-centered supports —relational, instructional, and environmental —that can be implemented with fidelity. The plan is documented, roles are assigned, and a follow-up date is set. A specific staff member is identified to oversee the plan's implementation and ensure communication and consistency.

Before the meeting ends, we close with one final, anchoring question for everyone at the table: *"What is one thing this student deserves from us going forward?"* It's a grounding moment. It brings us back to the reason we're here, not for compliance. Not to "fix" the child—but to restore connection.

The SiNoC process is not just a system; it is a comprehensive approach. It's a stance. A way of noticing. A refusal to let disconnection be the last word. Above all, it's a collective reminder that no one walks this work alone.

Why SiNoC?

We don't need another form. We need a process that helps us see students, hold them with consistency, and support them in ways that match both their history and their humanity. That's what the Student in Need of Connection (SiNoC) process offers.

The SiNoC process isn't a replacement for existing student support systems. It's a relational enhancement. A trauma-responsive tool that brings emotional insight and compassionate structure to the ways we respond when students show up in pain, disconnection, or dysregulation. It aligns seamlessly with MTSS, problem-solving teams, and restorative practices, strengthening those systems by centering relationships first.

When implemented well, the SiNoC process helps schools stop the cycle of behavior-referral-removal-repeat. It replaces quick fixes with long-term strategies grounded in trust, co-regulation, and student voice. Traditional student support processes often begin with behavior data. They ask: *What's the problem? What intervention fits?* The SiNoC process begins with a different question:

Who is this student—and what do they need to feel safe enough to learn, connect, and belong?

It reframes the conversation from what's wrong with a student to what's hurting, missing, or misunderstood. It centers the student's internal world, not just their observable actions.

It creates a space where team members collaborate around their strengths, not just their deficits.

Integrating the SiNoC Process Into Your Support Systems

The Student in Need of Connection (SiNoC) process doesn't need to stand alone. It works best when embedded within the structures your school already uses, enhancing them rather than replacing them.

In MTSS Tier 2 and Tier 3 meetings, the SiNoC Profile can reframe conversations about students who are repeatedly flagged for behavioral issues or disengagement. Rather than staying in a cycle of reactive planning, the team can begin asking different questions: *What relational needs aren't being met? Where might regulation and connection be breaking down?*

In problem-solving or care team discussions, the SiNoC interview or profile can be used early, before jumping into FBAs, behavior plans, or outside referrals. It invites a strengths-based, student-centered conversation about what's missing, not just what's misfiring.

Within restorative practices, the SiNoC process can be folded into circle work. Students can reflect on their profile over time, using it as a roadmap for self-awareness and growth. When students know what helps them feel safe, heard, and regulated, they are more likely to engage meaningfully in repair.

Even in formal systems like 504 or IEP teams, the SiNoC profile can offer language and insight often missing from paperwork, highlighting emotional needs, co-regulation strategies, and trust dynamics between students and adults. These often invisible factors are what determine whether a plan succeeds or falls apart.

When it comes to discipline, the SiNoC profile can serve as a necessary checkpoint before repeated removals. Regulation and reconnection should always precede removal, making it a routine process. If we haven't taken time to understand the root of the behavior, we shouldn't be reinforcing the rupture.

The process can be led by counselors, behavior specialists, trauma-informed team leads, or administrators. More important than the role is the mindset. The facilitator should be grounded in relational practice, have protected time to follow through, and be committed to working alongside teachers, students, and families.

Ideally, the SiNoC process becomes part of the school's early response system. It's not just triggered by data, but also by a teacher's concern, a student's withdrawal, or patterns of disconnection that may not always be documented formally.

This isn't about diagnosing. It's about understanding, connection, and planning for the future. Done right, it doesn't feel like a meeting about a student. It feels like a team gathering around one. Used consistently, the SiNoC process becomes more than a tool; it becomes a culture shift. It reminds us that we connect before we correct. That we notice patterns, not just incidents. That we build plans around strengths, not deficits.

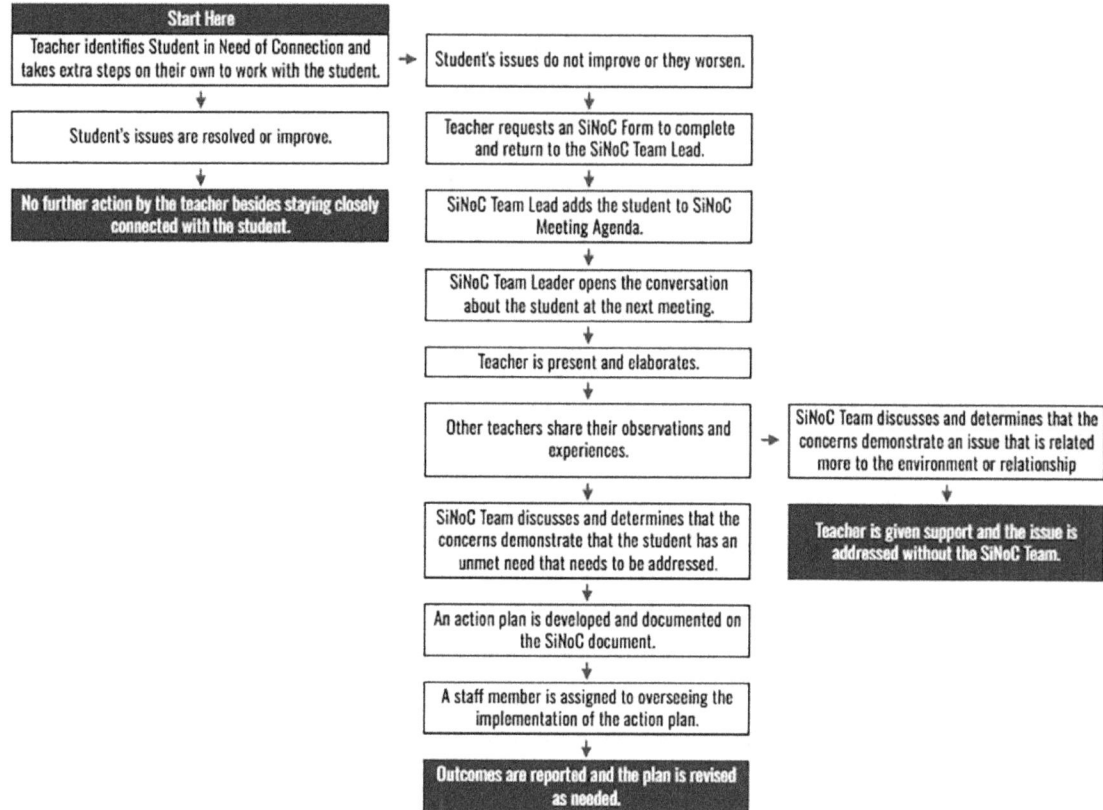

Most importantly, it reminds us that students don't heal from interventions. They heal from people. The SiNoC process ensures they're not just tracked, but truly seen. Not managed, but understood. Not talked about, but invited in.

The SiNoC Process Flow:

When a teacher notices a student struggling, the first step is always to establish a connection. The teacher leans in—offering extra support, presence, and care in hopes that the student's issues resolve with closer attention. Many times, this is enough. A child who feels seen and safe often begins to settle, and the teacher simply continues to nurture the relationship.

However, sometimes the concerns persist. In fact, they may deepen. When this happens, the teacher doesn't have to carry the weight alone. They complete a Student in Need of Connection (SiNoC) form and share it with the SiNoC Team Lead. This ensures the student is added to the agenda for the team's next meeting.

At the meeting, the conversation begins. The Team Leader introduces the student, and the referring teacher explains what they've observed. Other teachers and staff add their perspectives. Together, the team looks at the full picture.

From there, two different paths may emerge. Suppose the team recognizes that the concern stems more from the classroom environment or a strained relationship. In that case, the teacher is given guidance and support to address those dynamics directly—without needing a formal plan. Sometimes shifting the environment is enough to shift the student.

At other times, the team identifies unmet needs that run deeper. In those cases, the SiNoC Team creates a documented action plan. A staff member is assigned to walk alongside the student and oversee the implementation of the plan. The team doesn't stop there—they continue to track outcomes, adjusting the plan until it truly supports the student's growth.

In this way, the process honors both the power of individual connection and the strength of collective response. Teachers don't have to do it all alone, and students don't fall through the cracks. Every step is designed to ensure they are known, supported, and provided with what they need to thrive.

The SiNoC Profile: Seeing the Whole Student

The cornerstone of this process is the SiNoC Profile. This guided tool helps us move beyond anecdotal stories or reactive discipline records and instead craft a comprehensive portrait of the student as a person in context. In this section, we will explore the SiNoC process using Malik and his teacher as an example. You can also download a digital copy, as well as an example of a full SiNoC meeting featuring the profiles of all the students from the Book Companion. These profiles bring the theory to life and remind us: the most effective plans are never one-size-fits-all. They're shaped around each student's nervous system, identity, and relational landscape. Each profile includes the following components:

Student Information
> Basic demographics, strengths, known interests, trusted adults, and known barriers

Strengths and Interests
> Describe passions, talents, specific interests, and emotional, relational, and cognitive skills.

Areas for Growth and Teacher-Identified Goal
> Describe the emotional, relational, and cognitive areas where the student may need more support.

Resilience Factors Inventory
> Based on the Child and Youth Resilience Measure (CYRM-R): sense of belonging, self-efficacy, adult support, cultural connectedness[111]

Attachment Reflection
> Patterns of connection, signals of trust or fear, and relationship readiness

Perceived ACEs and Early Childhood Risk Factors
> Mark only what has been confirmed by reliable sources. Be aware of how implicit bias can affect interpretation.

Known Diagnoses or Labels

This section is not about assigning labels. It's about gathering context. A diagnosis can help explain patterns of behavior and guide more supportive, informed strategies.

The Regulation Fulcrum

Identify the factors of the regulation fulcrum: relationship, responsibility, rigor, and relevance.

Student Risk Screening Scale

Risk level for school disengagement, peer challenges, or unmet support needs

Behavior Patterns

What strategies have worked, what escalates, what's been tried (and how the student responded)

Regulation & Executive Function

Areas of strength and lagging skills across executive function skills, such as organization, working memory, and self-monitoring

General Concerns

What are the general concerns impacting emotional, relational, cognitive, and regulatory development and functioning?

Teacher Estimate of Achievement

Reflect intentionally on both past performance and expected future progress.

Intervention Planning Section

Identify what Tier 2/3 supports, roles for adults, environmental adjustments, and co-regulation plans that have been tried, and reflect on what has worked.

Directions for Completing the Student in Need of Connection (SiNoC) Profile

The Student in Need of Connection Profile is more than a form; it's a tool for seeing the whole child. It helps educators move beyond behavior into story, beyond reaction into reflection. To explore this process, we will use Malik's experience as a guide. Approach with curiosity, compassion, and a commitment to making sure no student goes unseen.

This profile should be completed when you are regulated and ready to reflect deeply on a student who may be signaling disconnection, distress, or unmet needs. It helps you document observations, interpret behaviors through a trauma-informed lens, and collaborate with your school team in a way that centers the student's humanity.

Student Information

Provide name, grade, and basic details.

Student in Need of Connection Profile

Student Name	Grade	Birthdate
Malik	9th	10/30/2011

Strengths and Interests

Every student has assets.

In coaching, I emphasize that identifying a student's strengths and interests is the gatekeeper to this process. If you cannot name what's good in a student, what lights them up, what they do well, you don't get to write about what's hard.

Pause. Observe. Build the relationship first.

If you're struggling to name positives, step away from the profile and spend two weeks intentionally connecting with that student. When you return, complete the Strengths and Interests section with optimism. Look for creativity, humor, compassion, grit, imagination, leadership, and kindness. Even in the mess, there is always something worthy of celebration.

Strengths	Interests/Passions
Malik is a creative thinker and observant. He has a sharp wit and shows strong visual-spatial intelligence when engaged.	He enjoys drawing, video games, and building things with his hands.

Core Needs and Growth Areas

Describe the emotional, relational, and cognitive areas where the student may need more support.

Areas for Growth	My goal for this child is...
Malik struggles to trust adults, avoids academic tasks, and has difficulty managing frustration without shutting down or acting out.	I want Malik to feel emotionally safe enough to ask for help, stay engaged in learning longer, and begin to believe he is capable of success.

Resilience Scale: The Child and Youth Resilience Measure (CYRM)

As you begin to complete the SiNoC Profile, it's important to deepen your understanding of the student's life *beyond the classroom*. Resilience-building practice calls us to see the whole child, not just the part that shows up in our room. This includes their relationships, environment, emotional safety, and the development of their identity.

To support this lens, we incorporate a modified version of the Child and Youth Resilience Measure (CYRM), developed by the Resilience Research Centre (2018).[112] This research-based tool is not used for diagnosis or categorization; instead, it helps us observe protective factors, identify areas of strength, and recognize where scaffolding may be needed.

This is a snapshot of resilience in context. Not just what a student can do, but what they have access to. Use the following items as a reflective checklist or conversation guide as you complete the SiNoC Profile. They can be used during observation, in collaboration with caregivers, or as a way to reflect on the supports available to a student, both in and outside of school.

Personal Resilience Indicator	Score
Cooperates/shares with people around them	1
Believes getting an education is important	2
Knows how to behave in different situations	1
Is fun to be with / liked by peers	2
Feels supported by friends	1
Feels they fit in at school	1
Has friends who care when times are hard	1
Is treated fairly	2
Given chances to show growing independence	2
Has chances to learn useful things	2
Total Personal Resilience	15/40

Relational Resilience Indicator	Score
Caregiver knows where they are	2
Caregiver knows what makes them happy/sad	1
Has enough to eat at home	3
Talks to caregiver about feelings	1
Family cares when times are hard	2
Likes how family celebrates things	2
Feels safe with caregiver	1
Total Relational Resilience	12/28

With a Personal Resilience score of 15/40, Malik shows only scattered signs of confidence, connection, and self-efficacy. He struggles to feel supported by peers, lacks a sense of belonging at school, and has few opportunities to experience autonomy or meaningful learning. His Relational Resilience score of 12/28 suggests inconsistent safety and emotional attunement at home. While some basic needs appear met, the deeper layers of relational connection-feeling seen, known, and emotionally supported-are thin. These scores don't just indicate low resilience; they reflect a young person who has learned to survive without depending on others. The path forward is not about fixing Malik, but about building the conditions-relationships, relevance, responsibility, and regulated environments-where resilience can grow.

Reflecting on Attachment Patterns

This chart is designed to help you reflect on a student's relational patterns and regulation needs through the lens of attachment, not as a diagnostic tool, but as a way to build insight and deepen your response.

Each row describes a specific area of behavior (e.g., classroom engagement, emotional awareness, stress response). Across the row, you'll see four descriptions aligned with general attachment styles: Secure, Insecure-Ambivalent, Insecure-Avoidant, and Disorganized.[113]

As you consider a student, highlight the description in each row that feels most representative of what you've observed. You may find yourself highlighting more than one box per row; that's expected. Most students don't fit neatly into one category, and their behavior can shift depending on the setting, the nature of the adult relationship, or their emotional state.

This isn't about labeling a child. It's about looking for patterns:

What shows up again and again?

Where do they seem to struggle?

What might help you better understand their stress, withdrawal, or significant reactions?

Approach this reflection with curiosity, not a conclusion. These insights are a starting point for empathy, not an endpoint for analysis.

Note: This tool does not determine attachment style. It helps us consider how early relational patterns may manifest in school behavior, and how we can respond with more connection, clarity, and care.

In my time working with Malik, I've come to see that his attachment patterns reflect a mix of avoidant and disorganized tendencies. He rarely seeks help and seems to operate from a place of deep self-reliance, often withdrawing emotionally and physically when he feels vulnerable or overwhelmed. At first glance, he appears "independent," but it's clear that this distance is a protective strategy-Malik has learned not to expect consistent emotional support from adults. When faced with correction or stress, he often shuts down or reacts unpredictably, swinging between disengagement and bursts of frustration. In the classroom, tasks that require emotional risk, collaboration, or self-reflection are especially hard for him. Malik needs more than academic support-he needs steady, attuned relationships that don't flinch when he pushes away, and co-regulation that honors the fear behind the behavior. Rebuilding his trust will take time, but I believe he is capable of forming safe, meaningful connections if we meet him with consistency, patience, and care.

Attachment Patterns

Area	Secure Attachment	Insecure-Ambivalent	Insecure-Avoidant	Disorganized Attachment
Caregiver Connection	Caregiver is consistent, attuned, and responds to emotional and physical needs	Caregiver presence is inconsistent—sometimes supportive, sometimes unavailable	Caregiver is often emotionally unavailable; the child learns not to rely on others	Caregiver is both a source of comfort and fear—the child experiences confusion, fear, or dysregulation
Relationship	Builds mutual, trusting relationships; engages well with peers	Craves connection but struggles with boundaries; may be overly dependent or fearful of rejection	Keeps emotional distance; may appear isolated or withdrawn	Struggles to form safe attachments; may show erratic, conflicted, or controlling behaviors in relationships
Emotional Awareness	Expresses a wide range of emotions and seeks support when needed	Emotionally expressive but may feel overwhelmed or anxious when emotions aren't reciprocated	Restricts emotional expression to maintain safety or self-sufficiency	May have difficulty identifying, naming, or managing emotions; emotional expression may be erratic or shut down
Classroom Engagement	Confident in classroom interactions; takes appropriate academic risks	May avoid tasks out of fear of failure or needing reassurance; perfectionism may emerge	Avoids vulnerability—tasks that require reflection or emotional engagement may be particularly difficult	Often struggles with trust, regulation, and task persistence; may appear oppositional or disengaged

Discipline Response	Responds well to relational discipline with clear boundaries and empathy	Needs consistent structure and emotional validation to engage with behavioral feedback	Withdraws or shuts down when confronted; responds better to quiet, non-punitive guidance	Reacts from survival brain; needs co-regulation and trauma-informed repair over traditional behavior correction
Stress Response	Uses adaptive, flexible coping skills; seeks support when overwhelmed	May internalize stress; blames self or over-apologizes	Appears "independent" but may suppress needs; avoids asking for help	Reacts with hypervigilance, aggression, or freezing; underlying fear and shame may drive behavior
Growth Needs	Benefits from opportunities for autonomy, connection, and mastery	Needs ongoing reassurance of worth, trust-building, and opportunities to succeed within a safe relationship	Needs relational safety to take emotional risks and build trust in others	Requires deep regulation work, co-regulation support, and safe, attuned relationships to begin healing
View of Personal Worth	"I am valued and capable. My needs matter, and others will respond to me with care."	"I am only lovable if I work hard to please others or stay close. If I'm not perfect, I may be left behind."	"I can't depend on others. I'm only safe when I'm strong and don't need anyone."	"Something is wrong with me. I'm too much, not enough, and unsafe in the world. I must protect myself at all costs."

Perceived ACEs and Early Childhood Risk Factors

This section of the SiNoC Profile helps educators reflect on how early adversity and biological beginnings may shape a student's regulation, behavior, and classroom engagement. It is not for diagnosis or confirmation of trauma, but for building compassionate awareness and guiding trauma-informed support.

Only mark ACEs (Adverse Childhood Experiences)[114] or early risk factors that have been confirmed through reliable sources (e.g., school records, caregiver reports, or direct disclosure). Do not speculate or ask students to complete ACE checklists.

Recognize that not all ACEs lead to trauma, and not all adversity is visible. This tool is meant to increase empathy, not define a student by risk. Use early childhood risk indicators (such as prenatal exposure, maternal stress, traumatic birth, frequent ear infections, or premature birth) to consider how a student's nervous system may have developed under stress. These are not deficits, but adaptations.

Reflect on the question: *What story was this student born into?* Let that shape your approach to safety, trust, and connection in the classroom.

Perceived ACES		Lowercase t Traumas/ Early Childhood Risk Factors	
Divorce/Abandonment	✔		
Experiencing Poverty	✔		
Caregiver Substance Abuse	✔	High Maternal Stress	no
Caregiver Mental Illness	?	Prenatal Exposure to Substances	✔
Violence in the Home	?	Traumatic Birth	no
Incarcerated Caregiver	no	Premature Birth	no
Death of Caregiver	no	Lowercase 't' Trauma:	?
Physical Neglect	?		
Emotional Neglect	?		
Victim of Abuse	?		
Total Number of Perceived ACEs	3+		

Malik's profile reveals a story shaped by instability, with confirmed experiences of divorce or abandonment, poverty, caregiver substance abuse, and prenatal exposure to substances. These early adversities likely taught his nervous system to stay on high alert, making trust, regulation, and learning more difficult.

His behavior in the classroom-shutting down, resisting help, or reacting with frustration-is not defiance, but an adaptation to a world that hasn't always felt safe. Understanding Malik's origin invites us to respond not with correction, but with connection-offering steady presence, relational safety, and learning environments that affirm his worth and potential.

Known Diagnosis

If a student has a known diagnosis related to behavior, attention, mood, or emotional regulation (such as ADHD, anxiety, depression, autism, ODD, or trauma-related challenges), you may include it in the "Known Diagnoses" section of the SiNoC Profile.

This section is not about assigning labels. It's about gathering context. A diagnosis can help explain patterns of behavior and guide more supportive, informed strategies, but it should never define a student or limit your expectations of what's possible for them.

Known Diagnosis	
ADD/ADHD	yes
Autism Spectrum Disorder	no
Generalized Anxiety Disorder	no
Depression	no
Oppositional Defiant Disorder	no
Conduct Disorder	no

Malik does have a diagnosis of ADHD. He does take medication, which has been successful when he is consistent with taking it as prescribed.

The Regulation Fulcrum

The Regulation Fulcrum invites us to look beneath the surface of student behavior and see motivation not as a fixed trait, but as something deeply shaped by relational safety, personal agency, and contextual relevance.

When students feel disconnected—from teachers, from tasks, or from their own sense of belonging—the fulcrum tips, and regulation becomes harder to access. Engagement doesn't begin with entertainment or compliance; it begins with trust. Students lean in when they feel seen, safe, and significant.

Motivation grows when they're offered real responsibility, not as a reward for good behavior, but as a pathway to connection and purpose. It deepens when learning feels relevant to their lives, when their voice and identity are valued, and when tasks are challenging yet achievable.

The Regulation Fulcrum	
Relationship	This child has no known adult relationships in school
Responsibility	The opportunity to positively contribute to the school community has been taken away from this child due to behavior
Relevance	This child's interests/passions/abilities are not reflected in classwork
Rigor	Most instructional tasks and activities are too difficult for this child

Malik comes to school already wary of adults, and his current experience offers little in the way of strong relationships. He floats through the day without a clear connection to any teacher or peer. While he's capable, he has few genuine responsibilities at school-many adults have stopped offering those opportunities because of his past behavior.

His academic work is often too difficult without proper scaffolding, making rigor another point of pain. Worse, Malik doesn't see any relevance in his assignments; they feel disconnected from his life and interests.

Malik's fulcrum is nearly flat; he lacks relationship, meaningful responsibility, and relevance, leaving him unregulated and disengaged. Restoring balance for him would begin with consistent adult connection, followed by intentional invitations to contribute meaningfully to his school community in non-academic ways, and then carefully adjusting the academic rigor to suit his needs.

At the heart of it all is the question: Can this student stay regulated enough to access their strengths? And if not, which part of the fulcrum—relationship, responsibility, rigor, or relevance—needs to be restored? When we rebalance that fulcrum, we don't just recover engagement; we reignite hope.

The Student Risk Screening Scale (SRSS)

The Student Risk Screening Scale (SRSS) is frequently used to identify students who are at risk for behavioral challenges.[115] By design, you would complete it for your entire class roster. Here, you'll use it for something more powerful, as a mirror for your perceptions. The SRSS asks you to rate how frequently a student displays behaviors such as:

Disruptive behavior

Aggression

Peer rejection

Low academic performance

Internalizing concerns like withdrawal or sadness

At first glance, it may seem like the goal is simply to "flag" high-risk students. However, remember that your ratings reflect your interpretation of their behavior, which may or may not tell the whole story.

How to Use the SRSS for Discernment

As you complete the SRSS, review your class data overall and reflect on it. As you review your risk ratings, pause for a moment and take note of your initial reactions. Which student behaviors triggered a strong response in you? Which ones made you instinctively rate a student as "high risk"? Now ask yourself: *Why?* What is it about this behavior that feels particularly threatening, concerning, or difficult to manage? Is it truly the behavior—or could it be your own stress, values, or personal history showing up in how you're interpreting it?

Sometimes, without realizing it, we extend more empathy to certain students than others—even when the behaviors are nearly identical. This is human. It's also a signal to reflect more deeply. Start by looking for patterns. Do you tend to rate certain types of students as higher or lower risk? Are cultural norms, implicit biases, or personal experiences influencing your lens?

Now, choose one or two students you rated as moderate or high risk and use the TEA Strategy to reflect more intentionally.

First, name your current perception. What behaviors have you been most focused on? Are you noticing disruption, defiance, withdrawal, or avoidance? Be honest with yourself. Then, walk through the TEA process:

What story are you telling yourself about this student or their behavior?
What emotions does this behavior stir up in you? Why those?
How have you been responding? Is that response helpful—or might it be adding fuel to the fire?

Finally, pause and reframe. Ask yourself:

What else might be true about this student's behavior?
What could they be feeling underneath the surface?
What would it look like to respond in a way that protects safety, belonging, and dignity—not just for them, but for you, too?

Shifting from Perception to Intention

Once you've completed the SRSS, reflect intentionally:

What did I learn about my lens through this process?
How can I reframe my next steps with students rated as "high risk"?
Am I seeing this student's behavior as a form of communication or simply as a problem?

Remember, the SRSS doesn't tell you who a student is; it tells you how you see them. Your goal is not simply to score students, but to reflect on the meaning you assign to those scores and to ensure that your future actions align with both compassion and purpose.

Student Risk Screening: Externalizing Behaviors	
Steal	1
Lie, Cheat, Sneak	2
Behavior Problem	2
Peer Rejection	2
Low Academics	2
Negative Attitude	3
Aggressive Behavior	3
15	

Student Risk Screening: Internalizing Behaviors	
Emotionally Flat	2
Shy, Withdrawn	2
Sad, Depressed	1
Anxious	1
Lonely	2
8	

I've been focused on Malik's *withdrawal, defiance,* and quick *frustration.* He shuts down, pushes back, and avoids help.

Reflect Using the TEA Strategy:
I sometimes catch myself thinking, "He just doesn't care. He's always pushing people away."
I feel frustrated and discouraged. It's exhausting trying to connect when he rejects every attempt.
I tend to either back off completely or approach him more forcefully, pushing him to engage-which usually backfires.

Pause & Reframe:
Malik's behavior might be a protective strategy. He may be afraid to trust because it hasn't been safe in the past. His "I don't care" attitude could be masking deep fear or hurt.
He's probably feeling *alone* and *vulnerable,* even if he won't show it openly.
I can respond by offering consistent, non-intrusive connection-small check-ins without pressure-and by staying predictable without taking his distance personally.

Considering Executive Function and Regulation Lagging Skills

This checklist is designed to help you reflect on the underlying skill gaps a student may be experiencing—especially when they struggle with behavior, emotional regulation, relationships, or task engagement. Rather than asking *"What's wrong with this student?"*, this tool invites you to ask: *"What skills might this student be lagging in, and how can we help them grow?"*

The word "lagging" here refers to skills that are delayed in comparison to what's typical for same-age, neurotypical peers. We recognize that this lens does not capture the full range of neurodivergent experiences—and that is intentional.

This checklist is designed to help identify skills that may be contributing to behavioral challenges, allowing us to respond with developmental sensitivity.Start with Observation. Think about what you consistently see from this student across the school day. Consider transitions, peer interactions, academic tasks, and responses to feedback or unpredictability.

Highlight or place a check mark next to any skill area where the student struggles in a way that appears to be developmentally atypical for their age. Leave it blank if the skill seems age-appropriate or is not impacting school functioning.

Executive Function & Regulation Lagging Skills

Cognitive Flexibility and Perspective-Taking

Difficulty shifting from original ideas, plans, or expected outcomes ✔

Difficulty understanding or considering other points of view

Difficulty recognizing how their behavior is affecting others ✔

Difficulty considering alternative solutions or strategies ✔

Emotional Regulation & Stress Tolerance

Difficulty managing emotional responses in the face of frustration ✔

Difficulty returning to baseline after perceived failure, correction, or peer conflict ✔

Difficulty tolerating unpredictability, ambiguity, or novelty ✔

Difficulty with chronic irritability or anxiety that interferes with problem-solving or focus ✔

Sensory Processing & Regulation

Difficulty with sensory and/or motor challenges that interfere with participation, attention, or regulation

Difficulty filtering sensory input (e.g., overwhelmed by noise, texture, visual clutter)

Difficulty with movement-seeking or movement-avoiding behaviors that mask underlying sensory needs

Impulse Control and Future Thinking

Difficulty considering potential outcomes or consequences before acting ✔

Difficulty slowing down in the moment to think before responding ✔

Difficulty adjusting behavior when a previous strategy didn't work

Difficulty persisting through frustrating, boring, or non-preferred tasks

Communication & Self-Expression

Difficulty identifying and expressing emotions or needs with words. ✔

Difficulty initiating conversations, entering peer groups, or sustaining interactions

Difficulty asking for help or clarification

Difficulty using appropriate tone, timing, or social cues in communication

Attention & Social Perception

Difficulty maintaining focus and following multi-step directions ✔

Difficulty noticing others' emotions, reactions, or boundaries

Difficulty differentiating between safe and unsafe situations or people

Difficulty taking into account the situational context when making decisions

Reviewing Malik's lagging executive function and regulation skills highlights how much of his behavior stems from overwhelmed systems-not defiance. He struggles most with emotional regulation, future thinking, and flexibility. When plans change, or he feels corrected or unsure, he often shuts down or escalates. He has difficulty expressing needs with words, predicting outcomes, or shifting his thinking when things don't go as expected. This shows up as resistance, but really, it's a sign that he lacks the internal tools to adapt in the moment.

Current General Concerns:

Use this section to identify current concerns that are impacting the student's well-being, learning, or behavior. Only check items that are supported by observation, caregiver report, or team documentation; avoid assumptions. This section is not a diagnostic tool, but a snapshot that helps you recognize patterns across emotional, academic, and relational domains. As you complete it, look for overlap between categories. A single challenge (like low frustration tolerance) may underlie multiple outward concerns.

Current General Concerns

Academic Struggles	✔	Gender Identity Issues	
Academic Overwhelm	✔	General Behavior Issues	
Alcohol Use		Homelessness	
Anxiety	✔	Identity Issues	
Attendance		Illness	
Abuse		Injury	
Changes in Appearance		Isolating from Peers	
Changes in Demeanor		Low Frustration Tolerance	✔
Dating Issues		Lack of Participation	✔
Death of a Family Member		Mental Health Issues	
Death of a Friend		Overreaction to Circumstances	✔
Depression or Extreme Sadness		Poor Decision-Making	✔
Destruction of Property		Poor Hygiene	
Domestic Violence at Home		Self-Injurious Behavior	
Drug Use		Student/Teacher Relationship	✔
Excessive Absences from Class		Threats to Others/Bullying	
Family Issues	✔	Too Many Tardies	✔
Friendship Issues		Witness to an Incident	
Other:		Other:	

Malik's profile reveals a cluster of interconnected concerns: academic struggle and overwhelm, anxiety, low frustration tolerance, poor decision-making, lack of participation, and strained student-teacher relationships. Taken together, these concerns suggest that Malik is not simply disengaged; he is chronically dysregulated.

Interventions Used and Formal Services in Place

Check all interventions and formal services that have been used to support the student. Be honest and thorough. This section is not about judging what has or hasn't worked, but about tracking efforts to support the student's needs. For each intervention, consider whether it was implemented consistently, whether the student responded positively, and whether it aligned with their strengths and challenges. In the "Formal Services" section, document only those supports that are officially in place (e.g., MTSS, medication, 504, or IEP plans). If no formal services exist, note this clearly; it may highlight a gap between the need and the support.

Interventions Used

2 x 10 Relationship Strategy	✔	Behavior Chart/Plan	✔
Regulation Room Breaks		Check-in / Check-out	✔
NeuroResilience Lessons		In-School Suspension	✔
Parent Conferences		Losing Privileges	✔
Peer Mentors		Out-of-School Suspension	
Restorative Circles		School Resource Officer	
Targeted Social Skill Instruction		Sensory Breaks	
Adult Mentors		Other:	

Formal Services in Place

Individualized Education Plan		MTSS Plan: Academic	
504 Plan		MTSS Plan: Behavior	✔
Medication	✔	Referred to Outside Services	

Malik has experienced multiple behavior-focused interventions-charts, check-ins, suspensions, and loss of privileges-but few that address his regulation or relational needs. Aside from one attempt at the 2x10 strategy, there's little evidence of co-regulation, restorative practices, or skill-building supports. Though he's on medication and has an MTSS plan, he lacks deeper system protections like a 504 or IEP.

Current and Past Academic Performance

Researcher John Hattie's meta-analysis of over 1,400 educational influences found that a *teacher's estimate of achievement*, a teacher's belief about how well a student is likely to perform, has one of the highest effect sizes on student learning outcomes (effect size = 1.29).[116] This means it's one of the most powerful predictors of student success. Simply put, what teachers believe about a student's potential shapes how they teach, what opportunities they provide, and how persistently they support that student through challenges.

In the context of the Student in Need of Connection (SiNoC) Profile, this is critically important. Many students referred for additional support, such as Malik, present with behavioral concerns, emotional dysregulation, or academic inconsistencies that can lead educators, often unconsciously, to lower their expectations for them. When educators internalize the belief that a student won't succeed, they may offer fewer challenges, overlook strengths, or shift into a mindset of containment rather than connection and growth.

Use this section to document the student's current academic performance across subjects. Include the student's most recent grades and any relevant teacher observations. Go beyond numbers, note how the student engages in each subject, their effort, patterns of avoidance, and any conditions that support or hinder success (e.g., time of day, relationship with the teacher, task type). This data helps the support team understand where breakdowns are occurring and where strengths can be leveraged. Remember: grades alone do not reflect capacity; behavioral and emotional barriers often mask academic potential.

Teacher Estimate of Achievement

Summary of Past Performance and Progress	Expected Level of Success if Supported
Core Content Areas:	**Core Content Areas:**
Malik has mainly remained on target in core academic areas when emotionally regulated and supported. His academic challenges appear to stem more from dysregulation and avoidance than from a lack of ability.	Malik is likely to remain on target academically if provided with consistent regulation support, relationship-based scaffolding, and alternative pathways for demonstrating mastery.
Socially:	**Socially:**
Below expectations. He tends to isolate or react defensively, which limits his opportunities for meaningful relationships.	With adult guidance, relational modeling, and structured opportunities for positive peer interaction, Malik can begin to build healthier social connections.

Emotionally:
Below expectations. Malik's emotional expression is restricted, with anger serving as his primary mode of communication. He has difficulty identifying, articulating, or regulating complex emotions.

Emotionally:
With a safe, predictable environment and access to co-regulation strategies, Malik has the potential to increase emotional awareness and develop more adaptive coping skills.

Behaviorally:
Malik has had multiple office referrals, including incidents involving physical aggression. These behaviors appear rooted in dysregulation and mistrust rather than willful defiance.

Behaviorally:
Given consistent, trauma-responsive intervention and relational accountability, Malik can make meaningful progress in reducing reactive behaviors and increasing classroom engagement.

Academic Performance

Class/Subject	Current Grade	Teacher	Teacher Comments
ELA	D+	Mr. Thomas	Malik struggles with written tasks and often fails to complete assignments. He shuts down during independent work but engages more in group discussion if prompted gently. He resists asking for help but shows insight when verbally processing.
Math	C-	Ms. Perez	Malik is inconsistent-some days he completes tasks, other days he refuses. He demonstrates an understanding of concepts but struggles with multi-step problems. Frustration leads to disengagement. He requires frequent check-ins and opportunities for revision.
Science	C	Mr. Lewis	Malik participates when projects are hands-on. He's curious but avoids formal assessments. Often distracted and slow to start tasks. Performs better when allowed to move or engage in peer collaboration.

Social Studies	F	Ms. Grant	Malik has stopped turning in assignments and rarely responds in class. He appears anxious when asked to read aloud or complete worksheets. He benefits from visual aids but needs one-on-one support to re-engage.
Art	B+	Ms. Jefferson	Malik thrives in this class. He completes all projects and often stays after class to work on details. He takes pride in his work and has positive interactions with his peers. This is a clear strength area.

Academic Assessments

District Assessments		State Assessments	
STAR Reading	7.4 - Below	ELA	275 - Approaching Proficiency
MAP Math	212 - Below	Math	273 - Approaching Proficiency
Writing Benchmark	2 - Basic	Science	277 - Approaching Proficiency
FastBridge ELA	31st Percentile	Social Studies	220 - Below Proficiency

The SiNoC Intervention Plan

In schools, it's easy to get overwhelmed by the sheer number of concerns we're holding for a student, such as academic gaps, behavioral challenges, social disconnection, and emotional dysregulation. It can feel like we need to fix everything, all at once—but when everything is a priority, nothing really is.

The Student in Need of Connection (SiNoC) Profile isn't just a reflection tool—it's a roadmap for meaningful intervention. Once completed, it allows educators and support teams to identify an intervention goal for the student by highlighting the most urgent or impactful area for growth. Whether it's emotional regulation, peer connection, academic persistence, or communication, any area marked as a lagging skill, executive function deficit, or current concern can become the focus of targeted support.

From there, we determine lag measures—the outcomes that will help us know if progress is being made. These might include reduced behavior referrals, increased assignment completion, or improved peer interactions. To influence those outcomes, we choose lead measures—the consistent adult actions we will take to support growth, such as daily check-ins, visual supports, co-regulation strategies, or restorative connection circles. The beauty of the SiNoC Profile is that it moves us from guessing to *planning*—from reacting to *responding*. It ensures our goals are personalized, our interventions are intentional, and our progress is measurable.

Setting an Intervention Goal

That's where the SiNoC Intervention Goal process comes in. This goal helps us focus our energy on what matters most for a student's growth. The concept originates from FranklinCovey's *4 Disciplines of Execution* model, which teaches that clarity and focus are essential for achieving meaningful progress—especially in complex systems. Rather than trying to solve every problem, this process calls us to choose one powerful goal that can serve as a lever for change.[117]

For students like Malik, who carry histories of adversity, patterns of mistrust, and skill gaps across multiple domains, a single goal helps us prioritize connection over correction, and progress over perfection. It brings clarity to a plan that might otherwise feel chaotic or reactive.

For students in the SiNoC process, the WIG serves as the anchor point for all adult action. We don't guess at what to do; we align around one goal and build our support around it with intention. A good SiNoC Intervention Goal is...

Specific and observable
Rooted in the student's actual needs and strengths
Relational, not just results-driven
Grounded in what's possible with the proper support

SiNoC Intervention Goal

Support Malik in strengthening his academic participation and emotional regulation by increasing his use of self-regulation strategies, improving relational consistency, and expanding his sense of agency in learning.

Lag Measures: How Will We Know It's Working?

Once the goal is set, we determine what evidence will show us we're moving in the right direction. These are our lag measures, the outcomes we hope to influence over time. Lag measures answer the question, "How will we know it's working?" These measures are outcome-based and measurable over time, such as improved assignment completion or reduced behavior referrals, which reflect change after sustained effort. They're called "lag" because they trail behind the actions we take; they show up later.

To drive those results, we focus on lead measures, the consistent actions we, as adults, will commit to. Lag measures indicate whether our student is making progress. Lead measures tell us what *we* will do to help make that growth possible. They are both predictive and influential, meaning that if we implement them with fidelity, we increase the likelihood of positive outcomes. Lag measures must also be measured frequently; often, this means keeping daily or weekly data.

Importantly, lead measures are not about fixing the student. They focus on adjusting the environment, strengthening relationships, and implementing resilience-building strategies to support the student's regulation and readiness to learn. These actions are the heartbeat of the SiNoC Intervention Plan.

Lag and Lead Measures
Lag Measure #1: Increased Academic Participation in Core Classes Measured weekly by assignment completion and participation logs in ELA, Math, and Social Studies

Lead Measure 1a:	Lead Measure 1b:
Teachers implement at least two scaffolded, choice-based assignments per week that incorporate creative or hands-on elements. Designed to increase relevance and reduce shutdowns related to task overwhelm.	Mr. Thomas to conduct advisory check-ins 3 times per week, prompting Malik to review progress and set a micro-goal for one class each day. Builds accountability, confidence, and a sense of ownership in his learning.

Lag Measure #2: Decrease in Dysregulation and Reactive Behaviors Measured biweekly using behavior referrals, observational notes, and Malik's self-monitoring tool

Lead Measure 2a:	Lead Measure 2b:
Malik maintains the use of his visual regulation card across ELA, Science, and Social Studies. Teachers review it daily and respond using co-regulation strategies. Supports emotional awareness and helps staff intervene before escalation.	One adult anchor (Ms. Jefferson or counselor) checks in weekly with Malik to celebrate progress and troubleshoot triggers. Sustains relational support as check-in frequency fades and student ownership increases.

The SiNoC Goal Process in Action

Begin by reviewing the SiNoC Profile to determine the most pressing goal for the student, one that is grounded in their strengths, needs, and current concerns. Write this goal using language that emphasizes growth and capacity, rather than compliance or correction. Then, identify one or two lag measures—indicators that will show whether the student is making progress toward that goal. For each lag measure, create one or two lead measures that focus on consistent adult action, ensuring responsibilities are shared across team members so the plan doesn't fall on just one person. Track progress weekly using a simple log, check-in, or quick reflection routine. Finally, revisit and revise the plan at your next SiNoC team meeting, typically every 4–6 weeks.

When we use this process with intention, we change the story. We move from *"What's wrong with this student?"* to
"What's one powerful thing we can do to support them right now?"
It gives us direction. It builds shared ownership. Most importantly, it sends a message to the student:

We see you.
We're not giving up.
We're walking this road with you, one step at a time.

Facilitating the Meeting

Once a student has been referred through the Student in Need of Connection (SiNoC) process, the team lead, typically the school counselor, MTSS coordinator, or social worker, convenes the support team for a formal meeting. This meeting is designed to bring clarity, compassion, and coordination to the support plan.

The meeting begins with a review of the completed SiNoC Profile, which serves as the foundation for the discussion. The team uses the profile to explore the student's lagging skills, regulatory patterns, strengths, behaviors, and known stressors, providing a more comprehensive picture of the child, not just as a student, but as a human being navigating a complex world.

From there, the group collaboratively determines which interventions are most appropriate based on what this specific student needs, not based on what's convenient or standardized, but what is relationally and developmentally aligned. This could include adult mentoring, co-regulation strategies, instructional accommodations, trauma-informed discipline shifts, or peer support structures.

Each section of the SiNoC Profile gives insight to what skills the student needs support in developing, what obstacles are impeding progress, and what interventions might be most effective. Use this information to set your goals, lead, and lag measures. This is how we customize plans that will work for the individual.

Before adjourning, the group sets a follow-up meeting date, typically within 4–6 weeks, to review progress, reflect on what's working, and revise the plan as needed. This cycle continues until the student has consistent support, strengthened relationships, and a clear pathway toward success.

The SiNoC meeting is not a final answer. It's a first, intentional step toward making sure the student is no longer alone in their struggle and toward ensuring every adult in the room shares responsibility for helping them reconnect, regulate, and thrive.

SiNoC Meeting Notes

Date	September 10
Focus	Initial Referral & Profile Review

Team Members
Mr. Thomas (ELA/Advisor), Ms. Shandy (School Counselor), Ms. Roberts (Assistant Principal), Mr. Erickson (MTSS Coordinator)

Discussion Points
Mr. Thomas completed the SiNoC Profile and shared concerns about Malik's emotional regulation, lack of participation, and defiant behavior in ELA.
Malik frequently arrives late, avoids academic tasks, and escalates quickly when redirected.
Review of academic data shows Malik is on target in comprehension but underperforming in written tasks due to avoidance.
Ms. Jefferson (Art) shared informally that Malik is engaged, creative, and cooperative in her class.
MTSS behavior plan is currently in place, but interventions have focused on compliance rather than connection.

Action Items
Begin daily morning check-ins with Mr. Thomas in his advisory role.
Add Malik to Art Club as a non-academic strength-based engagement point.
Counselor to reach out to caregiver to establish rapport and gather family context.
Identify one other teacher willing to implement relational strategy (2x10) for connection.

- - -

Date	October 12
Focus	Intervention Adjustment & Relationship Mapping

Team Members
Mr. Thomas (ELA/Advisor), Mrs. Vaught (School Psychologist), Mr. Erickson (MTSS Coordinator), Ms. Jefferson (Art), Ms. Wilson (School Social Worker)

Discussion Points
Mr. Thomas reports Malik is responding better during advisory-less guarded and more talkative during non-academic interactions.
In-class resistance remains, especially with writing tasks and group assignments.
Ms. Jefferson offered to model strategies for creative task design-shared how choice-based projects increase Malik's engagement.
Counselor's contact with caregiver revealed a history of prenatal exposure and early adversity; caregiver receptive but overwhelmed.

Action Items
Pilot co-created "choice board" writing assignment in ELA with Art-based integration.
Add visual regulation cue card to Malik's desk-developed with Malik during check-in.
Referral made to school-based mental health provider for screening.
Begin restorative connection circle 1x/week.

Date	November 7	Focus	Academic & Behavioral Progress Review

Team Members
Mr. Thomas (ELA/Advisor), Ms. Roberts (Assistant Principal), Mr. Erickson (MTSS Coordinator), Ms. Jefferson (Art), Ms. Wilson (School Social Worker)

Discussion Points
Office referrals have decreased, though Malik had a hallway outburst last week after a peer teased him. Teacher responded with de-escalation and redirection.
Check-ins with Mr. Thomas remain consistent. Malik initiated a conversation last week about missing an assignment and was supported in completing it.
Peer interactions improving slowly-still reactive at times, but less isolating.
ELA performance is still low, but Malik turned in his first complete assignment of the quarter.

Action Items
Reinforce positive behaviors with private praise and leadership opportunities (e.g., art room assistant).
Coach Mr. Lewis (Science) on calm entry and soft redirection strategies to reduce dysregulation at the start of class.
Counselor to schedule check-in with caregiver to update on progress and gather input for next steps.
Maintain weekly team updates via email-next formal check-in in four weeks.

Date	December 12	Focus	Mid-Year Review & Support Planning

Team Members
Mr. Thomas (ELA/Advisor), Ms. Roberts (Assistant Principal), Mr. Erickson (MTSS Coordinator), Ms. Wilson (School Social Worker)

Discussion Points
Malik has not had any major incidents in the past month. Still struggles with writing output, but is now consistently beginning tasks.
Peer relationships improving-initiated two partner activities in Science.
Morning check-ins now led by Malik independently using a "self-check card."
Caregiver has asked about tutoring support and expressed interest in Malik participating in a weekend community art program.

Action Items
Refer Malik for after-school tutoring (Math & Writing Lab) with peer mentor support.
Provide caregiver with info and contact for community art group.
Begin a fade-out plan for daily check-ins, transitioning to three times a week with increased student ownership.
Plan student-led parent conference in January to celebrate growth and set personal goals for spring semester.

One Student, One Connection at a Time

The SiNoC process is not just another tiered intervention or compliance checklist; it is a relational roadmap. It asks us to slow down, see clearly, and respond with intention. At its heart, the Student in Need of Connection process is about remembering the humanity behind the behavior and choosing connection over control.

When we sit down with a profile like Malik's, we aren't just reviewing data; we're reading a story. A story of resilience and rupture. A story still in progress.—and we get to be part of the next chapter. This process reminds us that healing doesn't happen through suspension, stickers, or one-size-fits-all behavior charts. It occurs when one adult becomes consistent, when one teacher believes in the possibility of growth, when one team commits to the long, slow, sacred work of co-regulation and belonging.

The SiNoC process gives us structure, but it's not the form that changes lives. It's the fierce hope behind it. The daily acts of care. The refusal to give up on a student because we understand what shaped them.

We do not need to change everything overnight. We start with one student. One plan. One meaningful goal. From there, we build a school where every child, especially the most disconnected, knows they matter.

katherinadonald.org/book-companion

Visit the book companion
site for additional
materials related to this
chapter.

Book Companion Resources

- **Student in Need of Connection Profile Template**
- **Student in Need of Connection Process resources**

❧ reflection ❧

Before you move on, follow the QR code to the sample Student in Need of Connection (SiNoC) Profile. Bring to mind a specific student, someone who lingers in your thoughts, who seems shut down or on edge, who hasn't yet found safety or belonging in your classroom.

As you fill out the profile, resist the urge to rush or judge. Pause at each section. Reflect deeply. When you don't know the answer, make a plan to find out, through observation, conversation, or collaboration.

This isn't just paperwork. It's an act of relational practice.

Use the ROOTED IN HOPE framework to guide your lens:

Resilience – Where does this student show signs of strength, even if it's hard to see?

Origin – What experiences may have shaped the behaviors you're noticing now?

Openness – What assumptions are you willing to challenge or release?

Trust – Who in the building is best positioned to begin a steady relationship?

Engagement – What helps this student stay connected, even briefly?

Discernment – What patterns are emerging across their school day?

Intentionality – What support actions are feasible, consistent, and impactful?

Neuro-Informed – What does this student's nervous system need to feel safe?

Hope – Where do you see even the slightest flicker of potential?

Ownership – How can you involve the student in setting goals and making choices?

Purpose – Why does showing up for this student matter to you?

Empowerment – How can your support build this student's sense of agency?

Let the process change how you see the student and how you see yourself. This is the work. Not just identifying disconnection, but choosing to meet it with presence, clarity, and care.

katiemcdaniel.org/book-companion

Visit the book companion site for additional materials related to this chapter.

❧ thirty ☙
Considerations for Whole School Implementation

Creating a resilience-building school is not a checklist; it's a cultural shift. It's the decision to root every practice in relationship, to build systems that support healing rather than punish pain, and to hold space for both the student's and the adult's nervous systems to feel safe, seen, and supported. While an individual educator can create meaningful change, sustainable transformation requires that the *whole school* come along.

Whole-school implementation ensures consistency, equity, and alignment throughout the school. When resilience-building practices are woven into every hallway, classroom, and leadership decision, students and staff alike experience the calm and clarity that regulation brings. Such a shift doesn't happen organically. It takes structure, support, and a shared commitment to something more profound than behavior management: belonging.

Building a Leadership Team

Successful implementation begins with people, specifically, a core group of educators who hold both vision and influence. This leadership team should be diverse in terms of role and perspective, comprising administrators, teachers, support staff, paraprofessionals, and mental health providers. The most effective teams also include those "informal leaders," the people others go to for advice, support, or guidance.

This team becomes the nervous system of the initiative. Their role isn't just about logistics; it's about culture. They model reflection, facilitate feedback, and carry the relational heartbeat of the work. Protected time to plan, reflect, and assess is vital, but so is permission to evolve. Their leadership is not about perfection; it's about presence.

Reaching the 75% Commitment

Change doesn't require unanimous consent. Research shows that once 75% of the staff commit to a new way of being, transformation becomes self-sustaining. Commitment isn't built through mandates; it's cultivated through meaning.[118]

Schools that reach this tipping point start by clarifying the "why." They ground the work in shared values, equity, belonging, and student success, rather than mere compliance or buzzwords. They create space for honest conversations, honor staff fears and frustrations, and encourage early adopters to share their stories. Progress becomes visible, not because everyone gets it right, but because enough people believe it matters.

Resilience-building leadership fosters open-mindedness, allowing for questions and discomfort, and promotes a culture of inquiry and growth. It doesn't expect staff to be experts overnight. It simply asks for open hearts, curious minds, and a willingness to reflect and grow.

The Inevitable Frustrations Along the Way

Even with strong leadership and growing buy-in, this work is not without struggle. As schools begin to shift toward trauma-informed practices, many experience an unexpected surge of frustration or anxiety. That's not a sign of failure. It's a sign of progress.

As we learn the science of trauma and resilience and begin integrating these strategies into our classrooms and policies, new awareness brings new visibility. We start noticing behaviors that were previously dismissed or misinterpreted. This can feel overwhelming, like things are getting worse before they get better.

Increased Behaviors

Once we understand the neurobiological roots of dysregulation, we begin to see them everywhere. Behaviors that once felt like defiance now read as distress. While this awareness is essential, it can also feel disheartening. You might find yourself wondering, *Why are things escalating now that we're trying to do the right thing?* Honestly, two things are happening.

The first phenomenon is known as the Baader-Meinhof phenomenon, also referred to as the frequency illusion.[119] It happens when something you've just noticed or learned suddenly seems to appear everywhere. You buy a white Jeep Cherokee, and suddenly the whole neighborhood has one. Your brain just can't unsee it. It's not that the thing is more common—your awareness has simply increased, so your brain is now tuned in to it more. This happens because of two cognitive processes:

Selective attention – Once you notice something new, you unconsciously keep an eye out for it.

Confirmation bias – You begin to interpret encounters with the item as evidence that it's everywhere.

You started to notice students were experiencing high levels of stress and trauma, and now you are looking for it and finding it.

The second is that you've increased students' sense of safety. As school climates become more relational, students may begin to reveal the very pain they previously concealed. It's not regression—it's trust. So, yes, Marisol might never have been the student to throw a chair - but after seeing Malik do it and get his needs met, she learned it might be the only way to be seen. Jayden isn't going to learn to throw chairs - his needs are already met. Our job is to hold steady.

A Sense of Less Accountability

Another common tension arises around discipline. As we move away from punitive responses and toward restorative practices, some staff may worry that "there are no consequences anymore." This concern is valid, but often rooted in a misunderstanding. Restorative does not mean permissive. Accountability still exists, but it takes on a different form. It sounds like repair. It feels like reflection. It requires us to redefine what it means to hold someone accountable while still showing care.

When frustrations rise, reflection is key. Pause to ask:

What is working?

Where have we seen relational wins, moments of regulation, or minor shifts in behavior?

Are there policies or practices still operating within a punitive framework that may require attention?

Celebrate those moments when a student names their feelings, uses a strategy, or the class returns to a regulated state. Celebrate when a teacher tries a new co-regulation script or when a hallway conflict is resolved with conversation instead of suspension. These moments are the seeds of something bigger.

Most importantly, support your staff. This work takes emotional labor. Without attention to adult nervous systems, even the best trauma-informed plans will falter. Make space for staff wellness, self-regulation, and relational connection. Provide professional development that doesn't just inform—but nurtures.

The Role of Administration

No system can change without its leaders. The most resilient schools are led by administrators who live the work—not just talk about it. These leaders create space for vulnerability, protect time for reflection, and evaluate not just performance, but presence. They understand that adult wellbeing isn't separate from student success—it's foundational to it.

Administrators lead with curiosity, not control. They revise policies through a relational lens. They ask teachers what they need to feel safe and supported, and they treat staff dysregulation not as defiance, but as a call for care. When leadership aligns with the values of the work, staff are more willing to take risks and stay invested—because they're not just implementing a model; they're living in a community.

Keeping the Long View

Transformation doesn't happen overnight. There will be moments that feel messy, disjointed, or stuck. That's part of it. Building a trauma-informed school culture is a long-term commitment. Every small step—every reflection, every relational repair, every reframe—moves us closer to the kind of school where students don't just survive, but belong. Where educators aren't just managing behavior, but healing communities.

Professional Learning That Sustains

Trauma-informed practice is not a training. It's a mindset—and it must be nourished over time. Effective schools don't rely on one-off PD days. They create layered, ongoing opportunities for growth, coaching cycles, learning communities, reflection sessions, and peer facilitation. They ensure that the tools shared are practical, responsive, and immediately usable. They recognize that adult regulation is foundational. Professional learning should never overwhelm. It should model the very principles it promotes: clarity, connection, and compassion.

The extension of this book is the Rooted in Hope Train-the-Trainer Model, a structured pathway for schools ready to embed this work systemically. This training equips your in-house leaders to guide implementation, facilitate professional learning, and coach their colleagues through real-world application. It includes virtual or in-person training options as well as sustained coaching support throughout the year. If your team is ready to move from intention to integration, I invite you to visit katiemcdonald.org to explore bringing me in to lead a workshop, keynote, or year-long coaching partnership tailored to your school's needs.

✺ reflection ☙

If you are reading this book as part of a team, focus your reflection on your group as a whole. Otherwise, take a personal focus.

Where have you seen signs of resilience within your team and students?

What stories from your school's origin still shape your current culture—and which ones are ready to shift?

How are you building trust—between leadership and staff, staff and students, and among staff themselves?

What does intentionality look like in implementation? Are your practices aligned with our values?

How are you supporting both student regulation and adult well-being in our learning structures?

What is your long-term purpose—and how are you measuring progress beyond behavior charts?

Who in your building is ready to lead—and how can you empower them?

Whole-school change begins not with perfection, but with a shared commitment to hope, grounded in connection. With the proper support, reflection, and relationships, that hope becomes a culture.

❧ part four reflection ❧
From Insight to Implementation

In this section, we shift from internal insight to external application—from understanding trauma to transforming the spaces where it manifests. Because students don't just experience school through curriculum or conversation, they experience it through hallways and lighting, tone of voice, and tap-out systems, as well as who shows up for them and how they are allowed to return after a hard moment. Every space speaks. So we asked: What story is our environment telling us?

This section also reminded us that regulation isn't instinct; it's instruction. It must be taught, modeled, and supported across all tiers, with strategies such as emotional check-ins, breathing tools, and grounding exercises integrated into daily routines. When dysregulation does happen (because it will), our response becomes the most powerful intervention. Through the co-regulation process, we learned how to walk with students, moment by moment, until their nervous systems return to a state of safety and trust.

Finally, we transitioned from a general strategy to individualized support through the Student in Need of Connection (SiNoC) Process, a tool that encourages us to view the whole child, not just their behavior. Not as a label, but as a nervous system in context —a story in motion.

You're not expected to implement all of this overnight. This work is layered. Ongoing. A practice of discernment, not perfection. What matters most is this: you are already creating spaces that heal. Every time you notice, adjust, reflect, or offer your calm, you are shaping an environment where regulation, restoration, and reconnection are possible.

Use the Part Four ROOTED IN HOPE Reflection found in Part Five on page 284 or by scanning the QR code below to organize your thinking to organize your thinking and start planting seeds of change in your practice.

Visit the book companion site for additional materials related to this chapter.

Book Companion Resources

- **Part FourReflection**

✺ part five ✺
Rooted Reflections

Insight without action just stays in our head.
Transformation resides within our bodies, our classrooms, and our relationships.

This final section may look like the end, but it's something you've been building all along. As you moved through the science, self-reflection, and student stories, you've been quietly assembling a guide — one grounded in your values, shaped by your experiences, and rooted in what you've learned. Now, we gather those pieces.

This section holds space for you to reflect more deeply, connect the dots, and turn intention into action. It includes guided reflections for each part of the book, along with step-by-step tools to help you apply the ROOTED IN HOPE framework and the Student in Need of Connection (SiNoC) process to real students, in real classrooms, with your real nervous system and capacity in mind. Whether you complete each reflection as you go or return here at the end to look back on your journey, this part is yours.

Not to perform, but to practice.

Not to fix, but to show up.

Not to perfect, but to grow.

Let's continue...

✺ thirty-one ✺

Reflecting on Culturally Responsive Teaching Through a Trauma-Responsive Lens

You've done the hard work. You've confronted systems. You've cracked open your own habits and reactions. You've sat with discomfort, wrestled with language, and invited student voice when it would have been easier to default to control. Now, here's the next question: Where are you now?

The Continuum: A Map for Reflection, Not Perfection

In Part One, you explored the Cultural Competence Continuum, not as a ladder to climb, but as a map to help us locate ourselves honestly. From cultural destructiveness to cultural proficiency, the continuum offers language for growth, not shame.

The truth is that most of us live in multiple places on the continuum, depending on the day, the student, and the trigger. You might operate with cultural proficiency when planning curriculum, but fall into denial or incapacity when interpreting behavior. That's not hypocrisy. That's being human. The goal isn't to plant your flag in "competence" and stay there. The goal is to keep noticing. To keep adjusting. To stay awake to the impact of your beliefs, biases, and behaviors.

The Self-Efficacy Scale

To deepen this reflection, I invite you to use the culturally responsive teaching self-efficacy scale adapted from Siwatu (2007).[120] You'll rate your confidence across four core areas, each of which gives insight into how you show up, not just what you believe, but how you act.

Culturally Responsive + Trauma-Informed Practice Self-Reflection

Instructions: For each statement below, rate your current level of confidence (self-efficacy) or practice on a 1–5 scale:

　　1 = Strongly disagree / Not yet confident

　　3 = Some confidence / Sometimes practice

　　5 = Strongly agree / Consistently practice

After completing, pause at each domain to reflect: How does awareness of culture and trauma shape my choices? Where am I stuck? Where am I growing?

Domain 1: Curriculum & Instruction

I feel confident designing lessons that connect students' cultural backgrounds to content (e.g., histories, examples, stories).

I can teach students about their own culture's contributions to academic subjects (science, math, literature).

I use culturally familiar examples, analogies, or stories to make new content accessible.

I adapt instructional methods when students' home learning styles diverge from school norms.

How do I strike a balance between academic rigor and culturally affirming relevance? How might this sustain resilience for trauma-impacted learners?

Domain 2: Classroom Management

I am confident using discipline approaches that are culturally respectful and trauma-informed.

I can adapt behavioral strategies when cultural norms regarding authority, communication, or expression differ from my own.

I seek input from students and families when setting behavioral expectations.

I can manage classroom conflicts in ways that center students' dignity and story, not just compliance.

I feel able to reflect on—and interrupt—my own biases (or assumptions) when interpreting student behavior.

Do I default to control when I feel unsafe? How would trauma and cultural understanding change my response?

Domain 3: Student Assessment

I design class assessments that recognize multiple ways of demonstrating mastery (e.g., oral, creative, collaborative).

I can adapt assessments so they don't penalize cultural or linguistic differences.

I feel able to assess student understanding in culturally affirming ways (e.g., portfolios, narratives, interviews).

I review grading practices to ensure they reflect opportunity and growth, not only compliance.

I intentionally align assessments with scaffolds and supports before demanding independent performance.

How am I honoring cognitive resilience over conformity? What biases might be built into my grading norms?

Domain 4: Cultural Enrichment & Relationships

I welcome and include family and community perspectives in classroom learning and decision-making.

I demonstrate knowledge of students' cultural values, identities, and lived experiences in my pedagogy.

I promote student agency by inviting them to help co-create classroom norms, goals, or projects.

I feel confident facilitating discussions about identity, race, power, or trauma—even when they're difficult.

I engage in ongoing self-reflection to understand how my own cultural lens influences my teaching and relationships.

Where am I practicing cultural humility? Where do I still need to listen more deeply?

❧ reflection ❧

This tool is not about perfection. It's about becoming the kind of educator who holds the child's culture, identity, and resilience at the center of every choice, from instruction to discipline to belonging.

What patterns do you notice in your ratings? Are there domains where you consistently feel stronger or weaker?

Where do your level-3 (sometimes) items reveal growth potential? What concrete steps could move you toward level 4 or 5?

In what ways do these self-evaluations align with, or challenge, your placement on the Cultural Competence Continuum from Part One?

How might greater cultural competence deepen your ability to support students impacted by trauma?

༄ thirty-two ༄
The Continuum of Becoming

We don't become trauma-informed all at once. We become it through a hundred honest choices, daily discomfort, and the willingness to keep showing up differently.

Becoming a resilience-building educator is not a checklist. It's a continuum, a progression of practice, presence, and purpose. No one starts at the top. We grow by noticing where we are, naming where we want to be, and taking courageous, imperfect steps forward.

This chapter is not about labeling yourself. It's about getting honest, curious, and committed. You were first introduced to the resilience-building practice continuum back in the Intentionality chapter. There, it was a reflection tool, an invitation to look inward and examine how your beliefs and practices aligned with the science and spirit of resilience-building education.

Now, as we near the end of this journey, we'll take a closer look.

This time, you'll walk through the full version of the continuum, one domain at a time. The goal is simple: get clear on where you are now and where you hope to be one year from now. This is your opportunity to step back, breathe, and reflect not just on what you've learned, but on how you're living it out.

Why the Continuum Matters

This work is layered. You might feel strong in relationship-building but unsure how to support regulation. You might use trauma-sensitive language, yet still rely on punitive systems that erode safety. That's not failure. That's growth in progress. The continuum exists to help you:

See the whole arc of trauma-informed development

Reflect honestly on your current practices

Set an intention for where you want to move next

Take a system-wide view of what supports or undermines your growth

This is not about perfection. It's about presence. It's about showing up with integrity, even when it's messy.

About the Continuum

The full continuum in the next section outlines six facets critical to resilience-building schools:

Relationship Focus	Behavioral Approaches	Responsibility Beliefs
Regulation Practices	Academic Structures	Felt Safety

Each level includes key descriptors and "next steps," making this not just a diagnostic tool, but also a developmental roadmap.

What This Assessment Can Reveal

You might discover that:

Your classroom is trauma-aware,
    but your discipline policies are still trauma-indifferent.
Your heart is trauma-informed,
    but your systems haven't caught up.
Your students feel safe with you,
    but not necessarily with the school as a whole.

This tool is meant to surface those tensions, not to shame, but to clarify the gap between intention and impact. Much of this continuum doesn't just reflect your individual beliefs; it reveals what your systems are reinforcing. There might also be things that are outside of your control due to school district policy, state law, or federal guidance.

This might include grading policies, chronic absentee laws, or requirements for administering state assessments. In those cases, we ask ourselves,

"How do I uphold this policy in a way that promotes dignity, safety, and belonging and not shame, isolation, and threat?"

Use the continuum not just to reflect on yourself, but to advocate for the systemic shifts that support a truly trauma-informed culture.

The Resilience-Building Continuum

Instructions: Identify the Statement in Each Row That Best Reflects Your Current Practice
For each domain, choose the level that feels most accurate for your consistent daily practice, not your ideals or intentions. It's okay if you feel like you're between levels. Choose the one you lean toward most of the time.

Facet 1: Relationships
How do I prioritize and maintain relationships with students?

I rarely invest in relationships and may view emotional connection as secondary or irrelevant to learning.	I primarily interact with students on matters related to rules or academics. I haven't created intentional ways to build trust.	I value relationships, but I may struggle with consistency or repairing them when harm occurs.
I intentionally build trust, use student names, and check in emotionally. Students know I care about them.	I prioritize relationships even during conflict. I repair ruptures and maintain a consistent emotional presence.	My classroom culture centers on belonging. Every student knows they matter and feels emotionally safe in my presence.

Facet 2: Behavioral Approaches
How do I interpret and respond to student behavior?

I respond to misbehavior with control, shame, or exclusion. I assume students should know better.	I enforce rules but rarely explore what might be driving the behavior underneath.	I've started shifting my language and tone, but I still fall into reactive patterns under stress.
I pause to consider what the behavior is communicating. I offer choices, redirection, or a co-regulation strategy.	I consistently respond to behavior with curiosity, empathy, and clear boundaries rooted in safety.	I've moved from managing behavior to understanding and supporting nervous system needs. My response helps students build skills.

Facet 3: Responsibility Beliefs
How do I view student accountability, motivation, and willpower?

I often view students as lazy, disrespectful, or manipulative. I see defiance as personal.	I believe students just need to "try harder" or "make better choices" without considering skill gaps or stress responses.	I've begun to question willful interpretations of behavior, but still default to frustration.
I understand that dysregulated students often can't, not won't. I scaffold responsibility with support.	I hold students accountable through connection, skill-building, and reflection, not shame.	I create a culture where students feel safe to fail, take ownership, and grow from mistakes without fear of judgment.

Facet 4: Regulation Practices
How do I support regulation for students and myself?

I expect students to manage their emotions on their own emotions. I punish dysregulation.	I may acknowledge dysregulation, but I lack tools or see it as someone else's responsibility.	I recognize when students are dysregulated, but I still feel unsure how to help them regulate.
I employ co-regulation strategies, including tone, posture, and space. I provide opportunities for students to reset.	I proactively plan for regulations, both mine and those of others, and embed them into classroom routines.	I consistently model self-regulation, use co-regulation as my first response, and teach these skills explicitly.

Facet 5: Academic Structures
How do I view and support truly differentiated learning?

I use academic systems that create pressure, shame, or exclusion. Grades, deadlines, and tasks are used to control behavior or compliance.	I use traditional grading, deadlines, and instructional methods without adapting them for students who struggle with trauma, executive function, or regulation.	I'm beginning to recognize that trauma impacts attention, memory, and motivation. I try to be flexible, but sometimes worry about fairness or lowering standards.
I adjust expectations, timelines, and assessments based on student needs. I provide chances to revise, retry, or learn in multiple ways.	I intentionally design instruction to support the whole child. I offer students varied ways to access content and demonstrate understanding, and I value progress over perfection.	I embed flexibility, relevance, and belonging into my academic design. Learning is accessible, meaningful, and paced for regulation. Rigor exists without re-traumatizing.

Facet 6: Felt Safety
How do I ensure that students feel safe in their bodies, in their identities, and in my presence?

My tone, expectations, or environment may feel unpredictable or unsafe to students. I may unintentionally escalate fear, threat, or shame.	I assume safety is present if no one is visibly upset. I haven't yet considered how my systems, routines, or physical space might impact students' sense of safety.	I understand the importance of felt safety and notice when students appear withdrawn or hypervigilant, but I'm not always sure how to respond or prevent it.
I create structure, consistency, and relational warmth to help students settle. I adapt when I notice my routines or tone cause dysregulation.	I prioritize emotional and psychological safety in daily decisions. I check in regularly, use calming transitions, and adjust routines to reduce threat responses.	Felt safety is foundational. Every aspect of my space, structure, and relationships is designed to convey cues of safety, dignity, and belonging. I lead with regulation and repair.

Reflect on Your Patterns

Count and record the number of times you selected each box.

1.

2.

3.

4.

5.

6.

As you look over your results, resist the urge to grade yourself. This isn't about performance, it's about presence. Throughout this book, we've returned again and again to the practice of shifting from judgment to discernment, choosing curiosity over shame.

Let that mindset guide you here. What patterns do you notice across your responses? Are there domains where you feel consistently grounded and aligned with trauma-informed practice? Celebrate those. They're not small wins, they're signs of transformation. Are there areas where you feel stretched, unsure, or stuck? Don't panic. That's not failure, it's an invitation. These growth edges are where the work gets real. Instead of asking, *"Am I doing enough?"* try asking, *"What's one area I feel drawn to grow in next?"* Let this be a moment of clarity, not criticism.

Where you are is simply your starting point, not your identity. With that understanding, below you will find a description of each level within the continuum. Take a few moments to read through each level before completing the reflection below.

The Resilience-Building Continuum

Trauma-Inducing	**Trauma-Indifferent**	**Trauma-Aware**
Some of my current systems or responses may be unintentionally harming students. I now recognize how urgency, control, or punitive practices might be impacting emotional safety, and I'm ready to take steps toward change.	I haven't consistently considered how trauma affects student behavior, learning, or my practice. I'm beginning to connect the dots and want to become more intentional in my approach.	I understand that trauma matters, and I'm trying to integrate this awareness into how I teach and lead. I still feel unsure in some areas, but I'm committed to learning more and applying what I know.
Trauma-Sensitive	**Trauma-Responsive**	**Trauma-Informed**
I'm actively adjusting my practices to reflect what I've learned about trauma and the brain. I'm becoming more responsive and reflective, even though it doesn't always come easily.	I consistently integrate trauma-responsive strategies into my classroom. I focus on connection, co-regulation, and emotional safety, and I'm seeing the impact in my relationships and systems.	Trauma-informed practice is embedded in how I think, teach, and lead. My classroom and routines are designed with nervous system needs, relational trust, and student dignity at the center. I know this is a lifelong journey, and I remain committed to growing.

✌ reflection ✌

Which domain represents your current strength?

Which domain represents your stretch or growth edge?

What do you notice about how your nervous system responds to certain domains (e.g., behavior, regulation, accountability)?

What is one step you could take in the next 30 days to shift one domain forward?

✣ thirty-three ✣
Rooted Renewal

This work isn't just about changing what you do.
It's about changing how you see, how you show up, and how you stay connected to your purpose, especially when it's hard.

Reclaiming Your Mission, Redefining Your Practice

You've completed a deep journey through trauma, resilience, the nervous system, and what it means to be a teacher who is present, intentional, and Rooted in Hope. Now it's time to pull it all together, to define your next step with clarity, compassion, and courage.

This reflection will help you name a specific goal, grounded in what you've learned about yourself, your students, and your impact. It's also a space to acknowledge growth, set boundaries, and commit to continued alignment with your values and calling.

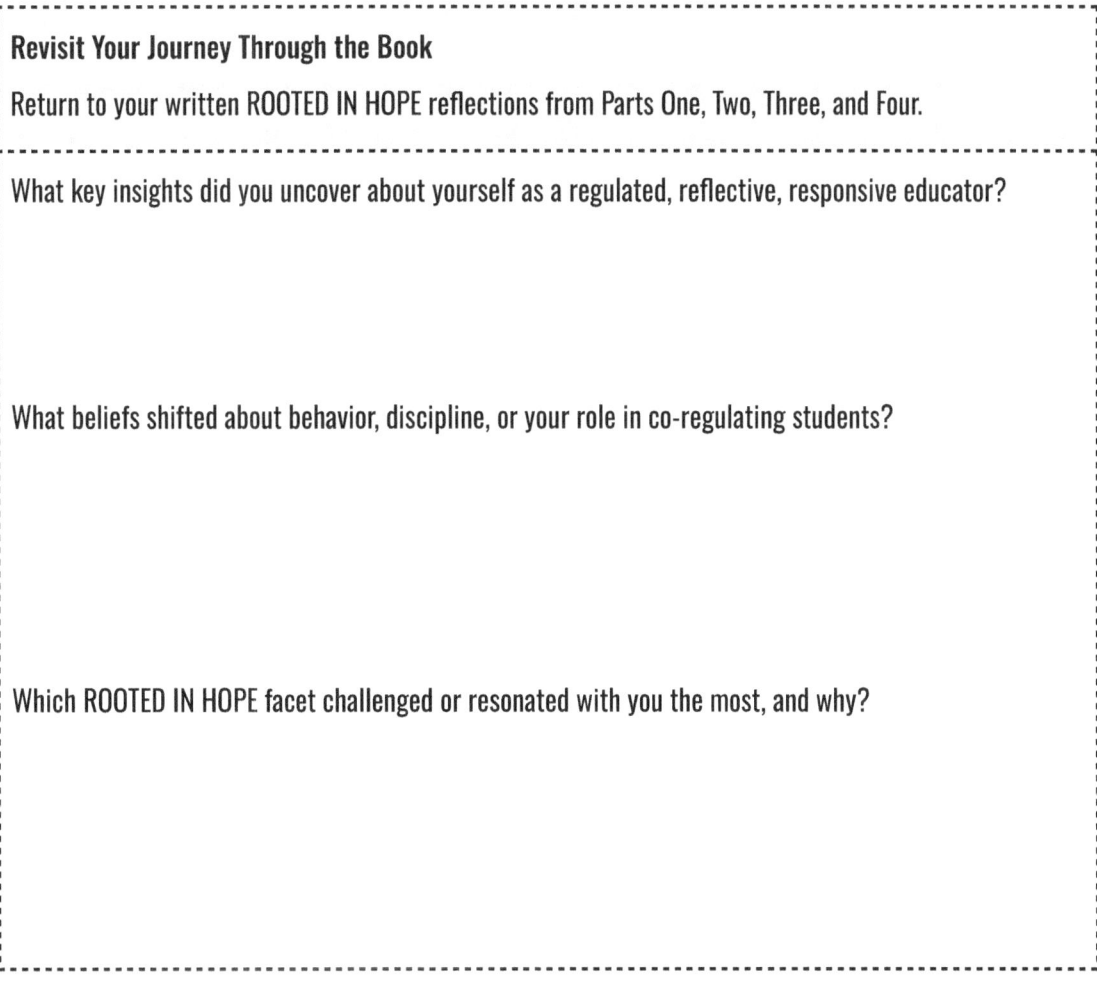

Revisit Your Journey Through the Book

Return to your written ROOTED IN HOPE reflections from Parts One, Two, Three, and Four.

What key insights did you uncover about yourself as a regulated, reflective, responsive educator?

What beliefs shifted about behavior, discipline, or your role in co-regulating students?

Which ROOTED IN HOPE facet challenged or resonated with you the most, and why?

Jot down 2–3 insights you want to carry forward into your next season of teaching.

1.

2.

3.

Part One Reflection: Foundations for a Rooted Practice

Resilience

- What is something new you've learned about how resilience is built (or interrupted)?
- How has your understanding of student resilience shifted from "grit" to "regulation"?
- What experiences in your own life have shaped your sense of resilience?

Origin

- What role do origin stories—family systems, early adversity, cultural identity—play in how students show up?
- How has learning about epigenetics or generational trauma expanded your perspective?
- How might your own origin story influence the way you interpret behavior?

Openness

- What beliefs or assumptions are you beginning to question?
- Where do you notice resistance in yourself, and what might that resistance be protecting?
- How are you practicing openness to student behaviors that previously felt confusing or frustrating?

Trust

- Why is trust a core component of resilience-building teaching?
- What types of trust (organic, contractual, relational) do you see at play in your classroom?
- What helps you feel safe enough to trust—and how might students need the same?

Engagement

- What stood out to you about the link between regulation and engagement?
- How might trauma or chronic stress affect a student's capacity to engage?
- What are ways you can foster engagement through connection, not control?

Discernment

- What's the difference between behavior and the story behind the behavior?
- How has learning about the stress response helped you better interpret student needs?
- When have you misread a student's behavior, and what might you do differently now?

Intentionality

- What classroom practices are you rethinking in light of the science?
- Where might you be unintentionally reinforcing shame or disconnection?
- What would it look like to align your teaching with what you now know about the brain?

_____
_____
_____
_____
_____
_____
_____
_____
_____
_____
_____
_____
_____
_____

Neuro-informed

- What surprised you about how the brain and nervous system operate under stress?
- How does this knowledge change your understanding of "willful" or "defiant" behavior?
- How can your classroom become a place that supports brain-aligned learning?

_____
_____
_____
_____
_____
_____
_____
_____
_____
_____
_____
_____

Hope

- How does understanding the science of trauma increase—not decrease—your sense of hope?
- What stories or moments from this section reminded you that healing is possible?
- What might it mean to become a *hope holder* for your students?

Ownership

- In what ways are you taking responsibility for your learning and growth as an educator?
- What myths about trauma or behavior are you ready to let go of?
- How does recognizing your influence—not control—over students shape your next steps?

Purpose

- Why does this work matter to you?
- What truths from this section do you want to carry forward?
- How is this foundation reconnecting you to your purpose as an educator?

Empowerment

- How does knowing the science behind behavior empower you as a teacher?
- How can this knowledge shift power back to students, especially those who have been most impacted by trauma?
- What's one way you can begin transforming your classroom into a space where students feel capable, seen, and safe?

Final Invitation:

Based on everything you've learned so far, what kind of educator do you want to become, and what kind of healing space do you want to build?

Part Two Rooted In Hope: Personal Reflection for Educators

Resilience

- What have you overcome that continues to shape how you show up for students?
- What's a strength you have that no one sees, but that you use every day?

Origin

- What early messages did you receive about learning, discipline, or belonging?
- How do your past school experiences influence how you teach and respond to students now?

Openness

- What kinds of students or behaviors challenge you the most, and what might that say about what you still need to understand?
- Where are you being invited to unlearn or grow?

Trust

- When do you find it hardest to trust students, families, or systems?
- What helps you feel safe enough to take emotional risks in your work?

Empowerment

- When do you feel powerful and purposeful in your teaching?
- Where do you feel silenced, restricted, or unseen, and how does that affect your energy?

_____

_____

_____

_____

_____

_____

_____

_____

_____

_____

_____

_____

Discernment

- What assumptions do you carry about behavior, effort, or trauma?
- How do you know when to intervene, when to hold space, and when to pause?

_____

_____

_____

_____

_____

_____

_____

_____

_____

_____

_____

_____

_____

_____

Intentionality

- What are your core values, and do your daily decisions reflect them?
- Where are you reacting instead of responding with purpose?

Neuro-Informed

- What do you understand about your stress responses, and how they show up in the classroom?
- How do you support co-regulation, and where might you unintentionally escalate stress?

Hope

- What vision keeps you going in hard seasons?
- Where is hope present in your classroom, even if quietly?

Ownership

- What part of the school culture do you shape, through action or inaction?
- What do you need to take responsibility for to be more aligned with healing and justice?

Purpose

- Why did you choose this profession, and what do you want to remember about that?
- What story do you want students to tell about their experience with you?

Engagement

- Who in your classroom or school feels like they're on the outside, and what are you doing to bring them in?
- When do you feel most alive and connected in your work?

Final Invitation

This work begins with you, but it doesn't stay with you. What you heal, shift, or reclaim in yourself will ripple into your classroom, your community, and your legacy.

Part Three Reflection: A Rooted Response

Resilience

- How has your understanding of resilience shifted from grit and compliance to regulation and connection?
- Which student's story made you reconsider how resilience forms, and who gets to be seen as resilient?
- What's one way you are already helping students bounce back that you hadn't named as resilience before?

Origin

- How has learning about trauma, neurodiversity, and cultural context helped you soften toward your students' struggles?
- What assumptions are you releasing about why students act the way they do?
- How are you beginning to view your students' behaviors as part of their origin stories, rather than their destinies?

Openness

- What does openness look like when you don't have all the answers?
- How are you creating space for students and families to speak into the plan instead of being handed one?
- What are you learning when you stop leading with assumptions and start leading with inquiry?

Trust

- What does trust require in your classroom, not just from students, but from you?
- How have you begun to demonstrate to students that your word, tone, and presence are consistent and trustworthy?
- Where are you rebuilding trust that others may have broken?

Engagement

- Where are you replacing entertainment with meaning, and compliance with a sense of belonging?
- How are you designing learning to reflect who your students are, and who they might become?
- What changed in your understanding of engagement after seeing how trauma interrupts curiosity?

Discernment

- How has the transforming discipline process helped you slow down your reaction and see what's happening?
- Which story reminded you that behavior is communication, not defiance?
- What judgment are you ready to release in exchange for clarity?

Intentionality

- Where in your day are you choosing differently because you now understand the impact?
- What part of your practice used to be automatic but is now more aligned with your purpose?
- How are you showing up on purpose, especially when it's hard?

Neuro-Informed

- How has your view of the "misbehavior" changed now that you understand dysregulation?
- What do you notice in students' bodies, tone, and energy that you used to miss?
- How is your classroom becoming a safer place for nervous systems, not just rules?

Hope

- What small evidence of change have you given your students this week?
- How are you holding hope for a student who doesn't yet see it for themselves?
- How are you growing the kind of hope that's rooted in proof, not just positivity?

Ownership

- Where are you replacing consequences with reflection?
- How are you helping students feel proud, not just compliant?
- What new language are you using that helps students take responsibility without shame?

Purpose

- How have the student stories reminded you that purpose can be both powerful and present in our lives?
- What are you doing to help students see themselves as someone who matters, not just someone who performs?
- How are you redesigning assignments, roles, and relationships to reflect meaning, not just metrics?

Empowerment

- Where are you offering choices that students should never have lost?
- What strengths have emerged in students once they were given voice, trust, and space?
- How are you redefining your role, not as someone who manages, but as someone who equips?

Final Invitation:

What does it mean, for you, in this moment, to be a resilience-building educator ROOTED IN HOPE?

Part Four Reflection: From Insight to Implementation

Resilience

- What structures or routines in your environment help students recover and re-engage after a hard moment?
- When students dysregulate, how do you communicate: "You can come back from this"?
- How are you helping students *practice* resilience, not just expect it?

Origin

- In what ways do you consider how your students' origin, including early adversity, attachment patterns, or trauma, has shaped their behavior and coping strategies?
- Are your interpretations of behavior rooted in curiosity about a student's nervous system story, or assumptions about intent?

Openness

- Are you open to revising your perception of a student once you learn more about their story?
- How do you respond when a strategy you've used before doesn't work? Do you double down, or try something new?
- What information from the SiNoC profile surprised or challenged you?

Trust

- What systems or strategies are in place to build student trust during and *after* dysregulation?
- How do your actions communicate to students: "You're safe with me—even when it's hard"?
- Are your co-regulation efforts consistent and predictable enough to build safety over time?

Engagement

- Where are your students actively engaged, and what aspects of that space or task make it possible?
- How do you intentionally incorporate relevance, creativity, and choice into learning or regulation supports?
- Do you offer students authentic opportunities to *participate*, or just to comply?

Discernment

- Are you using behavior data to *understand patterns*, or simply to track incidents?
- Which interventions are truly meeting this student's needs, and which are simply maintaining adult control?
- What supports do you keep using out of habit, and which ones are backed by clear outcomes?

Intentionality

- How intentional are you about preparing *for* dysregulation before it happens?
- In the moment, do you respond from habit or with purpose?
- Where can you shift from reactive discipline to proactive design?

Neuro-informed

- How are your school environments aligned with what we know about the stress response, regulation, and sensory processing?
- Do students have daily opportunities to *practice* regulation, not just be redirected when they lose it?
- Are you considering executive functioning, nervous system sensitivity, and developmental readiness in my interventions?

Hope

- What might help your students believe that things can be different, whether at school, at home, or within themselves?
- How do your words and responses build (or chip away at) a student's sense of future possibility?
- Have you given this student a chance to succeed recently, in a way that *felt* successful to them?

Ownership

- What role do you play in creating or reinforcing conditions that lead to student overwhelm?
- What's one area where you can take more responsibility for the environment or system around a student, not just their reaction to it?
- How do you support students in building *self*-ownership, not just compliance?

Purpose

- What are your students' "whys," and how do you help them connect learning, relationships, or regulation to something meaningful?
- Are the expectations and routines in your classroom linked to something deeper than just order or efficiency?
- How do you help students see themselves as active participants in their future, not just subjects to be managed?

Empowerment

- Do your spaces and systems provide students with opportunities to access and direct their self-regulation tools, or do they rely solely on adult control?
- How do you invite student voice into the design and expectations of the space they spend time in
- What's one way you can support a student in feeling more capable, rather than more contained?

Final Invitation:

What one belief, practice, or system are you ready to shift—not because it's easy, but because it's necessary?

Set a Clear, Specific Goal

Let your goal reflect your learning, not to prove anything, but to live it out more intentionally.

What is one focused area of practice you want to grow in based on what you've learned?

How does this align with your purpose, your values, and your students' needs?

What small, meaningful shift would be a sign of real change?

Write your goal below:

Example: "I will revise one classroom routine to support regulation and predictability for my students and track student response weekly for six weeks."

Clarify Your Place, Pace, and Path

Where do you currently feel aligned in your teaching practice and school context?

Where are you overextending, overcompensating, or misaligned with your values?

What pace do you need to maintain to stay regulated, connected, and sustainable?

Reflect on Your Strengths and Calling

What do you know now about your nervous system and how it shows up at school?

What strengths do you bring, even when you are depleted?

Where do you feel your presence is making the most difference right now?

"My classroom feels most alive when I..."

"My students respond best when I..."

Anticipate Barriers and Enlist Support

How will you know your goal is making a difference?

What specific indicators will help you track this growth (e.g., fewer escalations, more connection moments, improved student response)?

What data or reflection tools will you use? (e.g., journal notes, co-regulation tracker, student check-ins)

Define Success and Monitor Progress

What patterns (self-judgment, urgency, perfectionism) might pull you off course?

What mindsets might you need to release to make room for growth?

Who can you check in with when you need encouragement, accountability, or just to be reminded you're not alone?

"When I get discouraged, I will...

"One colleague I can reflect with is...

Complete Your STOPLIGHT Reflection

	Prompt	Your Response
I'll Stop...	A practice, mindset, or system that no longer aligns	
I'll Change...	Something you'll adjust or approach differently	
I'll Start...	A new commitment aligned with your growth and your students' needs	

Identify Your Ongoing Learning Focus

Growth doesn't end with this book. Let it shape your next learning journey.

A ROOTED IN HOPE facet I want to deepen is...

A practice I want to embody, not just understand, is...

A topic I would like to explore in more depth is...

A student I want to stay rooted with, even when it's hard, is...

Recommit With Intention

Use this final space to write a set of commitment statements, declaring who you want to be moving forward.

"I will show up for my students with..."

"I will protect my peace by..."

"I will not confuse urgency with importance."

"I will keep practicing, even when it's messy."

Tape it in your planner. Put it near your desk. Let it remind you: You are not the same teacher who opened this book. You have already established roots; now you're ready to bloom.

❧ part five reflection ❧

Looking Back, Rooting Forward — A Reflection for the Journey Ahead

Resilience

What has this journey reminded you of your strength?

Where did you grow or bend without breaking?

Origin

How has your understanding of student behavior, trauma, and history deepened?

What roots have you reclaimed in yourself or recognized in others?

Openness

What assumptions have you released or re-examined?

How are you more open to difference, discomfort, or new ways of knowing?

Trust

What relationships have begun to shift because you chose to lead with trust?

How has trust in myself grown?

Empowerment

What are you now ready to claim, speak, or act on with confidence?

Where do you feel more agency—in my classroom, school, or system?

Discernment

What have you learned to notice more clearly—about power, patterns, or needs?

Where are you more intentional in my choices and responses?

Intentionality

      Where do you now act more on purpose, not just from habit or urgency?

      What is one practice you will carry forward deliberately?

Neuro-Informed

      How has understanding the nervous system changed the way you lead/teach?

      What regulation tools are now part of your rhythm?

Hope

      What does hope mean to you now?

      Where do you see signs of possibility—even in hard places?

Ownership

      What have you taken responsibility for in your leadership or relationships?

      What will you no longer ignore or defer to others?

Purpose

      What values feel sharper, deeper, or more urgent now?

      How do you want my work to impact the students and communities you serve?

Engagement

      Where have you stepped in more fully?

      How are you building spaces of belonging—not just attendance?

Dear Reader,

You've walked with me through stories, science, and strategies for trauma-informed, equity-centered leadership. Now, before you return to your daily work, I invite you to pause. Take a breath. Feel the ground beneath you. You are not the same person who opened this book. Honor that.

This is your moment to look back and root forward—to notice what has shifted in you, what you will carry on purpose, and what you will leave behind. The questions that follow are not assignments but invitations—prompts to help you mark this ending as a beginning.

Find stillness. Take a deep breath. Let your body settle. You are not who you were when you began this book. Honor that. When you're ready, close with one sentence, a statement, or a promise to yourself:

Let that be what keeps you **Rooted in Hope.**

With gratitude for the work you do,

Katie

✒ end notes ✒

Chapter 1:

1 Margaret Distler, quoted in John Harlow, "Anxiety Nation," *UCLA Magazine*, July 10, 2019, https://newsroom.ucla.edu/magazine/anxiety-stress-semel-institute-7-ways-cope.

2 Centers for Disease Control and Prevention, "About the CDC-Kaiser ACE Study," last reviewed April 3, 2023, https://www.cdc.gov/violenceprevention/aces/about.html.

3 American Psychological Association, "Trauma," APA Dictionary of Psychology, accessed July 31, 2025, https://dictionary.apa.org/trauma.

4 Center on the Developing Child at Harvard University, "Toxic Stress," 2019, https://developingchild.harvard.edu/science/key-concepts/toxic-stress/.

5 IBID

6 Robert F. Anda et al., "The Enduring Effects of Abuse and Related Adverse Experiences in Childhood," *European Archives of Psychiatry and Clinical Neuroscience* 256, no. 3 (2006): 174–86;

 Ruth C. White, "What ACEs Didn't Tell Us," *Medium*, May 4, 2019, https://medium.com/s/story/what-aces-didnt-tell-us-2f8b73f4f460.

7 Vincent J. Felitti et al., "Relationship of Childhood Abuse and Household Dysfunction to Many of the Leading Causes of Death in Adults: The Adverse Childhood Experiences (ACE) Study," *American Journal of Preventive Medicine* 14, no. 4 (1998): 245–258.

8 Centers for Disease Control and Prevention, "Children's Mental Health: Data and Statistics," last reviewed March 22, 2023, https://www.cdc.gov/childrensmentalhealth/data.html.

9 Substance Abuse and Mental Health Services Administration (SAMHSA), Adverse Childhood Experiences (ACEs): Behavioral Risk Factor Surveillance System (BRFSS), 2016, https://www.samhsa.gov/sites/default/files/programs_campaigns/childrens_mental_health/ace-brochure.pdf.

10 Centers for Disease Control and Prevention, "About the CDC-Kaiser ACE Study," last reviewed April 3, 2023, https://www.cdc.gov/violenceprevention/aces/about.html.

11 IBID

12 Rudd, Tom. *Racial Disproportionality in School Discipline: Implicit Bias is Heavily Implicated*. Kirwan Institute for the Study of Race and Ethnicity, 2014. https://kirwaninstitute.osu.edu/wp-content/uploads/2014/02/racial-disproportionality-schools-02.pdf

 Feletti, V. J., Anda, R. F., et al., "Relationship of Childhood Abuse and Household Dysfunction to Many of the Leading Causes of Death in Adults," *American Journal of Preventive Medicine* 14, no. 4 (1998): 245–258

 Ginwright, Shawn. *The Four Pivots: Reimagining Justice, Reimagining Ourselves*. Oakland, CA: Berrett-Koehler Publishers, 2022.

13 Kaiser Permanente and Centers for Disease Control and Prevention, "ACE Questionnaire," CDC-Kaiser ACE Study, 1998, https://www.cdc.gov/violenceprevention/aces/about.html.

Chapter 2:

14   Finkelhor, David. *"Screening for Adverse Childhood Experiences (ACEs): Cautions and Suggestions."* *Child Abuse & Neglect* 85 (2018): 174–179. https://doi.org/10.1016/j.chiabu.2017.07.016

15   PACEs Connection, "What Are PACEs?," accessed July 31, 2025, https://www.pacesconnection.com/g/aces-in-education/blog/what-are-paces.

16   Snyder, C. R., Lopez, Shane J., Teramoto Pedrotti, Jennifer. *Positive Psychology: The Scientific and Practical Explorations of Human Strengths.* 3rd ed. Thousand Oaks, CA: Sage, 2015

17   Shane J. Lopez, Making Hope Happen: Create the Future You Want for Yourself and Others (New York: Atria Books, 2013).

18   IBID

19   IBID

Chapter 3:

20   For foundational neuroscience and trauma theory, this summary draws on the work of Bruce Perry, Daniel Siegel, Stephen Porges, and Bessel van der Kolk.

21   Jennifer Sweeton, Trauma Treatment Toolbox: 165 Brain-Changing Tips, Tools & Handouts to Move Therapy Forward (Eau Claire, WI: PESI Publishing & Media, 2019).

22   Jay N. Giedd, "The Teen Brain: Insights from Neuroimaging," *Journal of Adolescent Health* 42, no. 4 (2008): 335–343, https://doi.org/10.1016/j.jadohealth.2008.01.007.

23   Perry, Bruce D., and Maia Szalavitz. *The Boy Who Was Raised as a Dog: And Other Stories from a Child Psychiatrist's Notebook.* 3rd ed. New York: Basic Books, 2017.

24   Porges, Stephen W. *The Pocket Guide to the Polyvagal Theory: The Transformative Power of Feeling Safe.* New York: W. W. Norton & Company, 2017.

25   Perry, Bruce D., and Maia Szalavitz. *The Boy Who Was Raised as a Dog: And Other Stories from a Child Psychiatrist's Notebook.* 3rd ed. New York: Basic Books, 2017.

26   Dr. Ruby K. Payne, Emotional Poverty in All Demographics: How to Reduce Anger, Anxiety, and Violence in the Classroom (Highlands, TX: aha! Process, 2018).

27   Robert M. Sapolsky, *Why Zebras Don't Get Ulcers: The Acclaimed Guide to Stress, Stress-Related Diseases, and Coping* (New York: W.H. Freeman, 2004).

28   IBID

29   Shelley E. Taylor et al., "Biobehavioral Responses to Stress in Females: Tend-and-Befriend, Not Fight-or-Flight," *Psychological Review* 107, no. 3 (2000): 411–29

30   IBID

31   Dr. Ruby K. Payne, *Emotional Poverty in All Demographics: How to Reduce Anger, Anxiety, and Violence in the Classroom* (Highlands, TX: aha! Process, 2018).

32   Attachment and Trauma Treatment Centre for Healing (ATTCH), "Understanding and Working with the Window of Tolerance," ATTCH Blog, 2019, https://www.attachment-and-trauma-treatment-centre-for-healing.com/blogs/understanding-and-working-with-the-window-of-tolerance.

33 Daniel J. Siegel, The Developing Mind: How Relationships and the Brain Interact to Shape Who We Are, 2nd ed. (New York: Guilford Press, 2012).

34 Pollack Peacebuilding Systems, "Understanding the Behavior Escalation Cycle," Pollack Peacebuilding Blog, accessed July 31, 2025, https://pollackpeacebuilding.com/blog/behavior-escalation-cycle/.

California Department of Education, "Understanding the Escalation Cycle," Positive Environments, Network of Trainers (PENT), accessed July 31, 2025, https://www.pent.ca.gov/pbis/tier3/escalationcycle.aspx.

Katie McDonald and Carmen Zeisler, Co-Regulation Cycle, originally developed in 2017 as part of the Equipping Resilience Coaches initiative at ESSDACK (unpublished training tool, adapted for this manuscript, 2025).

Kimberly D. Rosanbalm and Dana W. Murray, Caregiver Co-Regulation Across Development: A Practice Brief, OPRE Brief #2017-80 (Washington, DC: Office of Planning, Research, and Evaluation, Administration for Children and Families, U.S. Department of Health and Human Services, 2017).

35 Norman Doidge, *The Brain That Changes Itself: Stories of Personal Triumph from the Frontiers of Brain Science* (New York: Viking, 2007);
Bruce D. Perry and Maia Szalavitz, *The Boy Who Was Raised as a Dog: And Other Stories from a Child Psychiatrist's Notebook—What Traumatized Children Can Teach Us About Loss, Love, and Healing*, 3rd ed. (New York: Basic Books, 2017); Harvard University Center on the Developing Child, "Key Concepts: Brain Architecture," 2023, https://developingchild.harvard.edu/science/key-concepts/brain-architecture/.

Chapter 4:

36 Zaretta Hammond, Culturally Responsive Teaching and the Brain: Promoting Authentic Engagement and Rigor Among Culturally and Linguistically Diverse Students (Thousand Oaks, CA: Corwin, 2015).

37 Lisa Delpit, Other People's Children: Cultural Conflict in the Classroom (New York: The New Press, 2006).

38 Zaretta Hammond, Culturally Responsive Teaching and the Brain: Promoting Authentic Engagement and Rigor Among Culturally and Linguistically Diverse Students (Thousand Oaks, CA: Corwin, 2015).

39 Derald Wing Sue et al., "Racial Microaggressions in Everyday Life: Implications for Clinical Practice," American Psychologist 62, no. 4 (2007): 271, https://doi.org/10.1037/0003-066X.62.4.271.

40 Coleman and Pellitteri. Cultural competence continuum- characteristics. 2nd ed. 2013. Web. 17 June 2015.

Chapter 5:

41 Katie McDonald and Carmen Zeisler, Establishing Your Why, originally developed in 2017 as part of the Equipping Resilience Coaches initiative at ESSDACK (unpublished training tool, adapted for this manuscript, 2025).

Chapter 6:

42 Gabrieli, John D. E. "Dyslexia: A New Synergy Between Education and Cognitive Neuroscience." Science 325, no. 5938 (2009): 280–283. https://doi.org/10.1126/science.1171999.

Chapter 7:
43 James Moffett (school principal), in discussion with the author, June 20, 2025.

Chapter 8:

44   Beth Hudnall Stamm, The Concise ProQOL Manual, 2nd ed. (Pocatello, ID: ProQOL.org, 2010), https://proqol.org.

45   Adam Koenig, *Learning to Prevent Burning and Fatigue: Teacher Burnout and Compassion Fatigue* (master's thesis, Western University, 2017), https://www.csmh.uwo.ca/docs/Koenig-Rodger-Specht-2017.pdf.

46   Katie McDonald, unpublished data from 637 educator ProQOL assessments collected during professional learning sessions across multiple school districts, 2021–2024.

47   Stamm, Beth Hudnall. *The Concise ProQOL Manual*, 2nd ed. Pocatello, ID: ProQOL.org, 2010.

48   Charles R. Figley, *Compassion Fatigue: Coping with Secondary Traumatic Stress Disorder in Those Who Treat the Traumatized* (New York: Brunner/Mazel, 1995).

49   Beth Hudnall Stamm, *The Concise ProQOL Manual*, 2nd ed. (Pocatello, ID: ProQOL.org, 2010).

50   Compassion Fatigue Awareness Project, "What is Compassion Fatigue?" Accessed May 18, 2019. http://www.compassionfatigue.org/.

51   IBID

52   Shane J. Lopez, Making Hope Happen: Create the Future You Want for Yourself and Others (New York: Atria Books, 2013).

53   Haim G. Ginott, *Teacher and Child: A Book for Parents and Teachers* (New York: Macmillan, 1972), 15.

Chapter 9:

54   Parker J. Palmer, *A Hidden Wholeness: The Journey Toward an Undivided Life* (San Francisco: Jossey-Bass, 2004), 79–81.

55   Katie McDonald, Transforming Discipline, initially developed in 2023 as part of the Equipping Resilience Coaches initiative at ESSDACK (unpublished training tool, adapted for this manuscript, 2025).

Chapter 10:

56   Parker J. Palmer, *A Hidden Wholeness: The Journey Toward an Undivided Life* (San Francisco: Jossey-Bass, 2004), 79–81.

57   Brené Brown, Daring Greatly: How the Courage to Be Vulnerable Transforms the Way We Live, Love, Parent, and Lead (New York: Gotham Books, 2012).

Chapter 11:

58   Alice Miller, For Your Own Good: Hidden Cruelty in Child-Rearing and the Roots of Violence, trans. Hildegarde and Hunter Hannum (New York: Farrar, Straus and Giroux, 1983).

59   Adapted from the "River of Cruelty" metaphor, Family Peace Initiative Facilitator Training, 2023.

Chapter 12:

60   Katie McDonald, Self-Care Wheel, initially developed in 2018 as part of the Equipping Resilience Coaches initiative at ESSDACK (unpublished training tool, adapted for this manuscript, 2025).

Chapter 13:

61   Katie McDonald, Student in Need of Connection Process, initially developed in 2018 as part of the Equipping Resilience Coaches initiative at ESSDACK (unpublished training tool, adapted for this manuscript, 2025).

Chapter 14:

62   Karyn B. Purvis, David R. Cross, and Wendy Lyons Sunshine, The Connected Child: Bring Hope and Healing to Your Adoptive Family (New York: McGraw-Hill, 2007).

63   Center on the Developing Child at Harvard University, "Resilience," Harvard University: Center on the Developing Child, 2019, https://developingchild.harvard.edu/science/key-concepts/resilience/.

64   National Child Traumatic Stress Network, *Trauma-Informed Schools for Children in K-12: A System Framework*, 2017. https://www.nctsn.org/resources/trauma-informed-school-strategies.

65   Gallup Inc., "School Engagement Is More Than Just Talk," Gallup.com, July 24, 2018, https://www.gallup.com/education/244022/school-engagement-talk.aspx.

66   Child Welfare Information Gateway, *Protective Factors Approaches in Child Welfare*, Washington, DC: U.S. Department of Health and Human Services, Children's Bureau, 2014. https://www.childwelfare.gov/pubPDFs/protective_factors.pdf

67   Harvard University Center on the Developing Child. *Resilience*. Accessed September 11, 2025. https://developingchild.harvard.edu/science/key-concepts/resilience/

68   Search Institute, "The Developmental Assets Framework," Search Institute, 2019, https://www.search-institute.org/our-research/development-assets/developmental-assets-framework/.

Chapter 15:

69   Siegel, Daniel J. *The Developing Mind: How Relationships and the Brain Interact to Shape Who We Are*. 2nd ed. New York: Guilford Press, 2012

70   Megan Tschannen-Moran, "Trust Matters: Leadership for Successful Schools," Educational Leadership, vol. 60, no. 6 (2004): 52–55.

71   John Hattie, *Visible Learning: A Synthesis of Over 800 Meta-Analyses Relating to Achievement* (New York: Routledge, 2009); Brené Brown, *The Gifts of Imperfection: Let Go of Who You Think You're Supposed to Be and Embrace Who You Are* (Center City, MN: Hazelden Publishing, 2010).

72   Curt M. Adams and Patrick B. Forsyth, "The Nature and Function of Trust in Schools," Journal of School Leadership 19, no. 2 (2009): 126–152

Chapter 16:

73   Robert F. Anda et al., "The Enduring Effects of Abuse and Related Adverse Experiences in Childhood," *European Archives of Psychiatry and Clinical Neuroscience* 256, no. 3 (2006): 174–86;

74   Megan R. Gunnar and Adriana Herrera, "The Development of Stress Reactivity: A Neurobiological Perspective," Progress in Brain Research 167 (2008): 3–18, https://doi.org/10.1016/S0079-6123(07)67001-9.

75   Claire D. Coles, "Discriminating the Effects of Prenatal Alcohol Exposure from Other Behavioral and Learning Disorders," Alcohol Research & Health 25, no. 3 (2001): 153–159.

76   Mary C. Sullivan et al., "Behavioral and Emotional Adjustment of Healthy Low Birth Weight Children at School Age," Journal of Developmental and Behavioral Pediatrics 29, no. 4 (2008): 245–252, https://doi.org/10.1097/DBP.0b013e31817eb5c2.

77   Thomas R. Verny and John Kelly, *The Secret Life of the Unborn Child* (New York: Dell Publishing, 1981).

        Bessel van der Kolk, *The Body Keeps the Score: Brain, Mind, and Body in the Healing of Trauma* (New York: Viking, 2014), chap. 2.

        Gabor Maté, *Scattered Minds: The Origins and Healing of Attention Deficit Disorder* (Toronto: Knopf Canada, 1999).

78   Steven G. Feagans, Mary K. Kipp, and William H. Blood, "The Effects of Otitis Media on the Social and Academic Behavior of School-Age Children," Journal of Pediatric Psychology 19, no. 2 (1994): 203–217, https://doi.org/10.1093/jpepsy/19.2.203.

79   Geddes, Heather. *Attachment in the Classroom: The Links Between Children's Early Experience, Emotional Well-Being and Performance in School*. London: Worth Publishing, 2006.

80   Alan Sroufe and Daniel J. Siegel, "The Verdict Is In," Psychotherapy Networker 36, no. 4 (July/August 2012): 32–39.

81   For foundational attachment theory, this summary draws on the work of:

        Louis Cozolino, The Social Neuroscience of Education: Optimizing Attachment and Learning in the Classroom (New York: W.W. Norton, 2013).

        John Bowlby, A Secure Base: Parent-Child Attachment and Healthy Human Development (New York: Basic Books, 1988).

        Ruby K. Payne, Emotional Poverty in All Demographics: How to Reduce Anger, Anxiety, and Violence in the Classroom (Highlands, TX: aha! Process, Inc., 2018)].

Chapter 17:

82   Bessel van der Kolk, The Body Keeps the Score: Brain, Mind, and Body in the Healing of Trauma (New York: Viking, 2014).

83   Bruce D. Perry, "Applying Principles of Neurodevelopment to Clinical Work with Maltreated and Traumatized Children," Working with Traumatized Youth in Child Welfare (New York: Guilford Press, 2006), 27–52.

84   Bruce D. Perry and Christine L. Hambrick, "The Neurosequential Model of Therapeutics," Pediatric Clinics of North America 55, no. 6 (2008): 1289–1312, https://doi.org/10.1016/j.pcl.2008.08.003.

85   American Psychiatric Association, *Diagnostic and Statistical Manual of Mental Disorders*, 5th ed. (Arlington, VA: American Psychiatric Publishing, 2013).

86   Ross W. Greene, The Explosive Child: A New Approach for Understanding and Parenting Easily Frustrated, Chronically Inflexible Children, 6th ed. (New York: Harper, 2021).

        Ross W. Greene, Lost at School: Why Our Kids with Behavioral Challenges Are Falling Through the Cracks and How We Can Help Them (New York: Scribner, 2014).

87   Lives in the Balance. "Collaborative & Proactive Solutions (CPS)." Accessed August 4, 2025. https://livesinthebalance.org/.

Chapter 18:

88 Jim Sporleder and Heather T. Forbes, The Trauma-Informed School: A Step-by-Step Implementation Guide for Administrators and School Personnel (Boulder, CO: Beyond Consequences Institute, LLC, 2016).

89 Ted Wachtel, *Restorative Practices: Building Relationships and Community in Schools* (Bethlehem, PA: International Institute for Restorative Practices, 2016).

90 Katie McDonald, Transforming Discipline, initially developed in 2023 as part of the Equipping Resilience Coaches initiative at ESSDACK (unpublished training tool, adapted for this manuscript, 2025).

91 Melissa Sadin and Nathan Maynard, *The Trauma-Informed School: A Step-by-Step Implementation Guide for Administrators and School Personnel* (Hilliard, OH: Beyond Consequences Institute, 2018).

Chapter 19:

92 Edward L. Deci and Richard M. Ryan, *Self-Determination Theory: Basic Psychological Needs in Motivation, Development, and Wellness* (New York: Guilford Press, 2017).

93 Suzy Pepper Rollins, "Two-Minute Relationships for Ten Days Can Change a Student's Life," ASCD Express, vol. 11, no. 19 (June 2, 2016), http://www.ascd.org/ascd-express/vol11/1119-rollins.aspx.

Chapter 21:

94 Katie McDonald, Trauma-Informed Continuum Self-Assessment, initially developed in 2019 as part of the Equipping Resilience Coaches initiative at ESSDACK (unpublished training tool, adapted for this manuscript, 2025).

95 Family Peace Initiative, "Working Inside the Fence" The Art of Facilitation (unpublished training materials, 2018).

Chapter 22:

96 Charles R. Snyder et al., "The Will and the Ways: Development and Validation of an Individual-Differences Measure of Hope," Journal of Personality and Social Psychology 60, no. 4 (1991): 570–585.

97 Shane J. Lopez, "Making Hope Happen in Schools," in *The Oxford Handbook of Hope*, ed. Matthew W. Gallagher and Shane J. Lopez (Oxford: Oxford University Press, 2018), 261–272.

98 Shane J. Lopez, Making Hope Happen: Create the Future You Want for Yourself and Others (New York: Atria Books, 2013), [page number].

99 IBID

100 IBID

101 IBID

Chapter 24:

102 Héctor García and Francesc Miralles, *Ikigai: The Japanese Secret to a Long and Happy Life* (New York: Penguin Books, 2017).

Chapter 26:

103 Joe Brummer and Margaret Thorsborne, Building a Trauma-Informed Restorative School (Philadelphia: Jessica Kingsley Publishers, 2022), 52.

104   Jess Harris, "Doing the Work" Resilience Conversations Podcast, hosted by ESSDACK Resilience Team, Spotify, June 16, 2022, https://open.spotify.com/episode/5nrxFm9HZhO1T9UrngumGm.

Chapter 27

105   Marc Brackett, Permission to Feel: Unlocking the Power of Emotions to Help Our Kids, Ourselves, and Our Society Thrive (New York: Celadon Books, 2019).

106   Jill Bolte Taylor, *My Stroke of Insight: A Brain Scientist's Personal Journey* (New York: Viking, 2008), 139

Chapter 28

107   Kimberly D. Rosanbalm and Dana W. Murray, Caregiver Co-Regulation Across Development: A Practice Brief, OPRE Brief #2017-80 (Washington, DC: Office of Planning, Research, and Evaluation, Administration for Children and Families, U.S. Department of Health and Human Services, 2017).

108   IBID

109   Katie McDonald and Carmen Zeisler, Co-Regulation Cycle, originally developed in 2017 as part of the Equipping Resilience Coaches initiative at ESSDACK (unpublished training tool, adapted for this manuscript, 2025).

        Pollack Peacebuilding Systems, "Understanding the Behavior Escalation Cycle," Pollack Peacebuilding Blog, accessed July 31, 2025, https://pollackpeacebuilding.com/blog/behavior-escalation-cycle/.

        California Department of Education, "Understanding the Escalation Cycle," Positive Environments, Network of Trainers (PENT), accessed July 31, 2025, https://www.pent.ca.gov/pbis/tier3/escalationcycle.aspx.

Chapter 29

110   Katie McDonald, Student in Need of Connection Process, initially developed in 2018 as part of the Equipping Resilience Coaches initiative at ESSDACK (unpublished training tool, adapted for this manuscript, 2025).

111   Michael Ungar and Resilience Research Centre, *Child and Youth Resilience Measure (CYRM-R)*, Dalhousie University, 2018, https://resilienceresearch.org/research/resilience-measures/.

112   IBID

113   For foundational attachment theory, this summary draws on the work of:

        Louis Cozolino, The Social Neuroscience of Education: Optimizing Attachment and Learning in the Classroom (New York: W.W. Norton, 2013).

        John Bowlby, A Secure Base: Parent-Child Attachment and Healthy Human Development (New York: Basic Books, 1988).

        Ruby K. Payne, Emotional Poverty in All Demographics: How to Reduce Anger, Anxiety, and Violence in the Classroom (Highlands, TX: aha! Process, Inc., 2018)].

114   Kaiser Permanente and Centers for Disease Control and Prevention, "ACE Questionnaire," CDC-Kaiser ACE Study, 1998, https://www.cdc.gov/violenceprevention/aces/about.html.

115   Kilgus, Stephen P., Kathleen Lynne Lane, and Holly M. K. McDaniel. "Student Risk Screening Scale for Internalizing and Externalizing Behaviors (SRSS-IE): Technical Manual." University of Kansas, 2013.

116   John Hattie, Visible Learning: The Sequel – A Synthesis of Over 2,100 Meta-Analyses Relating to Achievement (London: Routledge, 2023).

117   Chris McChesney, Sean Covey, and Jim Huling, The 4 Disciplines of Execution: Achieving Your Wildly Important Goals (New York: Free Press, 2012).

Chapter 30

118   Jim Sporleder and Heather T. Forbes, The Trauma-Informed School: A Step-by-Step Implementation Guide for Administrators and School Personnel (Boulder, CO: Beyond Consequences Institute, LLC, 2016).

119   Arnold Zwicky, "The Frequency Illusion and Other Cognitive Biases," *Language Log*, Stanford University, August 7, 2005, https://web.stanford.edu/~zwicky/2005/08/frequency-illusion.html

Chapter 31

120   Kamau Oginga Siwatu, "Preservice Teachers' Culturally Responsive Teaching Self-Efficacy and Outcome Expectancy Beliefs," Teaching and Teacher Education 23, no. 7 (2007): 1086–1101, https://doi.org/10.1016/j.tate.2006.07.011